S0-CAT-847

AUGUSTINE'S LOVE OF WISDOM

**Purdue University Series
in the History of Philosophy**

General Editors

Arion Kelkel

Joseph J. Kockelmans

Adriaan Peperzak

Calvin O. Schrag

Thomas Seebohm

AUGUSTINE'S LOVE OF WISDOM

An Introspective Philosophy

Vernon J. Bourke

Purdue University Press
West Lafayette, Indiana

Copyright ©1992 by Purdue University Research Foundation,
West Lafayette, Indiana 47907. All rights reserved. Unless permission is
granted, this material shall not be copied, reproduced, or coded for
reproduction by any electrical, mechanical, or chemical processes, or
combination thereof, now known or later developed.

The Latin text of *The Confessions of St. Augustine,* edited by
John Gibb and William Montgomery, 1927, Book X, 272–305, is used
by permission of Cambridge University Press.

The English text of Saint Augustine, *Confessions,* translated by
Vernon J. Bourke, in the Fathers of the Church Series, volume 21,
© 1953, Book X, 263–301, is used by permission of The Catholic
University of America Press.

Printed in the United States of America

Book and cover design by Anita Noble

Library of Congress Cataloging-in-Publication Data
Bourke, Vernon Joseph, 1907–
    Augustine's love of wisdom : an introspective philosophy /
Vernon J. Bourke
       p.   cm. — (Purdue University series in the history of
philosophy)
    Includes bibliographical references and index.
    ISBN 1–55753–025–4 (hard : alk. paper) — ISBN 1–55753–
026–2 (pbk. : alk. paper)
      1. Augustine, Saint, Bishop of Hippo. Confessiones. Liber 10.
I. Title. II. Series.
BR65.A62B68 1992
242—dc20
                                         91–46448

CONTENTS

L. I. F. E. Bible College
LIBRARY
1100 COVINA BLVD
SAN DIMAS, CA 91773

039721

(ACW) *Ancient Christian Writers.* Westminster, Md.:
Newman Press, 1946–.

(BW) *Basic Writings of St. Augustine.* 2 vols. New York:
Random House, 1948.

(CUAP) *Catholic University of America Patristic Series.*
Washington, D.C., 1922–.

(EDIN) *The Works of Aurelius Augustinus.* Edited by
Marcus Pods. 15 vols. Edinburgh: Clark, 1871–1876.

(FOC) *Fathers of the Church.* New York-Washington:
Catholic University of America Press, 1947–.

(LCC) *Library of Christian Classics.* London-Philadelphia:
Westminster Press, 1953–55.

(LNPN) *Select Library of Nicene and Post-Nicene Fathers of
the Church.* 1887–1902. Reprint. Grand Rapids, Mich:
Eerdmans, 1956.

City *City of God*

Conf *Confessions*

83 Q *Eighty-Three Questions*

Epist *Letters*

Exp Ps *Expositions of the Psalms*

Free *Free Choice*

Gen Lit *Literal Commentary on Genesis*

Happy *The Happy Life*

Soul *Magnitude of the Soul*

Music *On Music*

Order *On Order*

Retr *Retractations*

Serm *Sermons*

Trin *The Trinity*

PART
ONE

Introduction

CHAPTER ONE | Life and Writings of Augustine

At the age of nineteen, while studying rhetoric in Carthage, Augustine read the *Hortensius,* a short introduction to philosophy written by Cicero. It deeply impressed him with a life-long love of wisdom. As Augustine describes the experience:

> In the regular course of study, I came upon the book of a certain Cicero . . . that book of his contained an exhortation to philosophy. It was called *Hortensius.* In fact that book changed my mental attitude . . . I yearned with unbelievable ardor of heart for the immortality of wisdom.[1]

The *Hortensius* is no longer extant in its original format, but we know some of its content from passages quoted by later writers, including Augustine.[2] Among other things, Cicero wrote: "If it is necessary to philosophize, then one must philosophize; if it is not necessary to philosophize, one must still philosophize, for it is only by thinking philosophically that one can show that it is possible to go beyond philosophy" (Müller, ed., frag. 12). Further, the *Hortensius* stressed the importance of a liberal education as a basis for the study of philosophy (frag. 23). Cicero also included a sketch of the history of philosophy; Thales, Socrates, Democritus, Aristotle, Theophrastus, Ariston of Chios, Posidonius, and Nicomachus of Tyre are briefly discussed. The four great ancient virtues (prudence, temperance, fortitude, and justice) are covered (frag. 64). Cicero, writing before the time of Christ, even suggests that the study of philosophy is an ideal preparation for death and a celestial life (frag. 97). Influenced by the dialogue *Eudemus* attributed to Plato (278c), Cicero popularized the saying, "All men desire to be happy," a conviction that we will frequently encounter in Augustine's writings.[3]

Thus, long before he was fully converted to Christianity, Augustine learned that the Greeks gave the name *philosophia* (the love of wisdom) to a special field of study. He was to seek wisdom *(sophia, sapientia)* throughout his next fifty-seven years, not only through philosophical reasoning but also on the basis of religious beliefs.

| Biographical Sketch

Born in North Africa at Tagaste (modern Souk Ahras in eastern Algeria) in A.D. 354, Augustine was the son of native African parents. His mother, Monica, was a Catholic and his father, Patricius, was only converted to Christianity in his last years. Augustine first attended school in Tagaste; he then studied grammar and the Latin classics at the nearby town of Madaura. With the financial assistance of a wealthy Tagastan businessman, Romanianus, the young Augustine was sent eastward along the north coast of Africa to do advanced studies in rhetoric at Carthage. Both his parents saw these studies as a preparation for a possible career as a government official in the Roman province of Numidia. As far as is known, Augustine never studied under a professor of philosophy or theology.

After teaching grammar at Tagaste for about a year (374–75/76) and rhetoric in Carthage for about seven years, Augustine decided to go to Rome during the summer of 383. He taught rhetoric there for a year, and then, after an audition with the imperial official Symmachus, he was sent north to Milan as a public professor of rhetoric in the schools of the imperial city. In 385 his mother, with a group from Africa (his brother Navigius; Augustine's common-law wife and his son, Adeodatus; his cousins Rusticus and Lastidianus; and Licentius, the son of Romanianus), joined Augustine in Milan.

Not yet a baptized Catholic, Augustine had become interested in Manicheism while living in cosmopolitan Carthage. This religion was started by the Persian prophet, Mani (ob. 277), who viewed all events, either cosmic or psychic, as a constant struggle between the forces of good and evil. When first at Rome, Augustine resided with a fellow Manichean auditor, and during their talks Augustine became increasingly convinced that the religion of Mani did not show the way to the wisdom that he sought. His disillusionment resulted in a short period of skepticism, during which he resolved to refrain from positive judgments on any of the basic questions of philosophy. In Milan he met some learned Christians and scholars, notably the Catholic Bishop Ambrose and the priest Simplicianus. They belonged to a local group that discussed the philosophy of Plotinus and Porphyry, a type of later Platonism developed chiefly in the schools at Alexandria—one of the main cities on the estuaries of the Nile river in Egypt. This Neoplatonism was to have a permanent effect on Augustine's philosophy.

By the summer of 386, Augustine had decided to end his teaching in Milan. He had undergone a profound religious experience that brought him close to a complete acceptance of Christianity (*Conf* 8.8.19–12.30), and a chest ailment made teaching and public speaking difficult. A fellow professor named Verecundus offered Augustine and his associates the use of a country-place at Cassiciacum, some distance north of Milan, and Augustine's fellow Africans moved there at the end of that summer. They were joined by at least two other Africans, Alypius and Evodius, well-educated former public officials. In this rural retreat during the fall and winter of 386/87, they relaxed and conversed about many philosophical and religious problems. From their discussions developed several of Augustine's early dialogues, which he edited later. He was preparing to be baptized by Bishop Ambrose in the cathedral of Milan.[4]

After his and his son's baptism on 24 April 387, Augustine and his family rested that winter at Ostia, the main port of Rome. His mother died at Ostia and was buried there (*Conf* 9.12.22). Augustine and his son returned to Africa in late summer of 388. On the few acres of land at Tagaste that Augustine inherited, he established a sort of monastery where the group could devote themselves to philosophical and religious development. One of his associates there and later in life was Possidius, who wrote a short account of Augustine's mature life.[5]

On a trip north to the coastal city of Hippo (today's Bône in Algeria) in 391, Augustine attended a service in the cathedral, where the congregation recognized him as a well-educated Catholic. They demanded that he be ordained as their priest. Bishop Valerius was Greek-speaking, and he welcomed the assistance of a man able to preach well in Latin, the language of the coastal cities of Roman Africa. By the spring of 394, Augustine was consecrated bishop, and from 396 on, after the death of Valerius, he presided over the diocese of Hippo Regius.[6]

For the next thirty-four years, until his death in 430, Augustine was busy with the affairs of his diocese at Hippo and frequently traveled to various meetings in North Africa.[7] A powerful speaker, he conducted many debates with representatives of various religious sects—Manicheans, Donatists, Pelagians, and others.[8] Despite these episcopal duties and frequent bouts of ill-health, Augustine managed to write an impressive number of treatises on philosophical and religious topics. (In terms of quality and quantity of work, one could say that Augustine is the greatest writer that Africa has produced.) At the time of Augustine's death in Hippo, the city was under siege from the invading Vandals.

| Major Philosophical Writings

The complete Latin writings of Augustine are about the size of a modern encyclopedia. The famous Maurist edition of the *Opera Omnia,* made by the Benedictines of the Abbey of Saint Maur (Paris, 1679), extends to eleven large folio volumes. Four years before his death, Augustine wrote a detailed review of his writings (the *Retractationes*) which covered everything except the *Letters* (of which about 250 are extant) and *Sermons* (of which several hundred are recorded). In the preface to the *Retractations* (literally "retreatment," not "retractions"), he admits that he wrote many works (*multa scripsi*), perhaps too many.[9] And he adds that, besides the works written down by scribes from his dictation, other talks that he gave were copied and not edited by him (*quae dictata non sunt, tamen a me dicta conscripta sunt*). Thus he usually composed orally, and his associates recorded what he said. This may explain why Augustine is among the most voluminous of philosophic writers; he did not have to write laboriously on wax tablets or papyrus.

In the decade before taking charge of the diocese of Hippo (386–96), Augustine produced a number of short works on philosophical and religious subjects. Some of these were dialogues in the style of Cicero. Augustine rejected skepticism in philosophy in *Against the Academics* (*Contra Academicos,* written in 386). The important theme of humanity's universal desire for happiness (mentioned again near the end of our key text from book 10 of the *Confessions*) is debated in the dialogue *The Happy Life* (*De beata vita*). *On Order* (*De ordine*), also written in 386, is a dialogue on the problem of evil and the supervision of the world by divine providence. Order (*ordo*) is a recurrent topic in Augustine's later works, for it covers his way of explaining the relation of physical events and human activities to their ends, a teleological process. The *Soliloquies* (*Soliloquia,* 386/87) record Augustine's nightly meditations at Cassiciacum on the workings of his rational soul in itself and in relation to his body. This is his first formal essay in introspective philosophy. Speaking to his own "reason" (*ratio*) as if it were another person, he explores some of his most private thoughts and feelings. A sequel to the *Soliloquies* is entitled *The Immortality of the Soul* (*De immortalitate animae,* 387). It argues that one's soul lives on forever after the death of its body but, as Augustine remarks in the *Retractations* (1.5): "it [*The Immortality of the Soul*] is very obscure" (*sic obscurus est*), and reading it tires him so much that he is unable to understand the little treatise. Yet it does contain some of the seeds of his later psychology. The development of Augustine's philosophical psychology is also evident in *The Magnitude of the Soul* (*De quantitate animae,* 387/88). It deals with the extent of the dynamic functions of the human soul, through its body, and on the higher level, of rational knowing, willing, and feeling. As giving life to its body, the soul is usually called *anima,* but when performing nonphysical actions, it is called *animus,* which we usually translate as "mind." Evodius discusses these problems of mental activity with Augustine.

A different sort of dialogue involves Augustine and his teenage son, Adeodatus, in their attempt to unravel the relation between teaching and learning. Such a discussion apparently did occur and is recorded in *The Teacher (De magistro,* 389). One of its main points is that the person who teaches does not really put new ideas into the mind of the pupil. Rather, the master serves as a sort of catalyst, or instigator, inducing the learner to reach new insights from the background of his own experiences. Obviously Augustine knew the views of Socrates and Plato on learning, as found in the dialogue *Meno,* even though he obtained this information from Latin authors and not from the original Platonic works. *The Teacher* is a very important source for the study of Augustine's early views on the philosophy of mind and epistemology. It introduces the theory of the divine illumination of the understanding, which we will meet later.

During these preepiscopate years, Augustine had planned to compose textbooks for the study of the seven liberal arts: grammar, rhetoric, and dialectic (the *trivia,* or the three ways to learning); and arithmetic, geometry, astronomy, and musical or poetic theory (the *quadrivium*). He never completed this project (for instance, we have no treatise from him on rhetoric, his specialty), but there is the dialogue *On Music (De musica,* 388–91). An artificial dialogue between master and student, this work devotes its first five books to detailed analyses of poetic speech and song. The structure, metres, verse forms, and rhythms of versification are examined. Then, after an apparent lapse of time, a sixth book was added. Book 6 addresses the problem of how we know the difference between prose and poetry. Do we have a special sense of rhythm? Is there a numerical relation between the parts of a verse? How do we know the basic meaning of numbers? What is the connection between musical tempo and time? We shall see that Augustine's famous "active" theory of sensation is present in the sixth book.

While waiting at the port of Ostia for the return to Africa, Augustine began the last of these philosophical dialogues, *Free Choice of the Will (De libero arbitrio voluntatis,* 388–394/95). It was not finished until after he had become a priest in Africa. He and Evodius begin the dialogue with the great problem of evil: How explain the occurrence of bad events in the world, and particularly of bad decisions and actions of humans if divine providence is overseeing all these things? In its three books, this study of decision making touches on many of the great problems of philosophy.[10] However, Augustine was to develop his own philosophy still further in the great works written during his period as bishop.

Some writings of the early period are primarily religious in orientation, but they contain passages important for the study of Augustine's philosophy. *The Morals of the Catholic Church and of the Manichaeans* (*De moribus catholicae et manichaeorum*, 387/89) and the work *Two Souls, against the Manichaeans* (*De duabus animabus contra manichaeos*, 392/93) offer some contributions to Augustine's early ethics and psychology. Similarly, *The True Religion* (*De vera religione*, 389/91) and *The Profit of Believing* (*De utilitate credendi*, 392) help to clarify his explanation of the relation between faith and reasoned knowledge (*fides* and *scientia*). Another anti-Manichaean work, *On the Nature of the Good* (*De natura boni*, 399–405) returns to the problem of evil and treats it in terms of its relation to goodness and its privations. The suggestion that all goods may be so by participation in one supreme Good stimulates many discussions in medieval philosophy from the time of Boethius (early sixth century).

The most influential works of Augustine start with the writing of the *Confessions* (*Confessionum, libri 13*, 397–401). His critics were already pointing out that, when Augustine left Africa to teach in Rome, he was not even a baptized Christian. Now he had returned, claiming to have been received into the Church in far-away Milan, and after a few years he was made a bishop. The first nine books of the *Confessions* tell the story of the good and bad things in his early life. His frank account has made it one of the most popular autobiographies in the history of world literature. But his aim in writing the *Confessions* was not so much self-justification. Rather, he wanted to show the wonders that divine providence worked for him. After some lapse of time, Augustine wrote book 10, in which he offered a profound analysis of the inner workings of his own consciousness. The section of book 10 that is the selected text printed in the present study is a prime example of Augustine's use of the introspective method, and the eleventh book continues this method to explain time as primarily a mental process. This portion of the *Confessions* is of cardinal importance to the understanding of Augustinian philosophy, for it is the hinge on which the door from his early Platonism opens to the more personal thinking in the great writings of his maturity. The last books of the *Confessions* (11–13) take a surprising turn: they are one of his several attempts to comment on the Old Testament book of Genesis. What is even more astonishing, he never gets beyond the first verses in this biblical account of the origin of the universe. Moses wrote, says Augustine, "In the beginning God created the heavens and the earth."[11] His meditations on this theme in the last three books introduce us to many of the basic ideas in Augustine's understanding of the created world of bodies and spirits.

There have been many attempts to explain the unity of the *Confessions;* on first view, it appears to be an autobiography with an alien appendix added to it. Augustine himself saw it as a hymn of divine praise, as this paragraph from the *Retractations* shows:

> The thirteen Books of my *Confessions* praise the just and good God from both my evil and my good actions and they stimulate (*excitant*) man's understanding and affection for Him. As for me, that is what they did when I was writing them and they still move me when they are read again. What other people think of them is their own affair; yet I know that they have pleased, and still please, many of my brethren. From the first to the tenth Book, they were written about myself: in the three last Books they are about Holy Scripture, from what is written: "In the beginning God created the heavens and earth," until the repose of the Sabbath.[12]

During the years around 400, when he was finishing the *Confessions,* Augustine began to write two other major treatises, one on what the Christians teach about the divine Trinity, and the other on the literal meaning of Genesis. Both writings, while basically religious in content, include important philosophical insights.

The Trinity (*De trinitate, libri 15, 399–419*) deals with that part of Christian doctrine which is a mystery for both believers and non-believers: How is it possible for one supreme God to be three divine Persons? How can one understand the Father, Son, and Holy Spirit? Since we are concerned in the present work with philosophy, not theology, we will not attempt to follow Augustine's explanation of what his Church teaches on this subject. There are, however, many philosophical observations running through all the books of *The Trinity.* In particular, to show how three items may also be one, books 9 to 15 explore many psychological triads within the unity of the soul. Mind, memory, and will (*mens, memoria, voluntas*) are but one of several such psychic trinities. These are viewed as "images" of God within the human spirit. Such data of introspection form the basis for the study of Augustine's mature philosophy of mind. The last books of *The Trinity* were finished in the second decade of the fifth century, when Augustine was in his sixties.

The other philosophically significant work of this period is the *Literal Commentary on Genesis* (*De Genesi ad litteram, libri 12, 401–15*). While Augustine was more interested in the world of the spirit rather than in the realm of physical bodies, and he knew very little about the *Physics* of Aristotle, he was not an idealist in the modern sense; he thought that God had created a really existing physical universe. As a result he treats, in the first eleven books of this treatise, topics such as unformed matter, the nature of light, the seedlike principles of living things (*rationes seminales*), the eternal archetypes (*rationes aeternae*) of all creatures, including all kinds of bodies, and the origin of the human soul. As is frequently the case in Augustine's writings, there is an added final book (12), in which he tries to explain how Paul was rapt up to the third heaven. He examines three levels of "seeing" (*visiones*): the lowest is through the corporeal eyes by sense perception; the second is within the spirit, where one knows by cogitating (*cogitare*) on the images of sense objects; and the third and highest level is intellectual vision, an imageless seeing of immaterial objects, such as the principles of mathematics, and ideals such as truth, justice, and peace (12.6.15–7.16).[13]

By far the longest work of Augustine, the *Expositions of the Psalms* (*Enarrationes in Psalmos*), is probably the least known. Desiderius Erasmus named the work when he edited it for printing in the Renaissance. Originally it had no special name but was simply a collection of meditations, notes, and recorded sermons on the Psalter. When Augustine first became bishop in 394, he began to jot down or dictate his thoughts on these songs of David. This series continued for twenty-five years or more; it would take about six modern volumes to print these *Expositions* (they have not been completely translated into English). Few people have read them all. They touch on practically all the fundamental themes of Augustine's philosophy and theology. We will have occasion to refer to some of them in the commentary below. It is not known precisely when he ceased recording these meditations; possibly it happened around the year 420.[14]

Two other collections include works composed during Augustine's mature years. About two hundred and fifty of his *Letters* (*Epistulae,* 386–430) are preserved in the *Opera Omnia*. Some of these are actually short treatises on philosophical subjects. The important ones are included in the bibliography of Augustine's writings below. There are also the ordinary *Sermons* (*Sermones,* 393–430) that he preached as priest and bishop, not only in the cathedral at Hippo but also in Carthage and many other North African centers. In addition to the 342 sermons printed in the *Opera Omnia,* more than fifty other sermons have been found and edited in recent times. Again, there is no complete English version of all of Augustine's sermons. These "serial" works (*Enarrations, Letters,* and *Sermons*) were not reviewed by Augustine in his *Retractations.*

Several short treatises on moral subjects are of some interest for the history of ethics. Noteworthy are two studies of the evil of telling lies: *On Lying* (*De mendacio,* 395) and *Against Lying, for Consentius* (*Contra mendacium, ad Consentium,* 420–22). Augustine stresses the importance of the intention of the person who lies but insists in both works that there is something objectionable in all lies. Other short works deal with virtues other than the classical four cardinal ones. *On Continence* (*De continentia,* 395); *The Good of Marriage* (*De bono conjugali,* 401); *Holy Virginity* (*De sancta virginitate,* 414); *The Good of Widowhood* (*De bono viduitatis,* 414); *On Patience* (*De patientia,* 418); and *Care for the Dead* (*De cura pro mortuis gerenda,* 421) are discussions of such virtues or states of life. A brief explanation of the theological virtues of faith, hope, and charity is found in *Enchiridion,* written in 421.

Christian Doctrine (*De doctrina christiana,* 396 and 426) was started in the early period, and a fourth book was added some thirty years later. It is significant for its views on teaching and theory of knowledge. Much the same is true of *Instructing the Unlearned* (*De catechizandis rudibus,* 400). The treatise on the Gospel of John (*In Joannis evangelium,* 414–17) has valuable information on the concept of spiritual or intellectual light. *The Origin of the Soul, a Letter* (*De origine animae, Epist* 166, written in 415) deals with a topic that was never completely settled in Augustine's psychology. On the same subject is a longer treatise, *The Soul and Its Origin* (*De anima et ejus origine, libri* 4, 419–20). Another letter, *The Presence of God* (*De praesentia Dei, Epist* 187, written in 417), treats a subject connected with our key text from the *Confessions.* One of Augustine's last writings is *Grace and Free Choice* (*De gratia et libero arbitrio ad Valentinum,* 426–27), in which he again addresses the problem of how free will can be reconciled with divine governance of human actions. A year before he died, Augustine wrote *The Gift of Perseverance* (*De dono perseverantiae,* 428/29).

Finally we come to a work that many regard as Augustine's greatest, the *City of God* (*De civitate Dei, libri* 22, 413–27).[15] In his preface to the first book, Augustine calls it "a big work and difficult" (*magnum opus et arduum*). The *Retractations* (2.43) explains how, after the fall of the city of Rome to the Goths (A.D. 410), many pagan critics attributed a weakening of Roman imperial power to the growth of Christianity. Augustine decided to answer this criticism by writing *City of God.* As early as the year 400, he had described two cities, one of evil people and the other of the holy, now living together in one mixed society but differing in their wills and only to be separated at the last judgment of mankind.[16] What he meant by the difference of wills is clarified in a lengthy passage from the *Literal*

Commentary on Genesis (11.15.20) that contrasts "two loves, the first holy, the second foul; the first social, the second selfish; the first consults the common welfare for the sake of a celestial society, the second grasps at a selfish control for the sake of arrogant domination."

The first five books of the *City of God* treat the early history of the great kingdoms of antiquity, the rise of the Roman Empire with its philosophical ideals. From books 6 through 10, Augustine examines the pagan theology and philosophies of the Greek and Latin thinkers. By far the best of these schools, in his estimation, is that of the Platonists, whom he praises as approaching most closely to the Christian concept of God (7.5). Much of his historical information comes from the encyclopedic work of M. Terentius Varro (116–27 B.C.). It is with book 11 (which attempts another of his partial commentaries on Genesis) that Augustine develops his more personal ideas on the character of the heavenly city as contrasted with the terrestrial city. There is no evidence that he ever contemplated the establishment of a Holy Roman Empire on earth. The last section of the *City of God,* books 18 and 19, are most important for the study of Augustine's philosophy of history and society.

Many of Augustine's writings are concerned with religious controversies that have philosophical overtones. Most of them can be identified easily from their titles. A quick look at the philosophical contents of the four most important of these polemics may be profitable.

For nine years, during his twenties, Augustine was interested in Manichaeanism. He was an "auditor" in this religion while in Carthage and when he first went to Rome. Shortly after his conversion to Catholicism, Augustine began a series of criticisms of the fundamental teachings of Mani.[17] The twenty-two books of Augustine's *Reply to Faustus the Manichaean* (397/98) are quite representative of his views on this religion, which extended its influence as far away as ancient China.

The central teaching of Mani (who was indebted to Gnosticism, Christianity, Zoroastrianism, and possibly Buddhism) held that there was an everlasting struggle between the forces of good and evil. Evil was associated with darkness, and good, with light. Throughout the cosmos, evil powers fought constantly against the good. Within each person, there existed a duality of evil and good wills. As Augustine understood Manichaeanism, each individual had two competing souls. One of his early treatises, the *Two Souls, against the Manichaeans* (392/93), addresses this topic. There was also a sort of illumination of the human mind in the psychology of Mani.

This Manichaean controversy stimulated two things in Augustine's philosophy: a serious consideration of the problem of evil and an increased stress on the unity of the human person. As we have seen, the dialogue *On Order* is one response to Mani's teachings, for much of it is devoted to explaining how divine providence can permit evils, either physical or moral, to occur. Philosophically, Augustine's explanation suggests that sickness and other such bodily ills are really negative defects, or deprivations, in the basic goodness of things. Such evils are not positive entities and require no cause. On the other hand, moral evils are caused by human wills, which are created free to choose lesser or greater goods; otherwise people would not be entitled to credit for good actions. God knows what a person's choices are to be, but He does not force one's will in either way. A quick survey of Augustine's youthful fascination with Manichaeanism is found in the fifth book of the *Confessions* (5.3–7).

The second heresy that Augustine faced was Donatism. This movement within the Christian Church started with a dispute (around A.D. 311) as to who was the real bishop in Carthage. One of the early claimants was named Donatus, and his name was eventually given to the group that challenged the Catholic bishop. Donatism was chiefly an African cult; it lasted for about a hundred years. In Augustine's time, there were roughly the same number of bishops representing Donatism and Catholicism.[18] Since Donatism sprang from an administrative dispute, there were few doctrinal differences between the two groups. There was some dispute about the practice of rebaptism. But, as far as philosophy is concerned, the anti-Donatist writings have little to offer.

Pelagianism, another heresy, occupied much of Augustine's time in his later years. It centered on the influence of divine grace on the freedom of one's will and on God's foreknowledge and predestination. Augustine explains this, when reviewing his dialogue *Free Choice* in the *Retractations* (1.9.3):

> That is why the new heretical Pelagians so describe the will's choice that they leave no place for the grace of God, since they claim that grace is given to us according to our merits; they may not glorify themselves as if I were a supporter of their cause, pretending that in these Books [*Free Choice*] I spoke only in favor of free choice, as the argument in these Books required.

Augustine continues this review by citing many passages from *Free Choice* in which he wrote that human freedom is exercised under the control of divine justice, but at this point in his career there was no need to speak of divine grace. Later, when he read Pelagius' treatise, Augustine wrote *On Nature and Grace* as a reply to the mistaken interpretation of *Free Choice*.[19] Pelagius' *On Nature* is criticized in several of Augustine's later letters (169.13; 177.6; 186.1).

There is no doubt that, as a mature thinker, Augustine tended to stress the role of divine foreknowledge and grace in the governance of people's decisions and moral actions, much more than he had done in his early philosophical dialogues. This does not mean, however, that the older Augustine became a supporter of moral determinism. He always insisted that people were free agents.[20] The Pelagian controversy thus contributed to the development of Augustine's psychology.

A fourth movement in Christianity that Augustine opposed in his final years was Arianism. Earlier he did not pay much attention to it, although Arianism was known to Augustine as early as his Milan period, for there were followers of Arius (fourth century) at the Milanese imperial court. It was just three years before his death that Augustine confronted an Arian bishop, Maximinus, who accompanied the Gothic army that ravaged North Africa and eventually set siege to Hippo. The elderly Augustine engaged in unsatisfactory debate with Maximinus and also with another Arian layman, Count Pascentius.[21] Several of Augustine's last letters *(Epist* 238–42) treat these meetings. There is also a record of the debate with Maximinus and a *Reply to Maximinus the Arian Bishop* (written in 428).

The dispute centered on the divine Trinity. Arius had taught that the Son, second Person of the Trinity, was not equal to the Father. It became a question of whether the Son is of the same substance (*homoöusios*) as the Father. The meaning of *ousia* (Greek for entity or substance) continued to be debated between representatives of the Greek Church and Latin-speaking theologians. Also the meaning of person (*persona*) in the Trinity was critical to the polemic with the Arians. There are brief mentions of such problems in the *Treatise on John's Gospel,* but, on the whole, this Arian dispute did not greatly influence the philosophy of Augustine.

In a sense, the *City of God* is a long critique of the theology of paganism. But, as Gerald Bonner remarks, this pantheistic religion was a "dying cult" in Augustine's time.[22] Porphyry had tried to revitalize pagan theology in the third Christian century; Augustine criticized him severely in the tenth book of the *City of God* (chaps. 21–30). However, this polemic made no important contribution to Augustinian philosophy.

From the foregoing survey of Augustine's writings, one can gather that his works are so extensive and diversified that no single treatise can represent his entire philosophy. But the interiorism of his introspective method runs through all his writings. That is why the key text to be studied below is chosen from the tenth book of his

Confessions. His profound analysis of the mind as memory in that text not only shows what his thoughts and feelings were around the year 400; it also recalls his earlier philosophizing and looks forward to the perfecting of his thinking on the bodily world, the human soul, the nature of society, and what little one can know about the source of all wisdom.

I NOTES

1. Augustine, *Confessions,* trans. V. J. Bourke (New York: Fathers of the Church, Inc., 1953), 3.4.7; See also *The Happy Life,* where he says: "From the age of nineteen, having read in the school of rhetoric that book of Cicero's called *Hortensius,* I was inflamed by such a great love of philosophy that I considered devoting myself to it at once" (4).

2. M. Müller gathered these fragments in a reconstituted edition, Ciceronis, *Hortensius,* in *Opera Omnia,* vol. 4 (Leipzig: Teubner, 1890).

3. See Maurice Testard, *Saint Augustin et Cicéron* (Paris: Etudes Augustiniennes, 1958), 1:20–34. Peter Brown, *Augustine of Hippo: A Biography* (Berkeley and Los Angeles: University of California Press, 1967), 40–41, relates this reading to Augustine's future career; see also A. Solignac, "Notes Complémentaires," in *Les Confessions,* BA, vol. 13 (Paris: Desclée de Brouwer, 1962), 667–68.

4. Many details on Augustine's early life are found in the first nine books of the *Confessions.* There is no evidence that Augustine was called "Aurelius" by his contemporaries, as is sometimes stated; none of his correspondents so address him.

5. See H. T. Weiskotten, ed. and trans., *Sancti Augustini vita scripta a Possidio* (Princeton, N.J.: Princeton University Press, 1918); a more recent translation is in FOC, vol. 15 (1952).

6. Information on Augustine's life as a bishop is found in his *Letters* and *Sermons* (especially *Serm* 355 and 356). In spite of his association with the Greek-speaking Bishop Valerius, Augustine never fully mastered the Greek language; see Gerald Bonner, *St. Augustine of Hippo: Life and Controversies* (Philadelphia, Pa.: The Westminster Press, 1963), 394–95.

7. An excellent study of Augustine's many travels is Othmar Perler, *Les voyages de saint Augustin* (Paris: Etudes Augustiniennes, 1969).

8. For the episcopal period, consult F. Van der Meer, *Augustine the Bishop,* trans. B. Battershaw (London: Sheed & Ward, 1961).

9. *Retractationes,* "Prologue," 2; and *Conf* 3.4.7.

10. At the advice of Etienne Gilson, Richard McKeon selected book 2 of *De libero arbitrio* as typical of Augustine's philosophy for his *Selections from Medieval Philosophy* (New York: Charles Scribners, 1925), 1:11–64. Three questions are addressed in book 2: By what reason is it manifest that God exists? Are all goods from God? Is free choice one of these goods?

11. "Let me hear and understand how in the beginning Thou didst make heaven and earth" (*Conf* 11.3.5).

12. *Retr* 2.6; my translation is intentionally very literal.

13. For a more thorough analysis of the philosophical content of *De Genesi ad litteram,* see V. J. Bourke, "God and the Created World," chap. 12 of *Augustine's Quest of Wisdom* (Milwaukee, Wis.: Bruce, 1945).

14. In his "Introduction Générale" to the works of Augustine, BA, 1:109, Fulbert Cayré dated the *Enarrationes* A.D. 391–420. But Perler says

that the chronology of these expositions is not settled (*Les voyages,* 247, notes 1 and 4).

15. Of the many introductions to the *City of God,* one of the best is John O'Meara, *Charter of Christendom: The Significance of the City of God* (New York: Macmillan, 1961); see also my analysis in "God and Society," chap. 13 of *Augustine's Quest,* 248–84.

16. "Duae . . . civitates, una iniquorum altera sanctorum . . . in die vero judicii separandae" (*Instructing the Unlearned* 19.31).

17. The most useful survey of these religious polemics is Bonner, *St. Augustine of Hippo,* but he does not pay much attention to philosophical content. See also Brown, *Augustine of Hippo,* 46–60, 212–25, 340–52.

18. For a more complete study, see W. H. C. Frend, *The Donatist Church* (Oxford: Blackwell, 1952).

19. "So there came into my hands the book of a certain Pelagius, in which he defends the nature of man with as much argument as possible, against the grace of God, whereby the impious are treated with justice and we stand as Christians" (*Retr* 2.42).

20. Cf. G. W. Forell, *History of Christian Ethics* (Minneapolis, Minn.: Augsburg Publishing House, 1979), 1:162–68.

21. On these debates see Bonner, 141–46.

22. Bonner, 140.

| **Background and Methodology**

Western philosophy took its origin from the quarrel between faith and reason in ancient Greece. From the time of Thales (6th century B.C.) on, the myths of Hesiod and Homer were challenged by those who demanded factual data and rational explanations. But it is also the case that religious tenets have nearly always influenced philosophers, either positively or negatively. In the case of Augustine, it is evident that he reacted against the cosmic dualism in the religion of Mani. It is also clear that Augustine was positively influenced by parts of both the Old and the New Testaments. He also owed a great deal to earlier philosophers who were neither in the Judaic nor the Christian traditions.

| Background of Augustinian Thinking

Old Testament influences on Augustine's philosophy primarily stemmed from two books. Genesis stimulated his thinking on the absolute origin of the universe from no material cause and directed his thinking to the role of light in both the physical and the immaterial world. The Psalms attracted Augustine by their literary and emotional appeal.[1] Perhaps their greatest philosophical impact was on his ethical and social views. The notion of high-minded love, of both God and His creatures (charity, *caritas*) and the concept of mercy are but two of many insights from the Psalms that tempered the rationalism of Greek and Latin moralists. Of course, the theme of two societies—one good, the other evil—runs throughout the Psalms (Ps. 17, 44, 85), as the *City of God* (17.16) shows.

Although Augustine wrote commentaries on several parts of the New Testament, he was most impressed by the opening lines of the Gospel of John: "In the beginning was the Word (*verbum, logos*), the Word was with God and the Word was God" (*Prologue,* 1:1). This again turned Augustine's attention to the problem of the origin of the universe and its creation by God. Moreover, he saw here some relation between the concept of the creative mind of God (the Word, *Ars Dei*) and the Platonic theory of an immaterial world of exemplary ideals or forms. We shall see that it is not too much of a simplification to suggest that Augustine put Plato's Ideal Forms into the mind of the Creator; and they became the eternal principles (*rationes aeternae*) of all parts of creation.

A few lines later in this gospel, Augustine read: "The Word was the true light (*erat lumen verum*) that enlightens all men." Together with the Old-Testament stress on light as the principle giving form to matter—as well as the frequent references in Greek and Latin philosophy to light as an aid to understanding—this verse from John inspired Augustine to work out his teaching on the light of the mind and the theory of divine illumination.

There is no formal philosophy in the books of sacred Scripture, but, as the noted historian of Christian philosophy Etienne Gilson has remarked, they "have been a constant object of meditation and of intellectual elucidation" for thinkers throughout the Middle Ages.[2] As a precursor of medieval philosophy, Augustine quite obviously gleaned many insights from his study of Scripture.

Ancient Greek philosophy was known to Augustine chiefly through his reading of Latin digests and quotations. He was taught some Greek in elementary school, but he never liked the language.[3] He does not seem to have read the original philosophical writings from Greece. From writers such as Cicero and Varro, he knew the major themes of the *Meno, Republic,* and *Timaeus* of Plato. But there is no evidence that he ever saw the texts of these dialogues, either in Greek or Latin. Yet Augustine wrote that "of the pupils of Socrates, Plato was so remarkable for his brilliance that he deservedly outshone all the rest."[4]

In an important letter (#118), written in 410 to a young Greek student who had asked several questions about Cicero's philosophy, Augustine gave the same high rating to the teachings of Plato and his followers.[5] Using the divisions of philosophy commonly found in ancient writings, Augustine says in this letter that the Platonists, in their ethical view of the good life, place the highest good in God. Those in the Platonic Academy who taught this, he says, are Archesilaus, Polemon, and Xenocrates. They were also the best thinkers in the philosophy of nature and in rational philosophy and showed a true understanding of the human person. As for the Presocratics, they were too materialistic—Anaximenes talking about air as identical with God; Anaxagoras taking mind (*mens, nous*) as the first source of all things; Democritus thinking that little pictures (*imagines*) of sense objects flow into our minds (*Letter* 118.23–27). Even the Epicureans limited reality to bodily atoms (28).

For several centuries before and during the time of Augustine, the two most popular schools of philosophy were Stoicism and Epicureanism. Although Augustine knew little of the original writings of these schools, he had a general knowledge of what they taught. Epicurean philosophy, with its theory of atoms as indivisible particles of matter, its epistemology of sense perception, and its hedonistic ethics, found little favor with Augustine. On the other hand, he recognized that, apart from its materialistic outlook, Stoicism (as represented by Seneca, for instance) had a good deal of respect for rational inquiry, a proper attitude toward the control of human emotions (love, hate, fear, and sorrow), and a commendable view of the happy life as a steadfastness of spirit depending on some ideals superior to human consciousness.[6]

Works such as the *Tusculan Disputations* and *De officiis* of Cicero were part of the advanced studies that Augustine did at Carthage. Varro's encyclopedic writings (now mostly nonextant) offered historical surveys and digests of philosophic authors. However, except for the short logical treatise *The Categories,* which he read as a student,[7] Augustine knew none of the works of Aristotle. For many centuries before and after Augustine, Aristotelian writings were not available to Western scholars; it was only in the twelfth century that they came to medieval Latin readers. Some indirect knowledge of Aristotelian psychology filtered through the Neoplatonists of the Hellenistic period (Plotinus and Porphyry), but Augustine made little use of it.

While he was teaching in Milan, Augustine met a group of scholars who shared an interest in Neoplatonism. Bishop Ambrose and the priest Simplicianus discussed this spiritual type of philosophy with others in Milan. Through them, Augustine heard of the writings and thought of Marius Victorinus, the fourth-century rhetorician and translator of parts of the *Enneads* of Plotinus and several treatises by Porphyry. These are the Platonists of whom he speaks favorably in his early dialogues, throughout the *Confessions,* and, in fact, in all his major works.

Like Augustine, Plotinus (circa A.D. 204–70) was a native of North Africa, but he came from the far eastern coast. He was born in Egypt and educated at Alexandria, the center for centuries of Greek culture and learning. Eventually Plotinus established his school of philosophy at Rome. His talks and discussions were recorded in Greek and edited by his pupil Porphyry (A.D. 232–301). These are in six books of nine chapters each (the *Enneads* or *Nines*). Fascinated with the religions of the Far East but well acquainted with

the great works of Plato and Aristotle, Plotinus perfected one of
the first introspective philosophies. One of his reasons for turning
inward was his partial blindness. More immediately, Plotinus
was influenced by the Jewish-Hellenistic teacher Philo of Alexandria (25 B.C. to circa A.D. 40).

Plotinus' metaphysics had three levels. At the top was the One,
a perfect unity unblemished by any attributes. It is debatable
whether Plotinus thought of the One as personal; sometimes he
called it "He" and spoke of it somewhat as Christians (whom he
knew) talked about God. The One took thought and thus emanated
to the next level, that of Intelligence (*nous*), which is also called
Logos (reason or word). A third and bottom level comes from the
emanation of a greater multiplicity called Soul (*psyche*), a cosmic
spirit resembling the World-Soul of Plato's *Timaeus*. Obviously
these emanations (spreadings-out) describe a process from complete
unity to a many. Beneath the World-Soul, at its lowest level, is the
world of bodies, where unity is almost dissipated. Material things
have almost no goodness in them, as Plotinus saw them. Sensing
them is not a profitable way of knowing reality. In the short *Life of
Plotinus,* written by Porphyry, the opening sentence is: "Plotinus
our contemporary philosopher seemed to be ashamed of existing in a
body."[8] Since emanation from the One is also a descent from good to
evil, the unsystematic ethics of Plotinus urges the soul's freeing of
itself from bodily attachments and returning in a mental ascent to
the One.[9] Evidently Augustine retained many of the teachings of
Plotinus.

Of the Greek and Latin Christian writers who preceded Augustine, most were concerned with religious and social issues. The early
Christian writers are quoted by Augustine, but they contributed
little to his philosophy.[10] Apart from Bishop Ambrose of Milan and
Simplicianus (whose Neoplatonic influence has been mentioned),
Augustine's most important immediate Christian predecessor was
Marius Victorinus. An African like Augustine, Victorinus started a
school of rhetoric in Rome about the year 340, some forty years before Augustine did. Around 355, Victorinus was baptized as a Christian; the story of his public baptism made a deep impression on
Augustine at Milan.[11] As he says in the *Confessions* (8.5.10): "I
burned to imitate him." It was chiefly from Victorinus' translations
that Augustine learned of the spiritual introspectionism of the
Neoplatonists.

| Augustine's Basic Philosophical Views

What Augustine gleaned from this background was not a system of
philosophy. Rather, his thinking moved from one insight to another,

often with disconcerting changes of theme. He used the rhetorical device called the *excursus,* a sudden switch to a different topic with the intention of eventually returning to the original theme. Because of this, any attempt at presenting his views in an organized, logically developed system of philosophy is doomed to end in distortion. Augustine's notion of "order" (*ordo*), which we will see in operation later, places some stress on symmetry but great emphasis on using a variety of inner discoveries in order to reach a desired end. In other words, order for Augustine is chiefly a teleological rather than a spatial balance. With this in mind, our present sketch of key points in Augustine's philosophy will cover five characteristic themes.

❙ Believing and Understanding

In the Septuagint version of Isaiah (7:9) Augustine read: "Unless you will have believed, you will not understand" (*nisi credideritis, non intellegetis*). This text inspired Augustine to work out a long-lasting explanation of the relation between faith and reasoned knowledge. He thought that one cannot offer proof for all personal convictions; there must be some starting points that are things accepted as true before reasoning can begin. Out of this developed the famous slogan of patristic and medieval thought, "faith seeking understanding" (*fides quaerens intellectum*).[12]

To believe, in Augustine's meaning of the term, is to assent on the basis of some authority to something that is not clearly evident. In the first of his dialogues (*Order* 2.9.26), he wrote, "With regard to the acquiring of knowledge (*scientia*), we are of necessity led in a twofold manner: by authority and by reason."[13] One accepts, for instance, the fact that two particular persons are one's parents (*Profit of Believing* 11.25); yet this is based on the credibility of witnesses such as midwives, nurses, and other attendants at birth (ibid. 11.26). All the facts of history before our time are accepted by faith in human testimony. Other items of belief are assented to on the basis of divine authority as grasped through the Scriptures and reliable interpreters.

Understanding (*intellectus*), on the other hand, is achieved through reason (*ratio*). There are two functions of human reason, as Augustine sees it. One is more properly called ratiocination (*ratiocinatio*), the process of discursively searching for (*inquisitio*) knowledge; the other is reason considered as the mind looking at (*mentis aspectus*) some object clearly seen by understanding.[14] Intuitive reason may look upward (*ratio superior*) to eternal truths or downward (*ratio inferior*) to what little is understandable in the physical world of change.[15] Much of the twelfth book of *The Trinity* is devoted to the distinction between knowledge (*scientia*) and wisdom (*sapientia*). Looking upward, the soul sees something of the immutable truths of mathematics, logic, morality, and religion. As retained by the consciousness, these verities constitute the partial wisdom that can be attained in this life. Augustine looked forward to the more perfect wisdom of the blessed souls (*beati*) in heaven. The downward gaze of the mind discovers and judges the things and events in the bodily world. The result of this is knowledge, a less perfect type of understanding that enables humans to regulate their actions and lives.[16] Augustinian wisdom is not only a cognitive quality of mind; it is also a volitional habit inclining its possessor to act rightly when faced with moral problems.

❙ Introspective Method: Interiorism

Augustine's way of doing philosophy involves a turning away (*aversio*) from distractions of sense experience to the inner actions and data of one's own consciousness, eventually rising within the mind to the realm of eternal truth. We will see much about this in reading our selected text from the *Confessions*. This was the methodology of Plotinus and other Neoplatonists, but Augustine personalized it in the light of his own experiences and religious convictions.

As A. C. Pegis has observed, there are two kinds of introspection, two "interiorisms" at work here:

> *There is the explicit interiorism born of Christian wisdom,* based on the primacy and the dynamism of supernatural faith and love. Out of its very nature this interiorism impels the soul towards the vision of God. . . . *But there is also in Augustinianism the implicit but equally real Plotinian interiorism,* born of a Platonic metaphysics and a Platonic conception of man and intended as a method by means of which the soul may discover progressively its own divinity as well as its divine prerogatives. It is from this second interiorism, *and not from the first,* that Augustinian thought has produced in the course of its history many celebrated and embattled doctrines.[17]

The italic emphasis in the above was inserted by Pegis (himself Greek-American and partly educated in Greece), with a fine feeling for the nuances of Platonism).

The philosophy of this second psychological interiorism underlies even the theological teaching of Augustine. But we find an almost pure example of it in one of Augustine's earliest letters (7, to Nebridius) written in 388/89, before he became a priest. Here he offered a purely philosophical account of the role of images in memory. Nebridius, Augustine's former student, had written (*Epist* 6, in Augustine's letters) asking whether Augustine thought that everything in memory came from images (*phantasiae*). Augustine's reply is negative:

Your thinking is that there is nothing in memory that is not connected with images but I think differently (*ego aliud existimo*). We must understand that not all things that we remember are from the past, some continue on into the present and future (*manentia*). When I remember my father who is dead I depend on an image from the past but my memory of Carthage is of something that still exists.

Later in this letter (sect. 4 and 5) Augustine distinguishes three kinds of presentations in memory: there are the images of things seen in the past; second, images of constructs of the imagination (mythological persons, for instance); and third, the "imaginations" (*imaginationes*) of numbers, geometrical figures, and many things learned in liberal-arts studies, things that the young Augustine hesitates to call images; rather they are presentations—internal data—of memory. Both Nebridius and Augustine are, at this time, obviously influenced by the Platonic theory of reminiscence. But the theory is based on the idea that thoughts are retained from a previous life on earth, which, as Christians, neither of them can now accept. This letter helps us to understand something of what Augustine's introspective method was like. In the two following letters, he and Nebridius turned to speculations on the interpretation of dreams.

The *Soliloquies,* in which Augustine records his nocturnal meditations at Cassiciacum, has Reason (*Ratio*) questioning Augustine, which shows some of the working of introspection during his early years. Actually, all of the dialogues written before the *Confessions* display this tendency to examine inner mental data.

Apart from the *Confessions,* among the later major treatises, *The Trinity* offers the most striking evidence of psychological interiorism. Books 1 to 7 provide an exposition of what Augustine sees as the Catholic doctrine on the divine Trinity. Without going into theological details here, we may summarize that Catholics believe that there is only one God, with three divine Persons, the Father, the Son, and the Holy Spirit. Whatever these Persons are, they are not three different Gods. Augustine admits, throughout *The Trinity,* that this is a mystery; it is impossible for the human mind, in this life, to grasp the Trinity's full meaning. However, starting with book 8 and continuing through 15, he makes a valiant effort to find some "trinities" in ordinary human experience that might offer partial and remote analogies of the divine Trinity.

For instance, Augustine finds three factors in the act of loving: the lover, that which is loved, and the love that unites them (*Trin* 8.10.14). Particularly when the object loved is the supreme Good (God), this triad does seem to show a faint "image" of divine threeness in One. But it is not a very good comparison, only a vestige. For one thing, the love triad contains one substance (the lover, a human mind) that is distinct from another substance (God). So Augustine tries another analysis of loving: the mind as lover, itself as object of self-love, and the combining love (*Trin* 9.2.2). Again, this is not quite satisfactory, for the mind (*mens*) must *know* itself in order to love itself. He turns next to another psychic triad: mind, love (*amor*), and knowledge (*notitia*). This cannot mean, as Augustine sees it, that the knowledge and love are "accidents" (in the sense of Aristotelian categories) of the mind-substance (9.4.4). He explains (9.4.6) that knowledge and love seem each to exist substantially (*substantialiter*), and this could not be true of the divine Persons: they are not distinct substances.[18]

In the tenth book of *The Trinity*, Augustine explores more carefully how the soul knows itself (10.3.5–7.9), and he finds that this requires it to be present to itself. (The Latin word *praesentia* means both "presence," that is, being with something in space or some other medium, and "present," that is, being with something in an instant of time or other duration.) This leads to a penetrating examination of what Augustine calls memory (*memoria*), a present awareness of many contents of one's mind: learning, understanding, recalling, recognizing, feeling, suffering. (This is a reprise of the lengthy essay on memory that he had written some fifteen or more years earlier in the tenth book of the *Confessions,* which we will examine later.) Among the things that Augustine finds in the treasure-house (*thesaurus*) of his memory are the eternal principles (*rationes aeternae*) that the divinely enlightened mind discovers at the peak of its consciousness (*Trin* 10.10.14). Here he makes a discovery (*inventio,* literally a coming-into) that the "interior man" is a unity of three functions: knowing, retaining, and willing (*mens, memoria, voluntas*). The same one soul (*animus*) is cognitive, retentive, and dynamic. This interior psychic triad brings one as close as is possible for human understanding to reach up to the divine exemplar, the creative ideal (*ratio aeterna*) of humanity, and of each individual human soul. These three psychic features are beyond doubt: "If one doubts, then one is alive (*si dubitat, vivit*) and to be alive as an immaterial being is to remember, to understand, to will, to think, to know, and to judge who may be doubting" (*Vivere se tamen et meminisse, et intelligere, et velle, et cogitare, et scire, et judicare quis dubitet*).[19]

One of the closest analogies, then, to the divine Trinity is the unity of knowing, retaining, and willing (*mens, memoria et voluntas*). "The mind of man we have discovered (*reperiebamus*)," Augustine says, "reaching its peak in the trinity of memory and understanding and willing." This conclusion of book 10 of *The Trinity* (12.19) is recapitulated in the last book (15.12.15), where the psychic triad is said to resemble remotely the divine triad of eternity (*aeternitas*), wisdom (*sapientia*), and beatitude (*beatitudo*). And these three unite in divine Wisdom, which is God (15.6.9). Thus introspection into the most intimate recesses of the human mind enables Augustine to approach, if not fully attain, the wisdom he had so long sought.

| Five Axioms on Causality

The term *causa* has many meanings for Augustine, and he often uses the word *ratio* (reason) where English writers would say "cause." Moreover, he does not seem to be familiar with the Aristotelian description of four causes (material, formal, efficient, and final). Yet Augustine has a theory of causality that owes a good deal to Plotinian metaphysics. It will be outlined here under five statements that are axiomatic in the sense that they assume immediate agreement as soon as they are understood.

A. *Every cause is efficient and every efficient is greater than its product.* This summarizes what Augustine says in several sentences. One of the questions that Simplicianus proposed to Augustine was: "Why did God will to make the world?"[20] We may quote Augustine's brief but important answer:

> The person who asks why God willed to make the world is asking for the cause (*causam*) of the will of God. Now every cause is efficient (*omnis causa efficiens est*). And every efficient is greater than what is produced (*majus est quam id quod efficitur*). But nothing is greater than the will of God. So its cause must not be sought (*non ergo ejus causa quaerenda est*).

It is clear that, for Augustine as for most modern thinkers, the primary sort of cause is productive. As J. A. Beckaert comments on this answer, Augustine does not exclude the fact that there is a purpose, a final cause, for creating the world, "but above all in the case of God this purpose is not distinct from the thinking and willing of God."[21] This brings us to our second summary axiom.

B. *Nothing is greater than the will of God: the cause of divine willing must not be sought.* Here we have the second part of Augustine's answer in question 28 (*83 Q*). Augustinian thinking is theocentric: it concentrates on God for the ultimate answer to all causal questions. If there were some cause higher than God, then that higher cause would be God. This is but one aspect of divine omnipotence (*City* 5.9). As the *Enchiridion* (26.100) puts it in simple words: "From the point of view of sinners, they are doing what God does not will," but from God's perspective, "they can do nothing against the divine will, because of God's omnipotence." This is more fully explained in the last book of the *City of God* (22.2), which begins with this sentence: "It is true that wicked men do many things contrary to God's will, but so great is His wisdom and power, that all things that seem adverse to His purpose do still tend towards those just and good ends and issues which He Himself has foreknown." Similarly, the attribute of divine immutability (which we encounter in *Confessions* 10.25.36) entails the conclusion that nothing can produce a change in God.

C. *Every event* (coming into or going out of existence, or changing) *must stem from an efficient cause.* Augustine thought that every product requires a producer; this is a universalization of the principle of efficient causality. As expressed in the *City of God* (5.9), "If the order (*ordo*) of things is certain, then the order of causes (*ordo causarum*) is certain; for nothing can be done (*non enim fieri potest*) that has not been preceded by an efficient cause." All created causes are secondary, deriving their power from the one primary Cause, God (*Trin* 3.9.16). As we read there:

> It is one thing to establish and administer creation from that innermost and highest turning-point (*cardine*) of all causes, because He Who does this is God, the only Creator. And it is a different thing extrinsically to bring about (*admovere*) some activity by virtue of the powers and capacities that He has distributed, so that at this time or that, in one way or another, some creature puts in its appearance. All these, in fact, have already been created originally and primordially in the texture of the elements. They appear when conditions are appropriate. For, just as mothers are pregnant with their unborn children, so is this world pregnant with the causes of things to be born. These are created in it only by that highest essential Being (*ab illo summa essentia*) in which there is neither origination nor termination, neither coming into existence nor going out of it (*nec incipit esse, nec desinit*).[22]

D. *No thing can fashion itself (formare seipsum), since nothing is able to give itself what it does not have.* This may seem to be a statement of formal causality, since the Latin uses the verb *formare* (*Free* 2.17.45). But the discussion of "formation" is expressed in terms of putting forms, or perfections, into things, which is a function of efficient cause. The sentence before the axiom quoted above gives this alternative explanation: whatever the thing is, if it already has a perfection (*formam*), then it does not need to get what it already has; and if, in fact, it does not have this perfection, then it cannot get from itself what it does not possess.

As Augustine sees it, there is no such thing as a cause of itself. God is not self-caused, since He neither comes into being, nor is He subject to change.

E. *Higher reality may move the lower, but the lower thing cannot move what is higher*. An axiom for this universal language does not appear, to my knowledge, in Augustine's writings. Yet it is at work throughout his philosophy. This view is typical of Plotinus' meta-physics, and Augustine takes it as self-evident. Augustine's active theory of sensation, found in *Music* (6.5.9–10), maintains that, in perceiving sense objects, the soul is not moved or impressed by some physical stimulus; rather the soul, or conscious mind, is on the alert for any changes in its body and, when such a bodily change occurs, the soul makes an image or record of it. This activity of the soul is the sensation. Similarly, if anything is done in the soul by an external cause, that event must be caused by a higher reality, God. We will examine this theory of sensation later.

The view that created souls cannot cause any change in a higher reality is, of course, based on the attribution of immutability to God. We will discuss this further when we come to the three levels of reality in Chapter Three.

| Importance of Order and Teleology

In the *City of God* we find this definition: "Order (*ordo*) is an arrangement of like and unlike things whereby each of them is disposed to its proper place." This was the classical notion of symmetry. Many years before Augustine wrote this, he had edited the dialogue *On Order*, in which his young interlocutor, Licentius, brought out a more specific feature of order (1.5.14–6.15). With Augustine's approval, Licentius stated, first of all, that God governs all things in an orderly way (*cuncta ordine administrare*). They had been discussing the problem of evil in the world and in human behavior. Licentius pointed to the many instances of symmetry and balance in all levels of nature; this is a sort of spatial ordering of parts in a whole. But there is another level of order, they agreed, where a succession of events leads to a desired good or goal (*quam ratis successionibus in nodos suos;* see *Order* 1.5.14). This kind of teleological order is used by human minds managing a series of actions to produce a certain result. But purposive order is best instantiated in God's governance of the whole universe (ibid. 6.15). Augustine comments on his student's perceptiveness and adds that, just as error has a cause and may be included in a series of causes with a good result, so is evil permitted by God as eventually serving to produce some important good or truth (ibid. 7.18). One person's evil is often another's good.

A passage in the *Morals of the Manichaeans* (7.9) relates the concept of order to perseverance in existing being (*manentia*). "To be means to persevere" (*esse enim ad manendum refertur*), Augustine writes; not all change is bad, but that which changes for the worse does not persevere. It becomes defective in being (*sed quia pervetebatur in pejus, id est ab essentia deficiebat*). Not remaining constant in the ongoing process of existing also involves a turning away (*aversio* or *perversio*) from moral goodness. This is explained as the text continues:

> Some things change for the better and thereby they tend to continue in existence. Nor by this sort of change are they said to be perverted, rather to be reverted and converted. Now perversion is the contrary of being orderly. In fact those beings that tend onward in existence (*quae tendunt esse*) also tend onward in order (*ad ordinem tendunt*). And to attain it is to attain the fullness of being (*ipsum esse*), to the extent that any creature can do so. For order leads to a kind of agreement with that which orders. And to be in existence is to be one.

This notion of purposive order runs through much of Augustine's thinking. We will see it working in the *Confessions,* where he speaks of "this very beautiful order of things which are very good" (*iste ordo pulcherrimus rerum valde bonarum*) (13.35.50).

I Absolute Origin of the Universe

All of Augustine's philosophical explanations eventually focus on God. We see this clearly in his discussions of the beginning of the whole universe. Theocentrism is an important part of his methodology.

In the twentieth century, scientists and philosophers are still debating how this universe, as we now know it, first came into existence. The best-known of contemporary theories is the "big bang" theory, whereby all substance originated from one giant explosion, and the resulting primitive "stuff" evolved over millions of years into the many different kinds of living and nonliving things that fill our world today.

Strangely enough, Augustine would not necessarily have rejected the Darwinian theory of evolution, had he known it. Several scholars have regarded him as an evolutionist.[23] In a book generally critical of answering all cosmic problems by reference to evolution, Etienne Gilson commented that "Augustine and his school understood that everything that ever had been, or would be, had been created under a latent form. . . . Since everything that developed came from that, we have here a true doctrine of e-volution, understood in its natural sense of the un-rolling of something already given."[24]

The point is that Augustine tried to find the original source of that primitive stuff from which things in their present species may have developed. Particularly in his several commentaries on Genesis, he continually pointed out that, if the start is from absolutely nothing, then nothing can be caused or developed. All things and events in the universe are caused. So Augustine's major question is: What caused the whole universe? His answer begins with the initial belief that an uncaused cause, God, made all creatures from nothing. How he came to understand this belief, in a philosophical way, is shown in an answer to question 46, in the *Eighty-three Different Questions*.[25] First, he gives a short account of Plato's ideal forms. "But if we call them 'reasons' (*rationes*)," he says, "we are departing from a strict translation: reasons are called *logoi* in Greek and not Ideas." Yet, to call them eternal reasons in the creative mind of God is "not far from their true meaning."[26] Augustine also knew that the Stoics had a theory of seedlike reasons (*logoi spermatikoi*), which was a source for his seminal reasons (*rationes seminales*).

Thus Augustine thought that the only possible ultimate cause of the universe had to be a Being that existed above the world of change, uncaused and eternal. That is God. For a short popular argument for God as creator, Augustine's *Sermon* on Matthew 11:25–26 is recommended. He points out that, just as any person in the church building where he is preaching could see that its intricate design came from the mind of a human architect, so anyone examining the world should be able to understand that it came from the mind of a supreme architect. Of course, this is an early formulation of what came to be called the argument for God's existence "from design."

These, then, are some of the principles (*principia*) or general starting points from which Augustine's philosophy flows. In the next section we will examine some more specific but basic insights in this sort of philosophy.

| NOTES

1. For Augustine's praise of the Psalms, see *City* 17.15–22.

2. Cf. E. Gilson, *History of Christian Philosophy in the Middle Ages* (New York: Random House, 1955), 3–6.

3. *Conf* 1.14.23: "Why, then, did I hate Greek literature . . . ?" A few lines later Augustine remarks on "the real difficulty of a foreign tongue." It appears, however, that Augustine improved his knowledge of Greek after the year 400; see Paul Henry, *Plotin et l'Occident* (Louvain, 1934), 133–37.

4. *City* 8.4, Doubleday Image edition, 148; also in BW 2:104, where Augustine's review of Plato's philosophy, here, runs from chap. 4 to 14.

5. *Epist* 118.15–18; FOC, vol. 18.

6. These judgments on the Stoics and Epicureans are sharply expressed in *Serm* 150 (PL 38:807–14), which is no. 14 in Quincy Howe's translation (*Selected Sermons of St. Augustine* [New York: Holt, Rinehart and Winston, 1966]).

7. See *Conf* 4.16.28, where Augustine says that he understood the meaning of the categories of substance and its nine accidents without the aid of any teacher. Actually this had little influence on his later thought.

8. Porphyry's *Life of Plotinus* is printed at the front of most editions of the *Enneads*. The critical edition is P. Henry and H-R Schwyzer, eds., *Plotini Opera*, 3 vols. (Paris: Desclée de Brouwer, 1951); English versions are Plotinus, *The Enneads*, trans. S. MacKenna and B. S. Page, 3d ed. (London: Faber & Faber, 1962); and trans. A. H. Armstrong, Loeb Classical Library, 7 vols. (London-New York: Heinemann-Harvard University Press, 1966–88).

9. For details and bibliography on Plotinian ethics, see Bourke, *History of Ethics*, 40–44.

10. On Augustine's predecessors, see Gilson, *History of Christian Philosophy*, 11–52; and Forell, *History of Christian Ethics*, 1:33–92.

11. For what Augustine says about Victorinus, see *Conf* 8.2–5.

12. Anselm's twelfth-century *Proslogion* is subtitled "Fides quaerens intellectum." Anselm has been called "another Augustine" (*alter Augustinus*). For one of Augustine's many citations of Isa. 7:9, see *Free Choice* 2.2.6.

13. Augustine's early refutation of skepticism, *Against the Academics*, 3.20.43, says: "Certainly no one doubts that we are impelled toward knowledge by a twofold force: that of authority and the force of reason." Cf. *Order* 2.9.26.

14. Speaking of discursive reason (*ratiocinatio*) and intuitive reason (*ratio*), Augustine says: "*Quare ista opus est ad quaerendum, illa ad videndum*" (*Soul* 27.63).

15. On the upward and downward gaze of the mind, see *Trin* 12.3.3; and at 12.7.10, he writes: "As we have said concerning the nature of the human mind (*humanae mentis*), when it devotes itself totally to the contemplation of truth, it is an image of God . . . but when it turns its attention wholly to lower actions (*inferiora agenda*), it is not an image of God."

16. For key texts on the difference between wisdom and knowledge see J. A. Mourant, *Introduction to the Philosophy of St. Augustine: Selected Readings* (University Park: The Pennsylvania State University Press, 1964), 105–220; Bourke, *The Essential Augustine* (New York: Mentor-Omega, 1964), 37–40; 123–38; and *Wisdom from St. Augustine: Collected Essays* (Houston, Tex.: University of St. Thomas, 1984), 53–105.

17. Anton C. Pegis, "The Mind of St. Augustine," *Mediaeval Studies* 6 (1944): 60.

18. The best study of this "trinity" of mind, love, and knowledge is M. Schmaus, *Die psychologische Trinitätslehre des hl. Augustinus* (Münster, 1927), 235–64.

19. Descartes' famous "I think, therefore I am" (*cogito ergo sum*) obviously owes something to Augustine, who says: "If I am deceived, I am" (*si fallor, sum*) (*City of God* 11.26).

20. See *83 Q* , question 28, in toto.

21. Cf. J. A. Beckaert, "Note complémentaire" (on question 28), BA 10:714.

22. See Bourke, *Augustine's View of Reality* (Villanova, Pa.: Villanova University Press, 1964), 125–34.

23. H. Woods, *Augustine and Evolution: A Study in the De Genesi ad litteram* (New York: Universal Knowledge Foundation, 1924); M. J. McKeough, *The Meaning of the rationes seminales in St. Augustine* (Washington, D.C.: Catholic University of America Press, 1926); and E. C. Messenger, *Evolution and Theology: The Problem of Man's Origin* (London and New York: Burns Oates & Washbourne, 1933).

24. E. Gilson, *From Aristotle to Darwin and Back Again,* trans. John Lyon (Notre Dame, Ind.: University of Notre Dame Press, 1984), 50.

25. There is no complete English version of *De diversis quaestionibus 83,* but this answer to question 46 is included in *The Essential Augustine,* 62–63.

26. This application of Platonic "Ideas" to creation had been made long before Augustine by Philo of Alexandria (25 B.C. to A.D. 40); see Norman Bentwich, *Philo-Judaeus of Alexandria* (Philadelphia, Pa.: Jewish Publication Society of America, 1910), 174–83. Cf. F. Copleston, *A History of Philosophy* (New York: Doubleday Image Books, 1962), 1:202–6. Augustine mentions Philo as an erudite Platonist in *Against the Academics* 2.15; and *Against Faustus* 12.39.

27. This *Sermon* (Mai 126, in *Miscellanea Agostiniana* 1:355–68) dated 425–30, is translated in Howe, *Selected Sermons,* no. 30.

| **Ten Key Views**

There are certain typical ways of looking at philosophical problems.
We will consider ten of these starting points of Augustinian philosophy. They help to understand the selected text from the *Confessions*.

I Three Levels of Reality

Like Plotinus, Augustine saw all existing beings arranged on three
distinct levels. At the top is the immutable God, subject to no
change, perfect in all ways. On the bottom is the world of bodies,
imperfect in their mutability, for they change continually, both in
place and time. At the middle layer of being are souls, subject to
change in time but not in place.

In an early letter (A.D. 390) to Coelestinus (*Epist* 18.2),we find
this scale of natures most clearly described:

> There is a nature which is susceptible of change with respect to
> both place and time (*per locos et tempora mutabilis*), namely
> the corporeal. Another nature is in no way susceptible of
> change with respect to place but only in regard to time, namely
> the soul (*ut anima*). And there is a third Nature which can be
> changed neither in respect to place, nor in respect to time: that
> is God. These natures of which I have said that they are mu-
> table in some way are called creatures. The Nature that is im-
> mutable is called Creator.

Augustine uses the word "nature" (*natura*) for any sort of beings,
because Ciceronic Latin lacked a term for "being" (*ens*), which was
coined in later Latin.

Bodies are inferior in all ways to immaterial things, but this
does not mean, for Augustine, that they are evil, as some earlier
Neoplatonists thought. The treatise *The Nature of the Good* (1–25)
offers a long explanation of how "every spirit and every body is naturally good" (ibid. 2). Augustine is not as interested, philosophically,

in physical things as he is in the spiritual realm. This is evident in one of his most mature writings, the *City of God* (8.5), where he speaks with great approval of Platonist philosophers because "they have transcended every soul and all changeable things in seeking the supreme. They have seen also that, in every changeable thing the form which makes it that which it is, whatever be its mode or nature, can only exist through Him who truly is, because He is immutable."

Causality on all three levels is discussed in a prior book (*City* 5.9). Divine causality is primary, the source of all existence and changes in inferior things. Created spirits, including human souls and angels, are voluntary causes. Their wills are created free, and so they may act for or against the divine will. Bodily natures possess no active causes; all that happens in the physical world is efficiently caused by God. Summing up this chapter (*City* 5.9), Augustine says:

> The cause of things, therefore, which makes but is not made, is God, but all other causes both make and are made. Such are all created spirits, and especially the rational. Material causes, therefore, which may rather be said to be made than to make, are not to be reckoned among efficient causes, because they can only do what the wills of spirits do by them.

In one sense, then, all things are divided by Augustine on two more basic levels: they are either immutable or mutable. Also they are either causes or simply caused. We will see this in the *Confessions* (10.25.36), where he simply places God above all else: "Thou dwellest as an immutable Being above them all."

| *Rationes:* Eternal and Seminal

The dual division mentioned above is also exemplified in Augustine's theory of the rational principles (*rationes*) that inform all things. Question 46 (*83 Q*) is answered by equating Plato's ideal forms with the eternal reasons (*rationes aeternae*) that exist as exemplars in the creative mind of God. As Augustine concludes:

> Now, if these reasons (*rationes*) for all things to be created, or already created, are contained in the divine mind, and if there can be nothing in the divine mind unless it be eternal and immutable, and if Plato called these primary reasons of things Ideas—then not only do Ideas exist but they are true because they are eternal and they endure immutably in this way; and it is by participation in these that whatever exists is produced, however its way of existing may be.[1]

A long section of *The Trinity* (3.8.13–19) deals with the other kind of "reasons," the seminal forms (*rationes seminales*). They are like seeds (*semina, germina*) created in the material elements. All plants and animals stem from these; some species appear only later in the course of time, but their seedlike reasons were made by God at the first instant of creation. Their growth and development follow the laws established by divine wisdom (*congruae rationes id faciunt, quae incommutabiliter vivunt in ipsa summa Dei sapientia,* ibid. 3.8.15).

Of course, this theory of seminal reasons runs throughout the *Literal Commentary on Genesis.* One explanation is found in 5.21.45):

> As the seed contains invisibly all that may appear in the tree during the course of time, so must we think, since God created all in the same instant, that the world received at this time all that was created in it; when the day was created, not only the sky with its sun, the moon and the stars . . . but also potentially in their cause, all those beings that water and earth have produced in the course of time, up to the moment that they appear as we see them now.

We have already seen that this teaching on seminal reasons does not mean that Augustine would reject modern views on evolution. All that he would require is that whatever various species of living things may appear in the course of time, all would come from seed-like forms implanted by God in the very texture of the elements. He observes (*Gen Lit* 9.17.32): "A bean does not grow from a grain of wheat . . . or a man from a beast . . . the Creator keeps to Himself the ability to make out of all these things something other than what their seminal reasons, as it were, contain—but not something that He did not place in them."[2]

All such changes in the kinds of things may occur in the course of time and they are governed by divine providence.

❙ The Immaterial Soul

On the level of created spirits, the human soul is a primary object of attention for Augustine. In all thirteen books of the *Confessions,* he insists that, while God is most knowable in Himself, as perfect Truth and Wisdom, and He is ever present to the human soul, there are those who do not know God, or who confuse Him with lesser beings. But one's own soul is intimately present to itself; all people have some awareness of the workings of their own minds. This view is typical of Augustine's introspective interiorism.

He considers his soul to exist substantially as a part, along with his body, of the whole human person. He rejects the notion that the soul is merely a harmonious arrangement (*harmonia, entelechy*) of the body's members. As he says in the *Immortality of the Soul* (2.2), if the soul were just some physical arrangement, it would be mutable as the body is, but the soul is identical with its reason (*ratio*), and reason is immutable (*Mutabile est autem corpus humanum, et immutabile ratio*). While Augustine himself did not think highly of this hastily written little work on immortality (*Retr* 1.5.2), it does offer some of his earliest definitions of the soul and its abilities. Human reason is there described as the "gaze of the rational soul" (*aspectus animi,* see *Immortality* 6.10; cf. *Soul* 27.53). As life-giving principle, it is usually called *anima;* as rational principle, it is *animus.*

A primitive formulation of Augustine's argument for the immortality of the human soul is presented in this early treatise (*Immortality* 4.5), written just before his baptism. There he says that, since the human soul is rational, and reason sees and holds in its knowledge certain eternal truths, such as many propositions of mathematics and logic, this container of immortal truth cannot cease to exist. It has a beginning but no termination.

More sophisticated is the argument for psychic immortality found in *The Trinity* (13.8.11). Since all people desire to be happy, and this cannot be accomplished in this short and changeable life on earth, then real happiness requires the soul to live on, without termination, in a future life. Augustine even suggests here that, if asked, all people would say that they will to be immortal. His argument is that a person who thinks carefully about the real meaning of happiness must come to realize that life is necessarily unending: For how can one be truly happy if one knows for sure that happiness cannot endure? As he puts it: "In order for one to live happily, he must be alive" (*ut enim homo beate vivat, oportet ut vivat*). Of course, this view is implied throughout the dialogue *The Happy Life,* and we will encounter it in book 10 of the *Confessions* (chaps. 20–22).[3]

In the *Magnitude of the Soul* (13.22), we find a formal definition of the soul. Evodius had asked, "What is the soul (*animus*)?" Augustine replied: "A certain substance, participating in reason, suited to the ruling of the body" (*substantia quaedam rationis particeps, regendo corpori accommodata*). This may be compared with an early definition of a human being (*homo*) in *Morals of the Catholic Church* (1.27.52), "a rational soul using a body that is mortal and earthly" (*anima rationalis est mortali atque terreno utens corpore*).

This apparent dualism of human soul and body is typical of Augustine's early thinking.[4] The more mature *City of God* (5.11) simply says that God made the human "a rational animal consisting of soul and body" (*fecit hominem rationale animal ex anima et corpore*). He never doubted the unity of the human person (see *Conf* 10.6.9).

On the question of the origin of the individual human soul, Augustine hesitated to give a definitive answer. In the *Confessions* (9.13.37), he speaks of his parents, Monica and Patricius, "through whose flesh Thou didst introduce me to this life, I know not how." What he means is that he does not understand how his own soul came into existence. Writing the *Literal Commentary on Genesis,* a decade or so later, Augustine devotes a good part of the seventh book (1.1–11.17, 22.33) to the competing claims of creationism and generationism. He is certain that the human soul is created, but what he is not sure of is whether God made all individual souls in the beginning days of creation or allowed them to be made later when there was an organism ready to receive a rational soul. His belief in the reality of Adam's original sin, the doctrine that all humans inherit some stain of sin from Adam's first fault, inclined Augustine to think that parents contributed something to the souls of their offspring.

Book 10 of the *Literal Commentary on Genesis* (10.6.9–23.19) presents two opinions on this question. One states that the soul of the first man was created by God and gave rise to all later souls; this is one version of the generationist theory, similar to the explanation of the origin of the body. The second opinion suggests that each soul is individually created by God and does not depend on the souls of parents; transmission of original sin would have to occur through the body.

In the year 415, a critic named Vincentius Victor attacked Augustine's handling of the problem of the soul's origin. A series of Augustine's replies were gathered into the four books of *On the Soul and Its Origin.* In this work, four different solutions to the problem are explained. Reviewing the matter in the *Retractations* (2.56), four years before he died, Augustine still confesses his ignorance (*me nescire confessus sum*). Since this is primarily a theological dispute, we will not go further into it here, but the modest restraint shown by Augustine is typical of his philosophical approach to other difficult questions.[5]

I Functions of the Human Soul

Augustine was not acquainted with the Aristotelian theory of potency and act nor the later Scholastic psychology of human powers as "faculties" or accidental potencies. He does speak of powers (*vires*) of the soul (*Soul* 14.24; *Free* 1.11ff.), but these are not distinct accidents. They are simply capacities, or even functions, of the soul, which is a substantial unit. Thus he often mentions the outer and inner human (*Conf* 10.6.9; *Trin* 12.1.1). When the soul acts by giving life to its body, or in sensing external features of bodies, this is the outward person (*homo exterior*). And when it turns in upon itself and its mental contents, this is the inner person (*homo interior*). These are simply two different ways in which the conscious soul may direct its attention. Thus we will see him speaking (*Conf* 10.7.11) of the force (*vis*) that gives life to the body and the force that senses through its body. We will consider the power of sense perception later (see pages 39–40 below).

Augustine's early dialogues use a number of words for the soul as knowing: *mens, ratio, intellectus, animus*. In the volitional area, *voluntas* (will) is generally the dynamic function of soul, but its tendencies toward inferior objects are called *libido* or *cupiditas*. Memory (*memoria*) is the general function of mental containment of thoughts and feelings; it provides the basis for the argument showing that the soul has no physical size. Just as small mirrors keep on a small scale the objects that they reflect, so does the soul's memory retain items of all sizes (mountains and mice), or no size at all (*Soul* 5.8). But an extended analysis of memory does not appear before the tenth book of the *Confessions*.

The most developed description of the three functions of mind, memory, and will is in the last books of *The Trinity* (9–15), where Augustine's purpose is to find something in his consciousness that is even remotely analogous to the divine Trinity. The fact that he selects this psychological "trinity" for comparison with the one God of Christianity shows emphatically that he does not regard mind, memory, and will as three distinct faculties. Rather, the mind (*mens,* or sometimes *animus*) is a cognitive function; the soul as memory (*memoria*) holds its thoughts, feelings, and desires (it is not merely the ability to recall past experiences); and the same soul as active and dynamic, in any way, is will (*voluntas*).

There are also three levels of cognitive awareness in Augustinian psychology. Between sense perception of changing objects and intellectual intuition of immutable truths lies an intermediate layer of thinking (*cogitatio*) in terms of the images of sense objects.[6] Augustine sometimes uses the word *imaginatio,* but he was not familiar with Aristotle's teaching on imagination in the *De Anima* (3.3.428a27–429a9). Much human thinking, as Augustine describes it, is conducted on this level of image thinking. A carpenter who knows the properties of a square in terms of the many "pictures" that he retains from his work may be said to cogitate when he is planning to make a tabletop. But a geometer rises above this sort of image thinking and understands the meaning of "squareness" without contemplating any particular squares. There is such a thing as "imageless" thought in Augustine's psychology. He does not teach that we can abstract universal meanings from sensory phantasms: that would be to get something from sense images that they do not possess (true understanding). Therefore, we must have a higher source for our knowledge of general ideas. (This will be examined in section six of this chapter, 40–42).

The psychological importance of feelings, emotions, and mental affections does not escape Augustine. Few men have written more touchingly about love, both erotic and highminded. The first nine books of the *Confessions* are filled with the contrast between fleshly love and charity, the love of God and of divine goods. He knew and used the four basic passions of Stoic philosophy, love, hate, fear, and sorrow.[7] But no special power is assigned by Augustine to feel these disturbances (*perturbationes*) of the soul. At the end of our selection from *Confessions* book 10, we will see him starting an inventory of his own desires and passions. He thinks that he now has most of them under control. The thirteenth-century Scholastic philosophy of sensory appetites as passive faculties of the soul is not found in Augustine.

Seven grades of soul power (*vis animae*) and action are described in the *Magnitude of the Soul* (33.70–79). This analysis provides a good example of the introspective method at work.

On the lowest level, the soul gives life to its body (*corpus vivificat*). Psychic energy unifies the human organism, providing for nourishment, growth, and reproduction. This grade of functioning is shared with all members of the plant and animal world.

Up one level, we come to what the soul can do through the senses (*quid possit anima in sensibus*, 33.71). It directs its attention to touching, savoring, smelling, hearing, and seeing objects that may be helpful or harmful to its body. It controls the movements of the body in place, and it works to reproduce offspring and to care for the young. Its power of habit formation (*consuetudinis vis*) gives the organism continuity from one sense experience to another and moves it through uninterrupted sequences of time. This is called memory (*memoria vocatur*). Such habitual retention on the sensory level is a primitive form of the more complete function of memory described in *Confessions* 10. All animals share to some extent in this second level of soul activity.

Ascending to the third level, Augustine comes to what is distinctive of human psychic activity, the use of reason. Think (*cogita*) of a memory, he says (72), that rises above merely repetitive habits and retains what we learn by direct observation and through signs.[8] Think of the many crafts and skills in agriculture, building, the visual and oral arts, in social intercourse, in the academic studies, and so on. The acquisition of such skills, either by the unlearned or the learned, is the mark of the human person as rational.

With ascent to the fourth level, the soul rises to the appreciation of goodness (*bonitas*) and all truly praiseworthy objects (*omnis vera laudatio*). This is what modern philosophers call the realm of values.

These are not the goods of the sense world. By withdrawing from sordid pleasures and by purifying itself, the soul comes to see the worth of goods such as justice and tranquillity (73). It becomes able to profit from the instruction of wise men and from the wisdom that God speaks through such people.

If the fourth level involves a constant struggle to get away from earthly attachments, the next is that of the purified soul enjoying the possession of its own greatness. At the fifth level, the soul conceives the extent of its own magnitude (*concipit quanta sit*). Its understanding ascends to the very contemplation of truth (*in ipsam contemplationem veritatis*). It reaches up toward God as Truth (74).

Evidently these grades of soul activity are upward-moving steps toward the highest wisdom. Nearly all ancient philosophers took wisdom to include not only high-minded knowledge but also the appetitive inclination to act in accord with the highest values. The wholly wise person not only knows what is right to do; the sage does it. Accordingly, Augustine places the desire (*appetitio*) for the soul's highest vision on the sixth level (75). "It is one thing," he says, "to cleanse the eye of the soul" (*mundari oculum ipsum animae*) and quite another "to direct its gaze on what must be seen" (*in id quod videndum est*).

The seventh and ultimate grade of soul activity is the perfect vision of Truth and the enjoyment of supreme Goodness (*perfructio summi et veri boni*). Augustine does not say, here, that this is heaven, but there is no doubt that is what he means (76). He has been criticized for excessive intellectualism, but his emphasis on good as that which satisfies desire and on the peak of human joy (*perfructio,* whose objects are *gaudia*) runs counter to the intellectualist charge. Augustine never separates intellect from will; the same unitary soul enjoys as it understands.

These seven steps in the ascent toward wisdom may seem to exceed the grasp of the philosopher, but, at least, this analysis shows the heights to which Augustinian introspection aspires. Many interpreters of the famous vision at Ostia (*Conf* 9.10), in which Monica and Augustine are described as "touching" the level of unfailing wisdom, think that Augustine had at least one mystical experience. But whether he was truly a mystic is much debated.[9]

I Active Theory of Sensation

Because of his axiom that lower things cannot cause any change in higher beings, Augustine is not able to say that physical stimuli cause a sense impression in human consciousness. This is why he gave a rather peculiar definition of sensation in the *Magnitude of the Soul* (23.41): "I think that sensation is the soul's not being unaware of what the body suffers" (*sensum puto esse, non latere quod patitur corpus*). A more developed description is found in the dialogue *On Music* (6.5.10):

> In brief, it seems to me that, when the soul senses something in the body, it does not suffer any action from the body but rather it acts more attentively in regard to the passive changes (*passionibus*) in the body; and the active responses in the body (*actiones*), easy or difficult depending on whether they are agreeable or disagreeable, do not escape it (*non eam latere*): this is the whole explanation of sensing.

No doubt this theory that the soul actively produces in consciousness a sort of record of certain changes in its body owes a good deal to the psychology of Plotinus.[10] But Augustine modifies the Plotinian explanation. As Charles Boyer says: "For Plotinus, the soul senses because it grasps itself creating the object of sensation; for St. Augustine, the soul senses because it grasps itself producing an *image* of the sense object."[11]

Unlike the explanation of sense perception by Descartes and his followers in the school of Occasionalism, where there is really no interaction between soul and body, Augustine's theory of sensation allows for one-way action from soul to body. However, if the Augustinian soul makes its own sense images within itself, then there could be epistemological difficulties with Augustine's explanation of sensing. What guarantees the correctness of such perceptions? Of course, Augustine thinks that true judgments are found only on the level of understanding.

I Divine Illumination of Mind

At first glance, it seems quite easy to understand the suggestion that there is some sort of immaterial light that enables the human mind to "see" higher truths, axioms, principles, just as there is a light to aid sense vision. But the illumination theory is one of the most debated matters among interpreters of Augustine's thought.[12]

Before looking at these interpretations, let us consider the main things that Augustine says about the light of the mind. *The Teacher* (12.40) deals with the problem of how a student comes to understand what a teacher says. Augustine suggests that the student must have some way of getting to know the meaning of the teacher's words:

> If it is a matter of the things that we observe in the mind (*quae mente conspicimus*), that is by understanding and reason, then our words certainly express what we intuit (*contuemur*) as present in that inner light of truth (*in illa interiore luce*

veritatis), that illumines and rejoices (*illustratur et fruitur*)
what is called the inner man (*homo interior*).

This is the first of many references to the light that brings understanding to the human mind. Augustine leaves no doubt that the
things so understood are seen in a light that comes from God (*Deo
intus pandente*).

A few years later, the dialogue *Free Choice* (not finished until
391) relates the objects seen to the meaning of numbers (2.8.22–24).
Augustine argues that all counting depends on understanding what
one is: all other numbers simply take one twice, thrice, and so on. We
do not know *one* from sensation, he argues, because all sense objects
lack unity, they have many parts and are not simply one (*corpus est
enim, et ideo habet innumerabiles partes*). So the meanings of all
numbers and the laws governing their use in calculation are seen "in
that inner light which bodily sensation does not know" (*in luce
interiore conspicitur, quam corporalis sensus ignorat;* see ibid.,
2.8.23). Immediately after this (2.9–12), Evodius and Augustine
agree that while it is difficult to put the meaning of wisdom into a
few words, it is one and the same in all sages; and it is known in
somewhat the same way that the laws of numbers are understood.
There are many immutable truths and they are knowable to all
people in common, by a light that is both private and public
(*secretum et publicum lumen,* sect. 33).

By the year 400, Augustine was expanding on this in the *Reply
to Faustus the Manichaean* (20.7). There he explains:

> Far different from the cogitation whereby I think about limited
> and familiar bodies, is that incomparably distinctive thinking
> in which I understand justice, chastity, faith, charity, good-
> ness, and whatever else is like these. Now tell me, if you can, in
> regard to this cogitation known by trustworthy evidence, what
> kind of illumination is identified with it, whereby all those
> things that are not this light are both distinguished among
> themselves and shown to be different from the light. Yet even
> this light is not the Light that is God: the former is created, the
> latter is the Creator (*et tamen etiam hoc lumen, non est lumen
> illud quod Deus est; hoc enim creatura est, Creator est ille*).

From this it is apparent that, at this time (when he was finishing
the *Confessions*), Augustine thought that, while God is the supreme light,
He provides another created light to aid human understanding.

Commenting on such illumination texts, before 1952, F. J.
Thonnard distinguished three different modern interpretations.[13]
First of all, Thomas Aquinas and some of his followers (for instance,
Charles Boyer) think that the intellectual light created by God rein-
forces the agent intellect, which abstracts the intelligible meanings
from images (*phantasiae*) acquired in sense perception. Not many

Augustine scholars today accept this Thomistic interpretation. Abstraction of intelligible species from phantasms is quite foreign to Augustinian thought.

A second interpretation noted by Thonnard holds that God impresses the human mind with certain truths that determine our understanding. Such impressions are not innate but are produced in the human mind when needed. This sort of explanation has been proposed by Eugène Portalié.[14]

A third interpretation is credited to scholars such as Etienne Gilson, Régis Jolivet, and Fulbert Cayré.[15] It suggests that Augustine says nothing about abstraction of intelligible forms from sense images. Rather, he meant that the human mind simply intuits some higher truths and uses them in judging the changes of the body that are perceived by the soul.

Further examination of such interpretations will be reserved for the commentary on book 10 of the *Confessions* below. The teaching on intellectual illumination that we will see in the major treatises written after the *Confessions* is an important key to the understanding of the whole analysis of memory and human consciousness.

I Time as Mental Extension

Book 11 of the *Confessions* contains a continuation of the introspective program of the preceding book, while attempting to explain the opening lines about creation in Genesis. At one point (11.28.37), Augustine distinguishes three "directions" in which the mind turns during its self-examination. It looks ahead, it attends, and it remembers (*nam et expectat et adtendit et meminit*). In other words, there is intellectual vision of the future, the present, and the past.[16] Obviously these ways of looking are based on a special theory on the nature of time (*tempus*).

The Latin word *tempus* has a double meaning: it may signify what would be called tempo or rhythm in music; or it may mean measurable duration. The early dialogue *On Music*, in its first five books, studied all sorts of spoken or chanted rhythms (*tempora*) and investigated their numerical structures. We speak of three-four time and two-four time, and so on, in music. Clearly such time is based on a personal, psychological experience. Drummers who keep to a regular beat are said to keep good time. Augustine, as a trained master of rhetoric, was well aware of what we might call mental time. He did not deny the existence of time as the physical duration of bodies from past to future. The early books of the *City of God* recount what Augustine knew about the different times in the history of the world and humanity long before he came into existence.

However, from chapter 12 to the end of book 11 of the *Confessions,* Augustine works out a theory of time as a distending of personal life (*distentio est vita mea,* 11.29.39). In contrast to God's experience of all events as happening in an eternal present, Augustine thinks of human consciousness as necessarily spread out, distended, through past, present, and future. As he expresses this: "In thee, O mind of mine, I measure periods of time" (*tempora metior,* 11.27.36). This he sees as far more important than any physical measurement, or account, of time. He says: "Let no one tell me that periods of time (*tempora*) are equivalent to the movements of the heavenly bodies" (11.23.30).[17]

In the commentary on *Confessions* 10 below, we will see more about the relation of time to eternity.

| Natural Desire for Happiness

Much of Augustine's practical philosophy, his ethics and social thinking, stems from his conviction that all human beings have a natural desire for happiness. This was a commonplace dictum in ancient philosophy. Seneca, for instance, began his *De vita beata* with the sentence, "All people wish to live happily" (*Vivere omnes beate volunt*). Augustine's own dialogue on the subject, *The Happy Life,* presupposes the universality of this popular desire and proceeds to inquire into the nature of true happiness. He concludes there (*Happy* 5.33): "To be happy is nothing other than to lack nothing, that is to be wise" (*nihil est aliud quam non egere, hoc est esse sapientem*). This is immediately followed by an expanded definition of wisdom: it is "a measured quality of mind" (*modus animi*) "whereby the mind balances itself" (*sese librat*), "so that it never goes to excess and never is reduced below its proper fulfillment."

Within a year, the rather Stoic conclusion of the *Happy Life* is modified so as to include appetitive satisfaction. In the *Morals of the Catholic Church* we read: "We all certainly desire to live happily.... But the title "happy" cannot in my opinion belong either to him who does not possess what he loves, or to him who has what he loves, if it is harmful" (1.3.4). Then he argues that the object that will make all persons happy is the very best good (*bonum optimum*), that is God.

A striking sermon of the year 403 expounds on the religious context of true happiness. "All men love happiness, and therefore men are unreasonable in wanting to be wicked without being unhappy" (*Exp Ps* 3.15–16). And he reviews, here, many of the "goods" that people prize: money, estates, worldly magnificence, honors, physical beauty, health, or some perfection of the soul. Later in this sermon, Augustine advises his listeners to "look for something better than your soul itself. . . . Look for anything better, if you can find it: God keeps Himself for you" (3.16).

Preaching ten years later (*Serm* 150.3.4) he relates this insistence on God as the supreme Good to philosophy:

> Listen first to the common aim of all philosophers. . . . It is characteristic of all philosophers that, through their study, inquiry, discussion, their very life, they have sought to possess a happy life. This alone was the cause of philosophising (*Haec una fuit causa philosophandi*). Furthermore, I think that the philosophers even have this search in common with us. For, if I should ask you why you believe in Christ, and why you have become Christians, every man will answer truthfully by saying: for the sake of a happy life. The pursuit of a happy life is common to philosophers and to Christians.[18]

That *modus animi,* the moderating quality of the human soul, reaches its peak in the habit of wisdom. "The wise man is so united in his mind to God (*sapiens sit Deo ita mente conjunctus*), that nothing comes between them (*nihil interponatur*)." This statement in the *Profit of Believing* (15.33) plainly shows how theocentric Augustine's ethics is. Much later *The Trinity* (15.5.7) will review the many divine perfections attributed to God, and then reduce them all to wisdom (*ipse sapientia est*).

The conviction that all persons desire to live happily stands out in all the major writings of Augustine. A quite philosophical discussion of happiness (*beatitudo, felicitas*) occurs in *The Trinity* (13.3.6–9.12). Cicero plays an important role in Augustine's argument that the basic reason why people should strive to do what is right, to act ethically, to organize human societies that provide for peace and the context of well-being, is this volitional inclination toward happiness. It is the key to understanding Augustine's practical philosophy. This natural desire is presupposed in book 10 of the *Confessions*.[19]

I Virtues and Moral Character

We have just seen how chapter 3 of the *Morals of the Catholic Church* suggests that happiness depends on attaining the highest good. A later chapter (6) adds this: "No one will doubt that virtue makes the soul perfect" (*virtus animam faciat optimam*). Farther on, Augustine explains how the acquisition of virtue leads to a happy life (*virtus ad beatam vitam nos ducit*, 15). The greatest of the Christian virtues is charity, the highest love of God (*summum amorem Dei*).[20] The four great virtues of the ancient philosophers, temperance, fortitude, justice, and prudence, are but four affective parts of love:

> Temperance is love giving itself completely to that which is loved; fortitude is love readily bearing all things for the sake of what is loved; justice is love serving the loved object only, and therefore ruling rightly; prudence is love wisely making choices between what helps and what hinders.

The object of such high-minded love is not simply any good: it is God, the highest good, the highest wisdom, the highest peace of heart (*summi boni, summae sapientiae, summaeque concordiae*).

Prudent reasoning (practical wisdom) requires attention to the difference between goods that are to be *used* and those that are to be *enjoyed*. This is the important distinction between *uti* (to use) and *frui* (to enjoy). Question 30 in the *Eighty-three Questions* explains this.

> Just as there is a difference between a good-in-itself (*bonum honestum*) and a useful good (*utile*), so also is there a distinction between enjoying (*fruendum*) and using (*utendum*). Although one might try to show by subtle argument that every useful good is a good-in-itself, nevertheless it is more correct and in keeping with good usage to say that *honestum* means what ought to be sought after for its own sake (*propter se ipsum*), while *utile* designates that which is desired because it is directed to something else. . . . Thus every instance of human perversion (we could also say vice) consists in willing to use the objects of enjoyment (*fruendis uti velle*) or in willing to enjoy the objects of use (*atque utendis frui*). So, all good ordering (*omnis ordinatio*), in other words, all virtue, requires that the objects of joy be enjoyed (*fruendis frui*) and those of use be used (*et utendis uti*).

Immanuel Kant will echo one part of this distinction between ends and means in his third formulation of the categorical imperative: "Act so that you treat humanity, whether in your own person or in that of another, always as an end and never as a means only."[21]

The three theological virtues, faith, hope, and charity, are partly beyond the scope of philosophical study. Augustine's description of them depends on the New Testament. But the *Enchiridion,* in two places (2.7–8, 30.114–31.117), simply says that faith is the acceptance of things unseen, hope is the expectation of things of the future not yet attained, and charity is the pure love of God and of others as God's creatures. Many other Christian virtues, such as piety and patience, are dependent on the theological ones and are known through divine illumination.[22]

A lengthy section of book 19 in the *City of God* (19.4) treats the four great virtues described by the ancient philosophers:

> I speak especially of temperance—*sophrosyne,* as the Greeks
> call it—which must bridle our fleshly lusts, if they are not to
> drag our will to consent to abominations of every sort. . . . Take
> next, the virtue called prudence. Is not this virtue constantly
> on the lookout to distinguish what is good from what is evil, so
> that there may be no mistake in seeking the one and avoiding
> the other? . . . Then there is justice. Its task is to see that to
> each is given what belongs to each. . . . Look now, at the great
> virtue called fortitude. Is not its very function to bear patiently
> with misfortune—overwhelming evidence that human life is
> beset with unhappiness, however wise a man may be?[23]

These four virtues of the ancient philosophers are seen by Augustine
as good qualities of character, but he does not think that they assure
the attainment of happiness unless they are related to the love of
God.

Of course, Augustine speaks not only of virtue in his ethics; he
also has a good deal to say about moral laws, as we will see in the
Confessions (10.29.40). In a very early *Exposition of Psalm* 145, Augustine comments on the first verse: "Praise the Lord, my soul."[24]
Among the many things for which the human soul should be grate-
ful, Augustine dwells upon the view that the rational soul is situated
in the middle, between the Creator above and the world beneath
(*habens supra se Conditorem, infra se quod sub illo conditum est*).
And so human reason receives a law: "Cling to the superior, rule the
inferior" (*haerere superiori, regere inferiorem*). Practical understanding (*consilium*) of what should be done is what the soul works
out for itself, from God's light (*ex luce Dei*), through the rational
mind (*per rationalem mentem*). Augustine is thinking of moral conscience. This is one of the earliest and clearest expressions of what
he thought about the relation between God's eternal law and that
part of it that people are able to see with natural reason. The natural
moral law is a partial sharing by rational creatures in the supreme
law of the Creator.[25]

At about the same time (394/95), Augustine was editing *Free
Choice.* The discussions with Evodius therein compare the laws of a
state with the eternal law and debate how freedom, particularly in
the case of wicked people, may be restricted by such laws (1.5.13).
Augustine and Evodius then proceed to the relation of all temporal
laws to the law that is called the highest reason (*illa lex quae summa
ratio nominatur,* 1.6.15). It is summed up thus: "To explain in a few
words the basic meaning of eternal law (*aeternae legis notionem*),
that is impressed on us, it is that whereby all things are perfectly
ordered (*omnia sint ordinatissima*), so that the right thing (*justum*)
is done." Notice how Augustine ties justice in with the notion of
proper order (*ordo*). Order means not only the quasi-spatial placing

of God above soul, and soul above bodies, but also the notion of an organized and rational planning of the use of proper means to achieve a good end. Augustine rarely uses the term "natural law" (but see *Exp Ps* 118.4 for *"lex ista naturalis"*). But he does think, especially in the early writings, that orderly laws of living are impressed on all people's minds by the light that comes from God's reason. Typical is the answer to question 31 (*83 Q*), where he starts with Cicero's definition of virtue from *De inventione rhetorica* 2.53: "Virtue is a habit of the soul, in conformity with the measure of nature and with reason." All four philosophical virtues are fitted under this general definition, but, in the case of justice, Augustine stresses that it takes its origin from nature (*initium est ab natura profectum*). "That is right by nature (*natura jus*) which opinion does not generate but which an innate power has implanted," as Augustine sees it.

However, at the end of the first decade of the fifth century, Augustine began to hear of the teachings of the British Christian scholar Pelagius.[26] This man had his own views on many religious issues, but the one that disturbed Augustine was the idea that God had made people good, and so they have the power to do good actions, even without the special help of divine grace. In reaction to what might be called the ethical naturalism of Pelagius, several later writings of Augustine placed great stress on the need for special assistance from God, divine grace, so that human agents could perform really meritorious moral actions.[27] (It is necessary to understand this, for we will see the problem already developing in *Confessions* 10.29.40, where Augustine asks for God's help in doing what is right).

The treatise *On Nature and Grace* (circa 415) is characteristic of this more mature emphasis on the role of God's will in the governance of human affairs. This is what some commentators have called the ethical voluntarism of the older Augustine.[28] In any case, the virtues are more important in Augustinian ethics than any general theory of law.

| Two Cities: Terrestrial and Celestial

The *City of God* is, of course, Augustine's most important treatise on human society. If it were his only work, Augustine would still be entitled to an important place in world literature.[29] It is much more than a study of political philosophy, or as some have called it, a theology of history. This work brings Augustine's practical thinking, his ethics, to a mature peak.

One anticipation of the basic theme of the *City of God* is present in the much earlier *True Religion*. Two kinds of individual persons are there distinguished (26.49). There is what is popularly called the "old man," the outer person (*homo exterior*), the earthly person (*terrenus*), who lives for the goods or satisfactions of this created world. Some terrestrial people continue in that sort of life from birth to death; others turn at some point to immaterial goods and reform their lives. Then there is the "new man," the interior person, the celestial person, who prizes spiritual goods from early in life and makes progress through six stages in the unification of mind and body. Then the celestial person is ready for the seventh step, the eternal life of perpetual happiness (*Septima enim jam quies aeterna est, et nullis aetatibus distinguenda beatitudo perpetua*).

Following this (*True Religion*, 27.50), two different kinds of people are described, two societies of human beings. The one is holy (*pius*), the other is not holy (*impius*). Notice how the division into two societies arises from the psychological distinction of two sorts of persons, those of good will and those who desire inferior goods. To some extent, Augustine sees them as representative of two divisions of human history: the people whose minds are devoted to earthly goods and the ones dedicated to a supreme God. Both may last together from Adam to the end of time.

Several of the Psalms mention two cities of people and, of course, Augustine picks up this societal division in his *Expositions of the Psalms*. Sometimes the impious city is called Babylon and the pious one is Jerusalem (*Exp Ps* 64.1–2). Augustine says that Babylon means confusion (*confusio*) and Jerusalem signifies the vision of peace (*visio pacis*). They are contrary in their notions of what is good and right, but they live, all mixed together (*permixtae sunt*), throughout the course of time. Three years later, commenting on Psalm 142 (sect. 3), Augustine suggests that the city of God (*civitas Dei*) took its origin from Abel and the evil city (*mala civitas*) stemmed from Cain. Similar descriptions of the two cities appear in the *Expositions of Psalms* 98 (sect. 4) and 121 (sect. 4).[30]

The *Literal Commentary on Genesis* (11.15.20) has a famous text that describes the two cities in terms of different loves (*duo amores*):

> These are the two loves: the first is holy, the second foul; the first is social, the second selfish; the first consults the common welfare for the sake of a celestial society; the second grasps for a selfish control of social affairs, for the sake of arrogant domination. . . .They also separate the two Cities founded among the race of men, under the wonderful and ineffable Providence of God, administering and ordering all things that have been created. . . . Perhaps we shall treat, God willing, these two Cities more fully in another place.

Although this is from the penultimate book of the *Commentary on Genesis,* and that work is usually dated 401–15, its closing sentence in the quotation indicates that it was written before the *City of God* (usually dated 414–26).

If one can read only a part of the *City of God* (it is a large work), book 19 is the most rewarding for the student of philosophy. A good example of its content is the much-quoted description of peace as the "tranquillity of order." Note how the concept of *ordo* applies to many levels of human living. Augustine writes (19.13):

> The peace of the body consists in the duly proportioned arrangement of its parts. The peace of the irrational soul is the harmonious repose of the appetites, and that of the rational soul is the harmony of knowledge and action. The peace of body and soul is the well-ordered and harmonious life of the living creature. Peace between man and God is the well-ordered obedience of faith to eternal law. Peace between man and man is well-ordered concord. Domestic peace is the well-ordered concord between those of the family who rule and those who obey. Civil peace is a similar concord among citizens. The peace of the celestial City is the perfectly ordered and harmonious enjoyment of God, and of one another in God. The peace of all things is the tranquillity of order (*pax omnium rerum, tranquillitas ordinis*).

In our commentary below, we will see several other insights from the *City of God.* Augustine did not plan or foresee the establishment of a Christian empire on earth. He thought that the good people are destined to live with the wicked all through the centuries. Nor was he thinking of the separation of Church and State. The two cities are groups of people whose hearts are turned in opposing directions. This distinction is as much a product of introspection as any other Augustinian insight.

❙ NOTES

1. For an English version of Q. 46, see *TEA,* 62–63.

2. The paragraph (17.22) from *De Genesi ad lit.* 9 is translated in *TEA,* 103.

3. See Mourant, *Introduction to the Philosophy of St. Augustine,* 130–35.

4. Cf. V. J. Bourke, "The Body-Soul Relation in the Early Augustine," *Collectanea Augustiniana,* edited by J. C. Schnaubelt and F. Van Fleteren, 1:435–50 (Bern: Peter Lang, 1990).

5. Some details on Augustine's views on the origin of the soul are given in Bourke, *Augustine's Quest of Wisdom,* 194; 235–36; 239–40.

6. On *cogitatio* as a sort of "collation," see *Conf* 10.11.18.

7. *City* (9.4) offers a treatment of the Stoic theory of the emotions as disturbances of the soul.

8. For a discussion of Augustine's theory of signs, see *The Teacher* (6.8–11); and *Christian Doctrine* (books 2 and 4). Cf. R. A. Markus, "St. Augustine on Signs," in *Augustine: A Collection of Critical Essays,* edited by R. A. Markus, 61–91 (Garden City, N.Y.: Doubleday, 1972); and B. D. Jackson, "The Theory of Signs in St. Augustine's *De doctrina christiana,"* ibid., 92–147.

9. That Augustine was truly a mystic is suggested in C. Butler, *Western Mysticism* (London: Constable, 1927), 46.

10. See Plotinus, *Enneads,* 5.1.6; 3.4.3.

11. Charles Boyer, *L'idée de verité dans la philosophie de saint Augustin* (Paris: Beauchesne, 1921), 171.

12. R. H. Nash, *The Light of the Mind: St. Augustine's Theory of Knowledge* (Lexington: University Press of Kentucky, 1969); see chaps. 7 and 8; Caroline E. Schuetzinger, *The German Controversy on St. Augustine's Illumination Theory* (New York: Pageant Press, 1960); Bourke, *Wisdom from St. Augustine,* 106–25.

13. Thonnard, "Notes Complémentaires" (to *De magistro* and *De libero arbitrio*) in BA 6:478–79.

14. Eugène Portalié, *A Guide to the Thought of St. Augustine,* trans. R. J. Bastian (Chicago, Ill.: Regnery, 1960), 112–13.

15. For Gilson, consult *The Christian Philosophy of St. Augustine,* 289–91 and the criticism in R. Nash, *The Light of the Mind,* 94–97; see also R. Jolivet, *Dieu, Soleil des esprits* (Paris: Bibliothèque Augustinienne, 1934); and F. Cayré, *Les sources de l'amour divin* (Paris: Bibliothèque Augustinienne, 1933), 38–40.

16. These three types of conscious attention are further explored in *Conf* 11.29–30.

17. See J. F. Callahan, *Four Views of Time in Ancient Philosophy* (Cambridge, Mass.: Harvard University Press, 1948), 149–87.

18. In "The Mind of St. Augustine," 10–11, Pegis comments on Sermon 150 and shows how it leads to a discussion of moral value.

19. Some of the best secondary works on Augustine's practical thinking are not available in English: Ragnar Holte, *Béatitude et sagesse: Saint Augustin et la fin de l'homme* (Paris: Etudes Augustiniennes, 1962); J. Mausbach, *Die Ethik des heiligen Augustinus,* 2d ed. (Freiburg: Herder, 1929); Bernard Roland-Gosselin, *La Morale de saint Augustin* (Paris: Rivière, 1925).

20. See John Burnaby, *Amor Dei: Augustine on the Love of God as the Motive of Christian Life,* 2d ed. (London: Hodder & Stoughton, 1947).

21. I. Kant, *Foundations of the Metaphysics of Morals,* in L. W. Beck, ed., *Critique of Practical Reason and Other Writings* (Chicago, Ill.: University of Chicago Press, 1949), 80.

22. *De Gen. ad lit.* 12.31.59; for the English version, see TEA, 97.

23. This translation of *De civitate Dei* 19.4 is from G. G. Walsh, et al. (Doubleday Image, 1958).

24. *Exp Ps* 145.5 (Ps. 146 in some editions).

25. See Gilson, *Introduction à l'étude de s. Augustin,* 3d ed. (Paris: Vrin, 1949), 168ff. Consult also A. M. Chroust, "The Fundamental Ideas in St. Augustine's Philosophy of Law," *American Journal of Jurisprudence* 18 (1973): 57–79; and Joseph W. Koterski, "St. Augustine on the Moral Law," *Augustinian Studies* 11 (1980): 65–78.

26. The standard work on Pelagius is G. de Plinval, *Pélage: ses écrits, sa vie et sa réforme* (Lausanne: Payot, 1943); cf. Brown, *Augustine of Hippo,*

340–52; John Ferguson, *Pelagius: A Historical and Theological Study* (London: Cambridge University Press, 1956).

27. For Augustine's own remarks on Pelagius, see *Retr* 2.42.

28. Guido Fasso, *Storia della filosofia del diritto* (Bologne: Il Mulino, 1966), 196–200, contrasts the natural law of the early writings with the voluntaristic legalism of the anti-Pelagian works; but see Bourke, *Wisdom from St. Augustine,* 136–56; and *Joy in Augustine's Ethics* (1979).

29. E. Gilson, "Foreword," in *City of God* (New York: Doubleday Image, 1958), 13–35. Cf. O'Meara, *Charter of Christendom;* R. A. Markus, Saeculum: *History and Society in the Theology of St. Augustine* (London: Cambridge University Press, 1970).

30. Portions of these texts from *Enarrationes in Psalmos* are translated in *TEA,* 207–9.

PART TWO

Text

Confessions, 10.1–30, Latin and English

This selection is from Augustine's most widely read work, *Confessions,* book 10, chapters 1–30.

The Latin text is reprinted, with permission, from *The Confessions of Augustine,* edited by John Gibb and William Montgomery (Cambridge: Cambridge University Press, 1927), 272–305. (This text, with informative notes in English, does not differ significantly from the more recent critical edition of M. Skutella, 1934, reprinted in the Bibliothèque Augustinienne series, 1962, vols. 13 and 14; Skutella was revised but not substantially changed by H. Juergens and W. Schaub, 1969. Indeed, except for the footnote variants, the Gibb-Montgomery text differs little from the *Confessiones* in volume 1 of the Maurist edition of the *Opera Omnia,* 1679.)

The English version is reprinted, with permission, from St. Augustine, *Confessions,* translated by V. J. Bourke, Fathers of the Church Series, vol. 21 (Washington, D.C.: The Catholic University of America Press, 1953), 263–301. (This literal translation is intentionally close to the Latin of Augustine.) Phrases within quotation marks are from the Bible.

| Liber Decimus

| I.

(1) Cognoscam te, cognitor meus, cognoscam, sicut et cognitus sum. uirtus animae meae, intra in eam et coapta tibi, ut habeas et possideas sine macula et ruga. haec est mea spes, ideo loquor et in ea spe gaudeo, quando sanum gaudeo. cetera uero uitae huius tanto minus flenda, quanto magis fletur, et tanto magis flenda, quanto minus fletur in eis. ecce enim ueritatem dilexisti, quoniam qui facit eam, uenit ad lucem. uolo eam facere in corde meo coram te in confessione, in stilo autem meo coram multis testibus.

| II.

(2) Et tibi quidem, domine, cuius oculis nuda est abyssus humanae conscientiae, quid occultum esset in me, etiamsi nollem confiteri tibi? te enim mihi absconderem, non me tibi. nunc autem quod gemitus meus testis est displicere me mihi, tu refulges et places et amaris et desideraris, ut erubescam de me et abiciam me atque eligam te et nec tibi nec mihi placeam nisi de te. tibi ergo, domine, manifestus sum quicumque sim. et quo fructu tibi confitear, dixi. neque id ago uerbis carnis et uocibus, sed uerbis animae et clamore cogitationis, quem nouit auris tua. cum enim malus sum, nihil est aliud confiteri tibi quam displicere mihi; cum uero pius, nihil est aliud confiteri tibi quam hoc non tribuere mihi, quoniam tu, domine, benedicis iustum, sed prius eum iustificas inpium. confessio itaque mea, deus meus, in conspectu tuo tibi tacite fit et non tacite. tacet enim strepitu, clamat affectu. neque enim dico recti aliquid hominibus, quod non a me tu prius audieris, aut etiam tu aliquid tale audis a me, quod non mihi tu prius dixeris.

I Book Ten

I Chapter 1

(1) 'I shall know Thee,' O Knower of mine, 'I shall know Thee even as I am known.' Virtue of my soul, go deep into it and make it fit for Thee, that Thou mayest have and possess it 'without spot or wrinkle.' This is my hope and that is why I speak, and in this 'hope I rejoice,' when my joy is sound. As for the other things of this life: the more tears they receive, the less are they deserving of tears; the less tears are shed over them, the more do they deserve tears. 'For behold Thou hast loved truth,' since 'he who does the truth, comes to the light.' I desire to do this in my heart, before Thee in confession; and in my writing, before many witnesses.

I Chapter 2

(2) Even if I were unwilling to confess unto Thee, what could be hidden in me from Thee, O Lord, to whose eyes the abyss of human conscience is naked? I should but hide Thee from myself, not myself from Thee. Now, indeed, that my groaning is a witness that I am displeased with myself, Thou art refulgent, pleasing, lovable and desirable, that I may be ashamed of myself, reject myself and choose Thee, and that I may be pleasing neither to Thee nor myself, except on account of Thee.

Before Thee, then, O Lord, I lie unconcealed, whatever I may be. Yet, I have already said what is the fruit of my confessing to Thee. Nor am I doing it with fleshly words and speech, but with the words of the soul and the clamor of cogitation, which Thy ear doth recognize. For, when I am bad, to confess to Thee is nothing but to be displeased with myself; when I am good, to confess to Thee is simply not to attribute this to myself. For, Thou, O Lord, dost bless the just man, but first Thou dost rectify him from his impiety. And so, my confession, O my God, is made silently to Thee in Thy sight, yet not silently. It is silent in relation to noise, but, in the sphere of feeling, it cries aloud. Nor do I say any right thing to men which Thou hast not heard before from me, nor dost Thou hear any such thing from me which Thou hast not previously said to me.

| III.

(3) Quid mihi ergo est cum hominibus, ut audiant confessiones meas, quasi ipsi sanaturi sint omnes languores meos? curiosum genus ad cognoscendam uitam alienam, desidiosum ad corrigendam suam. quid a me quaerunt audire qui sim, qui nolunt a te audire qui sint? et unde sciunt, cum a me ipso de me ipso audiunt, an uerum dicam, quandoquidem nemo scit hominum, quid agatur in homine, nisi spiritus hominis, qui in ipso est? si autem a te audiant de se ipsis, non poterunt dicere: "mentitur dominus." quid est enim a te audire de se nisi cognoscere se? quis porro cognoscit et dicit: "falsum est," nisi ipse mentiatur? sed quia caritas omnia credit, inter eos utique, quos conexos sibimet unum facit, ego quoque, domine, etiam sic tibi confiteor, ut audiant homines, quibus demonstrare non possum, an uera confitear; sed credunt mihi, quorum mihi aures caritas aperit.

(4) Verum tamen tu, medice meus intime, quo fructu ista faciam, eliqua mihi. nam confessiones praeteritorum malorum meorum, quae remisisti et texisti, ut beares me in te, mutans animam meam fide et sacramento tuo, cum leguntur et audiuntur, excitant cor, ne dormiat in desperatione et dicat: "non possum," sed euigilet in amore misericordiae tuae et dulcedine gratiae tuae, qua potens est omnis infirmus, qui sibi per ipsam fit conscius infirmitatis suae. et delectat bonos audire praeterita mala eorum, qui iam carent eis, nec ideo delectat, quia mala sunt, sed quia fuerunt et non sunt. quo itaque fructu, domine meus, cui cotidie confitetur conscientia mea spe misericordiae tuae securior quam innocentia sua, quo fructu, quaeso, etiam hominibus coram te confiteor per has litteras adhuc, quis ego sim, non quis fuerim? nam illum fructum uidi et commemoraui. sed quis adhuc sim ecce in ipso tempore confessionum mearum, et multi hoc nosse cupiunt, qui me nouerunt, et non me nouerunt, qui ex me uel de me aliquid audierunt, sed auris eorum non est ad cor meum, ubi ego sum quicumque sum. uolunt ergo audire confitente me, quid ipse intus sim, quo nec oculum nec aurem nec mentem possunt intendere; credituri tamen uolunt, numquid cognituri? dicit enim eis caritas, qua boni sunt, non mentiri me de me confitentem, et ipsa in eis credit mihi.

▌ Chapter 3

(3) But, what business have I with men that they should hear my confessions, as if they could become the healers 'of all my diseases?' A race interested in finding out about the other man's life, slothful in amending their own! Why do they seek to hear from me what I am, when they do not wish to hear from Thee what they are? And how do they know whether I am telling the truth when they hear about me from myself, since no one 'among men knows what does on in a man, save the spirit of the man which is in him?' But, if they hear about themselves from Thee, they cannot say: 'the Lord is lying.' For, what is it to hear about oneself from Thee, but to know oneself? Who, then, can know himself and say: 'It is false,' unless he himself lies? But, because 'charity believes all things,' certainly among those whom it makes one, in intimate union with each other, I, also, O Lord, do even confess to Thee in such a way that men may hear, though I cannot prove to them that the things I confess are true. But, they whose ears charity doth open unto me, they believe me.

(4) Do Thou, however, my inner Physician, make clear to me with what profit I am doing these things. For, the confessions of my past evils (which Thou hast 'forgiven and covered up,' so that Thou mightest make me blessed in Thee, changing my soul by faith and Thy Sacrament) may, when they are read and heard, excite the heart so that it will not lie in a torpor of despair and say: 'I cannot,' but will rather wake up in the love of Thy mercy and in the sweetness of Thy grace, whereby every weak man is made strong, provided he becomes aware through it of his own weakness. It is a joy for good men to hear of the past evils of those who are now free from them; not that joy arises from the fact that there are evils, but from the fact that they were, but do not now exist.

With what profit, therefore, O my Lord, to whom my conscience confesses daily, being more secure in the hope of Thy mercy than in its own innocence—with what profit, I ask, do I also confess to men through these writings, in Thy presence, not what I have been, but what I am. Now, the profit of confessing of the past I have observed and noted. Yet, what I now am, right at this very time of my confessions, many people desire to know, both those who know me and those who do not. They have heard something from me or about me, but their ear is not close to my heart, where I am whatever I am. They wish, then, to hear me confessing what I am within myself, where neither eye nor ear nor mind can reach in; they wish this as believers, for how could they know it? Charity, whereby they are good, tells them that I do not lie in confessing about myself, and it, being present in them, believes me.

▌IV.

(5) Sed quo fructu id uolunt? an congratulari mihi cupiunt, cum audierint, quantum ad te accedam munere tuo, et orare pro me, cum audierint, quantum retarder pondere meo? indicabo me talibus. non enim paruus est fructus, domine deus meus, ut a multis tibi gratiae agantur de nobis et a multis rogeris pro nobis. amet in me fraternus animus quod amandum doces, et doleat in me quod dolendum doces. animus ille hoc faciat fraternus, non extraneus, non filiorum alienorum, quorum os locutum est uanitatem, et dextera eorum dextera iniquitatis, sed fraternus ille, qui cum approbat me, gaudet de me, cum autem inprobat me, contristatur pro me, quia siue approbet siue improbet me, diligit me. indicabo me talibus: respirent in bonis meis, suspirent in malis meis. bona mea instituta tua sunt et dona tua, mala mea delicta mea sunt et iudicia tua. respirent in illis et suspirent in his, et hymnus et fletus ascendant in conspectum tuum de fraternis cordibus, turibulis tuis. tu autem, domine, delectatus odore sancti templi tui, miserere mei secundum magnam misericordiam tuam propter nomen tuum et nequaquam deserens coepta tua consumma inperfecta mea.

(6) Hic est fructus confessionum mearum, non qualis fuerim, sed qualis sim, ut hoc confitear non tantum coram te secreta exultatione cum tremore et secreto maerore cum spe, sed etiam in auribus credentium filiorum hominum, sociorum gaudii mei et consortium mortalitatis meae, ciuium meorum et mecum peregrinorum, praecedentium et consequentium et comitum uiae meae. hi sunt serui tui, fratres mei, quos filios tuos esse uoluisti dominos meos, quibus iussisti ut seruiam, si uolo tecum de te uiuere. et hoc mihi uerbum tuum parum erat si loquendo praeciperet, nisi et faciendo praeiret. et ego id ago factis et dictis, id ago sub alis tuis nimis cum ingenti periculo, nisi quia sub alis tuis tibi subdita est anima mea et infirmitas mea tibi nota est. paruulus sum, sed uiuit semper pater meus et idoneus est mihi tutor meus; idem ipse est enim, qui genuit me et tuetur me, et tu ipse es omnia bona mea, tu omnipotens, qui mecum es et priusquam tecum sim. indicabo ergo talibus, qualibus iubes ut seruiam, non quis fuerim, sed quis iam sim et quis adhuc sim; sed neque me ipsum diiudico. sic itaque audiar.

| Chapter 4

(5) But, to what profit do they wish this? Do they desire to join me in giving thanks, when they hear how near I approach Thee through Thy grace, and to pray for me, when they hear how much I am retarded by my own weight? I will reveal myself to such people. For, it is no small profit, O Lord my God, that 'thanks will be given by many on our behalf,' and that Thou shouldst be implored by many for our sake. Let the brotherly mind love in me what Thou dost teach to be worthy of love, and lament in me what Thou dost teach to be worthy of lament.

Let the mind doing this be brotherly, not alien, not 'of strange children, whose mouth hath spoken vanity: and their right hand the right hand of iniquity,' but a brotherly one which, approving me, rejoices for me, disapproving me, becomes sad for me, because, whether approving or disapproving me, it loves me. To such people, I will reveal myself. Let them breathe easily over my good deeds, breathe anxiously over my evil ones. My good deeds are Thy arrangements and Thy gifts; my evil ones are my own offenses and Thy judgments. Let them breathe easily over the former and anxiously over the latter, and let hymns and weeping ascend in Thy sight from brotherly hearts, Thy censers. But do Thou, O Lord, delighted with the scent of Thy holy temple, 'have mercy on me according to Thy great mercy because of Thy Name, and, in no wise forsaking Thy undertakings, bring my imperfections to perfection.

(6) This is the fruit of my confessions, that I should confess, not what kind of man I was, but what kind I am; and this, not only before Thee in hidden rejoicing with trembling, and in hidden grief with hope, but even unto the ears of believers among the sons of men, of the companions of my joy and the colleagues of my mortality, of my fellow citizens and the pilgrims in my company, those who have gone before and those who go after, and those who share my company on the way. These are Thy servants, my brethren, whom Thou didst desire as Thy sons, my masters, whom Thou didst command me to serve, provided I wish to live with Thee and from Thee. And this Word of Thine would amount to little, if it prescribed to me by words only and did not first lead the way by deeds. I serve these men by words and deeds; I do so 'under Thy wings,' with every great risk, except for the fact that my soul is protected under Thy wings and my weakness is known to Thee. I am very little, but my Father lives forever and My Protector is adequate for me. For He is the same Being, He who has generated me and who protects me. Thou Thyself art all my goods, Thou omnipotent Being who art with me even before I am with Thee. So, I will reveal myself to such men, the

I V.

(7) Tu enim, domine, diiudicas me, quia etsi nemo scit hominum, quae sunt hominis, nisi spiritus hominis, qui in ipso est, tamen est aliquid hominis, quod nec ipse scit spiritus hominis, qui in ipso est; tu autem, domine, scis eius omnia, qui fecisti eum. ego uero quamuis prae tuo conspectu me despiciam et aestimem me terram et cinerem, tamen aliquid de te scio, quod de me nescio. et certe uidemus nunc per speculum in aenigmate, nondum facie ad faciem; et ideo, quamdiu peregrinor abs te, mihi sum praesentior quam tibi, et tamen te noui nullo modo posse uiolari; ego uero quibus temptationibus resistere ualeam quibusue non ualeam, nescio. et spes est, quia fidelis es, qui nos non sinis temptari supra quam possumus ferre, sed facis cum temptatione etiam exitum, ut possimus sustinere. confitear ergo quid de me sciam, confitear et quid de me nesciam, quoniam et quod de me scio, te mihi lucente scio, et quod de me nescio, tamdiu nescio, donec fiant tenebrae meae sicut meridies in uultu tuo.

kind whom Thou hast commanded me to serve—showing not what I was, but what I now am, and what I am still. However, 'I do not even judge myself.'

Thus, then, may I be heard.

| Chapter 5

(7) For it is Thou, O Lord, who dost judge me. Because, though no one 'knows the things of a man save the spirit of the man which is in him,' there is nevertheless something in a man which even the very spirit of the man does not know which is in him; but Thou, O Lord, knowest all about him, Thou who hast made him. In fact, though I despise myself before Thy sight and consider myself but earth and ashes, yet I do know something about Thee which I do not know about myself. Truly, 'we see now through a mirror in an obscure manner,' not yet 'face to face.' And so, as long as I am a wanderer away from Thee, I am more present to myself than to Thee, and yet I know that Thou canst in no way be affected from without. But, in fact, I do not know what temptations I may be strong enough to resist and what ones I cannot. Yet, there is hope, for Thou 'art faithful, Thou wilt not permit us to be tempted beyond what we can bear, rather Thou wilt also with the temptation provide a way out that we may be able to bear it.'

Therefore, I will confess what I know of myself and what I do not know of myself, since even what I do know about myself I know by virtue of Thy enlightenment of me, and what I do not know about myself I remain ignorant of, until my 'darkness shall become as the noonday' in Thy sight.

▌VI.

(8) Non dubia, sed certa conscientia, domine, amo te. percussisti cor meum uerbo tuo, et amaui te. sed et caelum et terra et omnia, quae in eis sunt, ecce undique mihi dicunt, ut te amem, nec cessant dicere omnibus, ut sint inexcusabiles. altius autem tu misereberis, cui misertus eris, et misericordiam praestabis, cui misericors fueris: alioquin caelum et terra surdis loquuntur laudes tuas. quid autem amo, cum te amo? non speciem corporis nec decus temporis, non candorem lucis ecce istum amicum oculis, non dulces melodias cantilenarum omnimodarum, non florum et unguentorum et aromatum suauiolentiam, non manna et mella, non membra acceptabilia carnis amplexibus: non haec amo, cum amo deum meum. et tamen amo quandam lucem et quandam uocem et quendam odorem et quendam cibum et quendam amplexum, cum amo deum meum, lucem, uocem, odorem, cibum, amplexum interioris hominis mei; ubi fulget animae meae, quod non capit locus; et ubi sonat, quod non rapit tempus; et ubi olet, quod non spargit flatus; et ubi sapit, quod non minuit edacitas; et ubi haeret, quod non diuellit satietas. hoc est quod amo, cum deum meum amo.

(9) Et quid est hoc? interrogaui terram, et dixit: "non sum"; et quaecumque in eadem sunt, idem confessa sunt. interrogaui mare et abyssos et reptilia animarum uiuarum, et responderunt: "non sumus deus tuus; quaere super nos." interrogaui auras flabiles, et inquit uniuersus aer cum incolis suis: "fallitur Anaximenes; non sum deus." interrogaui caelum, solem, lunam, stellas: "neque nos sumus deus, quem quaeris," inquiunt. et dixi omnibus, quae circumstant fores carnis meae: "dicite mihi de deo meo, quod uos non estis, dicite mihi de illo aliquid." et exclamauerunt uoce magna: "ipse fecit nos." interrogatio mea intentio mea et responsio eorum species eorum. et direxi me ad me et dixi mihi: "tu quis es?" et respondi: "homo." et ecce corpus et anima in me mihi praesto sunt, unum exterius et alterum interius. quid horum est, unde quaerere debui deum meum, quem iam quaesiueram per corpus a terra usque ad caelum, quousque potui mittere nuntios radios oculorum meorum? sed melius quod interius. ei quippe renuntiabant omnes nuntii corporales praesidenti et iudicanti

| Chapter 6

(8) I love Thee, O Lord, not with doubtful but with assured awareness. Thou hast pierced my heart with Thy Word and I have loved Thee. The heaven and earth, also, and all things which are in them, see how, on all sides, they tell me to love Thee. Nor do they cease to tell this to all men 'that they may be without excuse.' More profoundly, however, 'wilt Thou have mercy on whom Thou wilt have mercy, and wilt Thou show pity, to whom Thou wilt show pity:' otherwise, heaven and earth speak Thy praises to the deaf.

But, what do I love, when I love Thee? Not the prettiness of a body, not the gracefulness of temporal rhythm, not the brightness of light (that friend of these eyes), not the sweet melodies of songs in every style, not the fragrance of flowers and ointments and spices, not manna and honey, not limbs which can be grasped in fleshly embraces—these I do not love, when I love my God. Yet, I do love something like a light, a voice, an odor, food, an embrace, when I love my God—the light, voice, odor, food, embrace of my inner man, wherein for my soul a light shines, and place does not encompass it, where there is a sound which time does not sweep away, where there is a fragrance which the breeze does not disperse, where there is a flavor which eating does not diminish, and where there is a clinging which satiety does not disentwine. This is what I love, when I love my God.

(9) And what is this?

I asked the earth, and it answered: 'It is not I.' Whatever things are in it uttered the same confession. I asked the sea, the depths, the creeping things among living animals, and they replied: 'We are not Thy God; look above us.' I asked the airy breezes, and the whole atmosphere with its inhabitants said: 'Anaximenes is mistaken; I am not God.' I asked the sky, the sun, the moon, the stars: 'Nor are we the God whom you seek,' they said. And I said to all these things which surround the entryways of my flesh: 'Tell me about my God, since you are not He; tell me something about Him.' With a loud voice, they cried out: 'He made us.' My interrogation was my looking upon them, and their reply was their beauty.

Then, I turned to myself and said: 'Who art thou?' And I answered: 'A man.' Here are the body and soul in me, standing ready to serve me; the one without, the other within. From which of these should I have sought my God, whom I had already sought in the realm of body from earth to sky, as far as I could send out the messenger rays of my eyes? But, the better is what is interior. To it, indeed, as to an overseer and judge, all the messengers of the body send back their messages concerning the answers of heaven and

de responsionibus caeli et terrae et omnium, quae in eis sunt,
dicentium: "non sumus deus" et: "ipse fecit nos." homo interior
cognouit haec per exterioris ministerium; ego interior cognoui
haec, ego, ego animus, per sensum corporis mei. interrogaui
mundi molem de deo meo, et respondit mihi: "non ego sum, sed
ipse me fecit."

(10) Nonne omnibus, quibus integer sensus est, apparet haec
species? cur non omnibus eadem loquitur? animalia pusilla et
magna uident eam, sed interrogare nequeunt. non enim
praeposita est in eis nuntiantibus sensibus iudex ratio.
homines autem possunt interrogare, ut inuisibilia dei per ea,
quae facta sunt, intellecta conspiciant, sed amore subduntur eis
et subditi iudicare non possunt. nec respondent ista inter-
rogantibus nisi iudicantibus nec uocem suam mutant, id est
speciem suam, si alius tantum uideat, alius autem uidens
interroget, ut aliter illi appareat, aliter huic, sed eodem modo
utrique apparens illi muta est, huic loquitur: inmo uero omnibus loquitur, sed illi intellegunt, qui eius uocem acceptam foris
intus cum ueritate conferunt. ueritas enim dicit mihi: "non est
deus tuus caelum et terra neque omne corpus." hoc dicit eorum
natura. uident: moles est, minor in parte quam in toto. iam tu
melior es, tibi dico, anima, quoniam tu uegetas molem corporis
tui praebens ei uitam, quod nullum corpus praestat corpori.
deus autem tuus etiam tibi uitae uita est.

earth, and all things in them, which say: 'We are not God,' and: 'He has made us.' The interior man knows these things through the help of the exterior man; I, the interior man knew these things, I, I, the mind through the senses of my body. I asked the whole frame of the world concerning my God and it replied to me: 'I am not He, but He has made me.'

(10) Is not this beauty evident to all whose sense perception is intact? Why does it not speak the same thing to all men? Tiny and large animals see it, but they cannot interrogate it—for reason is not placed above the message-carrying senses in them, as a judge. But, men are able to ask, so that 'they may clearly see the invisible attributes of God, being understood through the things that are made, but through love they are made subject to these things and, being thus subjected, are not able to judge. These things do not reply to questioners unless these latter are capable of judging. Not that they change their voice, that is, their beautiful appearance, if one being simply sees, while another sees and interrogates, so that it appears one way to the first and another way to the second—but, appearing just the same to both, it is mute to one, while it speaks to the other. Rather, it speaks to all, but the latter understand, for they take in its voice from outside and compare it with the truth within. Now, the truth says to me: 'Thy God is neither sky, nor earth, nor any body.' This, their own nature states. Men see: it is a thing with bulk, smaller in its part than its whole. Now, you are better—I am talking to you, my soul—since you activate the bulk of your body, giving it life, which no body confers on a body. God, however, is even for you the Life of life.

I VII.

(11) Quid ergo amo, cum deum amo? quis est ille super caput animae meae? per ipsam animam meam ascendam ad illum. transibo uim meam, qua haereo corpori et uitaliter compagem eius repleo. non ea ui reperio deum meum: nam reperiret et equus et mulus, quibus non est intellectus, et est eadem uis, qua uiuunt etiam eorum corpora. est alia uis, non solum qua uiuifico sed etiam qua sensifico carnem meam, quam mihi fabricauit dominus, iubens oculo, ut non audiat, et auri, ut non uideat, sed illi, per quem uideam, huic, per quam audiam, et propria singillatim ceteris sensibus sedibus et officiis suis: quae diuersa per eos ago unus ego animus. transibo et istam uim meam; nam et hanc habet equus et mulus: sentiunt etiam ipsi per corpus.

I Chapter 7

(11) What, then, do I love, when I love my God? Who is He, above the head of my soul? I shall go up through my soul itself to Him. I shall pass beyond my life-force, whereby I cling to the body and fill its frame with life. I do not find my God by that force, for 'the horse and the mule, who have no understanding,' would find it likewise, since it is the same force by which their bodies also live.

There is another force, by which I not only vivify but also sensify my flesh which the Lord has framed for me, commanding the eye not to hear, the ear not to see, but assigning to the former through which I may see and to the latter through which I may hear and to the other senses, according to their organs and functions, their proper objects respectively. I, being one mind, do these different things through them. I shall also pass above this force of mine, for the horse and mule have this, too; they also sense through the body.

I VIII.

(12) Transibo ergo et istam naturae meae, gradibus ascendens ad eum, qui fecit me, et uenio in campos et lata praetoria memoriae, ubi sunt thesauri innumerabilium imaginum de cuiuscemodi rebus sensis inuectarum. ibi reconditum est, quidquid etiam cogitamus, uel augendo uel minuendo uel utcumque uariando ea quae sensus attigerit, et si quid aliud conmendatum et repositum est, quod nondum absorbuit et sepeliuit obliuio. ibi quando sum, posco, ut proferatur quidquid uolo, et quaedam statim prodeunt, quaedam requiruntur diutius et tamquam de abstrusioribus quibusdam receptaculis eruuntur, quaedam cateruatim se proruunt et, dum aliud petitur et quaeritur, prosiliunt in medium quasi dicentia: "ne forte nos sumus?" et abigo ea manu cordis a facie recordationis meae, donec enubiletur quod uolo atque in conspectum prodeat ex abditis. alia faciliter atque inperturbata serie sicut poscuntur suggeruntur et cedunt praecedentia consequentibus et cedendo conduntur, iterum cum uoluero processura. quod totum fit, cum aliquid narro memoriter.

(13) Ubi sunt omnia distincte generatimque seruata, quae suo quaeque aditu ingesta sunt, sicut lux atque omnes colores formaeque corporum per oculos, per aures autem omnia genera sonorum omnesque odores per aditum narium, omnes sapores per oris aditum, a sensu autem totius corporis, quid durum, quid molle, quid calidum frigidumue, lene aut asperum, graue seu leue, siue extrinsecus siue intrinsecus corpori? haec omnia recipit recolenda, cum opus est, et retractanda grandis memoriae recessus et nescio qui secreti atque ineffabiles sinus eius: quae omnia suis quaeque foribus intrant ad eam et reponuntur in ea. nec ipsa tamen intrant, sed rerum sensarum imagines illic praesto sunt cogitationi reminiscentis eas. quae quomodo fabricatae sint quis dicit, cum appareat, quibus sensibus raptae sint interiusque reconditae? nam et in tenebris atque in silentio dum habito, in memoria mea profero, si uolo, colores, et discerno inter album et nigrum et inter quos alios uolo, nec incurrunt soni atque perturbant quod per oculos haustum considero, cum et ipsi ibi sint et quasi seorsum repositi lateant. nam et ipsos posco, si placet, atque adsunt ilico, et quiescente lingua ac silente gutture canto quantum

I Chapter 8

(12) So, I shall also pass above this power of my nature, ascending by degrees toward Him who made me, and I come into the fields and broad palaces of memory, where there are treasures of innumerable images, brought in from all sorts of sense objects. There is stored away whatever we cogitate on, too, either by adding to, or taking away from, or changing in any way the things which sense perception has contacted, and anything else kept or put back there, which forgetfulness has not yet engrossed and buried.

When I am in it, I can request that whatever I wish be brought forward. Some things come forth immediately; others are hunted after for a longer time, yet they are dug out as it were from some more concealed containers; still others rush out in a mob, when something else is sought and looked for, jumping forth in the middle as if to say: 'Would we do, perhaps?' These I drive away from the face of my remembrance with the hand of my heart, until what I want becomes clear and enters into sight from the secret places. Other things come up as they are required, in easy and uninterrupted sequence. The first ones give way to those which follow and, in leaving, are stored up to come forth again when I desire it. All of this goes on, when I recite something memorized.

(13) In it, all things are kept distinct and classified. They are carried in, each by its own channel—light, for instance, and all colors and shapes of bodies through the eyes; through the ears all kinds of sounds; all odors through the channel of the nostrils; all flavors through the channel of the mouth; and then, by the sensitivity of the whole body, what is hard or soft, hot or cold, smooth or rough, heavy or light, whether outside or inside the body. All these the great recess of memory, and its indescribably hidden and mysterious chasms, take in, to be called to mind and reviewed, when need arises. All these things go in, each by its own gateway, and are there stored away. The things themselves do not go in, of course, but the images of sensible things are ready, there, for the cogitation which recalls them.

Just how these are fashioned who can say, though it is evident by which senses they are caught up and stored away within? For, even while I dwell in darkness and silence, I can, if I wish, produce colors in my memory, and distinguish between white and black and between any others as I wish. Nor do sounds rush in and disturb the object drawn in through the eyes, when I am considering it; yet, they are there, also, and lie hidden in separation, as it were. I can summon these, too, if it pleases me, and they are present at once; with tongue at rest and silent throat, I can sing as much as I wish. The

uolo, imaginesque illae colorum, quae nihilo minus ibi sunt, non
se interponunt neque interrumpunt, cum thesaurus alius
retractatur, qui influxit ab auribus. ita cetera, quae per sensus
ceteros ingesta atque congesta sunt, recordor prout libet et
auram liliorum discerno a uiolis nihil olfaciens et mel defruto,
lene aspero, nihil tum gustando neque contractando, sed
reminiscendo antepono.

(14) Intus haec ago, in aula ingenti memoriae meae. ibi enim
mihi caelum et terra et mare praesto sunt cum omnibus, quae
in eis sentire potui, praeter illa, quae oblitus sum. ibi mihi et
ipse occurro meque recolo, quid, quando et ubi egerim, quoque
modo, cum agerem, affectus fuerim. ibi sunt omnia, quae siue
experta a me siue credita memini. ex eadem copia etiam
similitudines rerum uel expertarum uel ex eis, quas expertus
sum, creditarum alias atque alias et ipse contexo praeteritis
atque ex his etiam futuras actiones et euenta et spes, et haec
omnia rursus quasi praesentia meditor. "faciam hoc et illud"
dico apud me in ipso ingenti sinu animi mei pleno tot et
tantarum rerum imaginibus, et hoc aut illud sequitur. "o si
esset hoc aut illud!" "auertat deus hoc aut illud!" dico apud me
ista et, cum dico, praesto sunt imagines omnium quae dico ex
eodem thesauro memoriae, nec omnino aliquid eorum dicerem,
si defuissent.

(15) Magna ista uis est memoriae, magna nimis, deus, penetrale
amplum et infinitum. quis ad fundum eius peruenit? et uis est
haec animi mei atque ad meam naturam pertinet, nec ego ipse
capio totum, quod sum. ergo animus ad habendum se ipsum
angustus est, ut ubi sit quod sui non capit? numquid extra
ipsum ac non in ipso? quomodo ergo non capit? multa mihi
super hoc oboritur admiratio, stupor adprehendit me. et eunt
homines mirari alta montium et ingentes fluctus maris et
latissimos lapsus fluminum et Oceani ambitum et gyros
siderum et relinquunt se ipsos nec mirantur, quod haec omnia
cum dicerem, non ea uidebam oculis, nec tamen dicerem, nisi
montes et fluctus et flumina et sidera, quae uidi, et Oceanum,
quem credidi, intus in memoria mea uiderem spatiis tam
ingentibus, quasi foris uiderem. nec ea tamen uidendo
absorbui, quando uidi oculis, nec ipsa sunt apud me, sed imagines eorum, et noui, quid ex quo sensu corporis inpressum sit
mihi.

images of colors, despite the fact that they are present, do not intervene or break in when another store, which has flowed in through the ears, is reviewed. Thus, I can remember at will the other things which have been taken in and piled up through the other senses. I can distinguish the fragrance of lilies from that of violets, while smelling nothing, and I can prefer honey to a decoction of musk, smooth to rough, and not by tasting or touching anything at the time, but by recollecting.

(14) I do this inside, in the immense palace of my memory. In it, sky, earth, and sea are present before me, together with all the things I could perceive in them, except for those which I have forgotten. In it, I even encounter myself and I bring myself to mind: what, when and where I did something, and how I felt when I did it. In it are all the things which I remember, either those personally experienced or those taken on faith. Out of the same supply, even, I can take now these, now those likenesses of things (whether those experienced or those derived from experience) and combine them with things of the past, and from these I can even think over future actions, happenings, and hopes—and all these, again, as if in the present. 'I shall do this or that,' I say within myself in this huge recess of my mind, filled with the images of things so many and so great, and this or that follows in consequence. 'Oh, if this or that could happen!' 'May God prevent this or that!'—I say these things to myself, and, while I say them, the images of all the things I am saying are present from the same storehouse of memory. I could not say anything at all about them, if they were lacking.

(15) Great is this power of memory, exceeding great, O my God, a vast and unlimited inner chamber. Who has plumbed its depths? Yet, this is a power of my mind and it belongs to my nature; I myself do not grasp all that I am. Is, then, the mind too narrow to hold itself, so that the questions arise: Where is this thing which belongs to it, and it cannot grasp? Would it be outside it, and not in it? How, then, does it not grasp it? A mighty wonder rises before me, and on this point astonishment seizes me.

Yet, men go to admire the mountains' peaks, giant waves in the sea, the broad courses of rivers, the vast sweep of the ocean, and the circuits of the stars—and they leave themselves behind! They feel no wonder that I did not see with my eyes all these things when I was talking about them. Yet, I could not have talked of them unless I could see within, in my memory, in their vast expanses, as if I were seeing them externally, the mountains, waves, rivers, and stars which I have seen, and the ocean which I take on faith. Yet, I did not, by vision, take these things into me, when I saw them with my eyes. They are not themselves with me, but just their images. And I know for each what was impressed on me by each sense of the body.

| IX.

(16) Sed non ea sola gestat immensa ista capacitas memoriae meae. hic sunt et illa omnia, quae de doctrinis liberalibus percepta nondum exciderunt, quasi remota interiore loco, non loco; nec eorum imagines, sed res ipsas gero. nam quid sit litteratura, quid peritia disputandi, quot genera quaestionum, quidquid horum scio, sic est in memoria mea, ut non retenta imagine rem foris reliquerim, aut sonuerit et praeterierit, sicut uox inpressa per aures uestigio, quo recoleretur, quasi sonaret, cum iam non sonaret, aut sicut odor dum transit et uanescit in uentos, olfactum afficit, unde traicit in memoriam imaginem sui, quam reminiscendo repetamus, aut sicut cibus, qui certe in uentre iam non sapit et tamen in memoria quasi sapit, aut sicut aliquid, quod corpore tangendo sentitur, quod etiam separatum a nobis imaginatur memoria. istae quippe res non intromittuntur ad eam, sed earum solae imagines mira celeritate capiuntur et miris tamquam cellis reponuntur et mirabiliter recordando proferuntur.

I Chapter 9

(16) These are not the only things which the vast capacity of my memory bears. Here, also, are all those things which have been grasped from the liberal disciplines and which have not yet been forgotten—put aside, as it were, in an inner place which is not a place. Nor do I carry the images of these, but the things themselves. For, what literature is, what skill in discussion is, how many kinds of questions there are, whatever things like this I know, are present in my memory in a special way. I have not left the thing outside and just retained the image—nor has it existed as a sound and then passed away, like a spoken word impressed through the ears, through a vestigial image, by which in recollection it again sounds, as it were, when it is not actually sounding—nor, as an odor, while passing and disappearing on the breezes, affects the sense of smell from which it sends in its image to the memory, for us to recall when remembering—nor, as food, which, of course, causes no taste when already in the stomach, yet is tasted, in a way, in memory—nor, as some object perceived by touching it with the body, which the memory pictures even when it is separated from us. In fact, these things are not introduced into the memory, but their images alone are grasped with marvelous speed, and are put away in wonderful compartments, and come forth in a wondrous way through remembering.

| X.

(17) At uero, cum audio tria genera esse quaestionum, an sit, quid sit, quale sit, sonorum quidem, quibus haec uerba confecta sunt, imagines teneo et eos per auras cum strepitu transisse ac iam non esse scio. res uero ipsas, quae illis significantur sonis, neque ullo sensu corporis attigi neque uspiam uidi praeter animum meum et in memoria recondidi non imagines earum, sed ipsas: quae unde ad me intrauerint dicant, si possunt. nam percurro ianuas omnes carnis meae nec inuenio, qua earum ingressae sint. quippe oculi dicunt: "si coloratae sunt, nos eas nuntiauimus"; aures dicunt: "si sonuerunt, a nobis indicatae sunt"; nares dicunt: "si oluerunt, per nos transierunt"; dicit etiam sensus gustandi: "si sapor non est, nihil me interroges"; tactus dicit: "si corpulentum non est, non contrectaui; si non contrectaui, non indicaui." unde et qua haec intrauerunt in memoriam meam? nescio quomodo; nam cum ea didici, non credidi alieno cordi, sed in meo recognoui et uera esse approbaui et conmendaui ei tamquam reponens, unde proferrem, cum uellem. ibi ergo erant et antequam ea didicissem, sed in memoria non erant? ubi ergo aut quare, cum dicerentur, agnoui et dixi: "ita est, uerum est," nisi quia iam erant in memoria, sed tam remota et retrusa quasi in cauis abditioribus, ut nisi admonente aliquo eruerentur, ea fortasse cogitare non possem?

| Chapter 10

(17) However, when I hear that there are three kinds of questions—
Whether a thing is? What it is? What kind it is?—I keep the images
of the sounds by which these words are constituted, of course, and I
know that they have passed away through the air, accompanied by
noise, and now do not exist. But, the things themselves, which are
signified by these sounds, I did not attain by any sense of the body,
nor did I see them anywhere else than in my mind; yet, I have stored
up in memory, not their image, but the things themselves.

If they can, let them tell me whence these things have come into
me. For, I have gone over all the entrances of my flesh and have not
found out by which one they came in. Of course, the eyes say: 'If they
are colored, we have reported them'; the ears say: 'If they emitted
sound, they have been made known by us'; the nostrils say: 'If they
were odorous, they passed through us'; so also the sense of taste
says: 'If it is not a matter of taste, do not ask me'; touch says: 'If it has
no bodily bulk, I did not touch it; if I did not touch it, I did not make
it known.'

From what source, and by what route, did these things enter
into my memory? I do not know how. When I learned these things, I
did not believe in another man's heart; rather, I recognized them in
my own and I approved them as true. I committed them to it as to a
repository, from which I could take them out when I desired. Therefore, they were there even before I learned them, but they were not
in the memory. Where, then, and why did I know them when they
were spoken, saying: 'It is so, it is true,' unless because they were
already in memory, but so far removed, buried in its deeper enclo-
sures, that, unless they had been dug out by something that suggested them, I should perhaps have been unable to think them.

▎XI.

(18) Quocirca inuenimus nihil esse aliud discere ista, quorum non per sensus haurimus imagines, sed sine imaginibus, sicuti sunt, per se ipsa intus cernimus, nisi ea, quae passim atque indisposite memoria continebat, cogitando quasi colligere atque animaduertendo curare, ut tamquam ad manum posita in ipsa memoria, ubi sparsa prius et neglecta latitabant, iam familiari intentioni facile occurrant. et quam multa huius modi gestat memoria mea, quae iam inuenta sunt et, sicut dixi, quasi ad manum posita, quae didicisse et nosse dicimur. quae si modestis temporum interuallis recolere desiuero, ita rursus demerguntur et quasi in remotiora penetralia dilabuntur, ut denuo uelut noua excogitanda sint indidem iterum—neque enim est alia regio eorum—et cogenda rursus, ut sciri possint, id est uelut ex quadam dispersione colligenda, unde dictum est cogitare. nam cogo et cogito sic est, ut ago et agito, facio et factito. uerum tamen sibi animus hoc uerbum proprie uindi-cauit, ut non quod alibi, sed quod in animo colligitur, id est cogitur, cogitari proprie iam dicatur.

▎XII.

(19) Item continet memoria numerorum dimensionumque rationes et leges innumerabiles, quarum nullam corporis sensus inpressit, quia nec ipsae coloratae sunt aut sonant aut olent aut gustatae aut contrectatae sunt. audiui sonos uerborum, quibus significantur, cum de his disseritur, sed illi alii, istae autem aliae sunt. nam illi aliter graece, aliter latine sonant, istae uero nec graecae nec latinae sunt nec aliud eloquiorum genus. uidi lineas fabrorum uel etiam tenuissimas, sicut filum araneae; sed illae aliae sunt, non sunt imagines earum, quas mihi nuntiauit carnis oculus: nouit eas quisquis sine ulla cogitatione qualis-cumque corporis intus agnouit eas. sensi etiam numeros omnibus corporis sensibus, quos numeramus; sed illi alii sunt, quibus numeramus, nec imagines istorum sunt et ideo ualde sunt. rideat me ista dicentem, qui non eos uidet, et ego doleam ridentem me.

▮ Chapter 11

(18) Therefore, we find that to learn things of this kind—whose images we do not acquire through sensation, but which we discern in themselves within us, without images and as they are—is nothing else than, by cogitation, to make a kind of collation of the haphazard and unarranged contents of memory, and, through one's act of awareness, to command that they be placed close at hand, as it were, in this same memory, where they formerly lay scattered about and unnoticed, that they may eventually come easily to the attention of a mind already familiar with them.

How many things of this kind my memory holds which are already found out, and, as I say, placed ready at hand, as it were—things which we are said to have learned and to know! If I cease to recall them to mind for even a short period of time, they are again submerged and slip off, as it were, into the more removed recesses, so that they must again be excogitated, as if new, from the same place as before—there is no other place for them—and they must be drawn together [*cogenda*] again, so that they may be known. That is, they must be collected as if from a condition of being dispersed; hence, one speaks of cogitating. For, *cogo* [draw together] and *cogito* [cogitate] are related as are *ago* [do] and *agito* [do constantly] and as *facio* [make] and *factito* [make frequently]. But the mind has made this word its own property, so that what is collated, that is, drawn together, in the mind, but not in any other place, is now properly said to be cogitated.

▮ Chapter 12

(19) Again, memory contains the reasons and innumerable laws of numbers and dimensions, none of which any bodily sense impresses; for, these are neither colored, nor resonant, nor odorous, nor tasty, nor tangible. I have heard the sounds of words by which they are signified when there is a discussion about them, but these sounds are one thing and the objects are another. For, the sounds are different in Greek from what they are in Latin, but the things are neither Greek nor Latin, nor do they belong to any kind of language. I have seen the lines of craftsmen—even the thinnest ones, like a strand from a spider's web; but these [mathematical lines] are quite different. They are not the images of those lines which my fleshly eye has reported to me. They are known by whoever recognizes them interiorly, without cogitation about any body whatever. I have perceived, also, the numbers which we

I XIII.

(20) Haec omnia memoria teneo et quomodo ea didicerim
memoria teneo. multa etiam, quae aduersus haec falsissime
disputantur, audiui et memoria teneo; quae tamenetsi falsa
sunt, tamen ea meminisse me non est falsum; et discreuisse me
inter illa uera et haec falsa, quae contradicuntur, et hoc memini
aliterque nunc uideo cernere me ista, aliter autem memini
saepe me discreuisse, cum ea saepe cogitarem. ergo et
intellexisse me saepius ista memini, et quod nunc discerno et
intellego, recondo in memoria, ut postea me nunc intellexisse
meminerim. et meminisse me memini, sicut postea, quod haec
reminisci nunc potui, si recordabor, utique per uim memoriae
recordabor.

reckon in all the bodily senses, but the ones *by which* we do the counting are quite different. They are not images of these, and so, they really exist. Let him laugh at my saying this, the man who does not see them. I shall pity him for laughing at me.

| Chapter 13

(20) I hold all these things in memory, and I also remember the way I learned them. I have heard and keep in memory the many things most falsely said against them in arguments. Now, even though they are false, the fact that I remember them is not false. I remember, too, that I distinguished between those truths and these errors which are said in opposition. In one way I see that I am now distinguishing these two things, and in another way I remember that I have often made this distinction when I cogitated on them. Therefore, I both remember that I have often understood these things and, as for the fact that I now perceive and understand them, this I store up in memory, so that afterwards I may remember that I now did understand. And so, I remember that I remembered, just as later, if I recall that I could now remember these things, I shall certainly recall it through the power of memory.

| XIV.

(21) Affectiones quoque animi mei eadem memoria continet non
eo modo, quo eas habet ipse animus, cum patitur eas, sed alio
multum diuerso, sicut sese habet uis memoriae. nam et
laetatum me fuisse reminiscor non laetus et tristitiam meam
praeteritam recordor non tristis et me aliquando timuisse recolo
sine timore et pristinae cupiditatis sine cupiditate sum memor.
aliquando et e contrario tristitiam meam transactam laetus
reminiscor et tristis laetitiam. quod mirandum non est de
corpore: aliud enim animus, aliud corpus. itaque si prae-
teritum dolorem corporis gaudens memini, non ita mirum est.
hic uero cum animus sit etiam ipsa memoria—nam et cum
mandamus aliquid, ut memoriter habeatur, dicimus: "uide, ut
illud in animo habeas," et cum obliuiscimur, dicimus: "non fuit
in animo" et "elapsum est animo," ipsam memoriam uocantes
animum—cum ergo ita sit, quid est hoc, quod cum tristitiam
meam praeteritam laetus memini, animus habet laetitiam et
memoria tristitiam, laetusque est animus ex eo, quod inest ei
laetitia, memoria uero ex eo, quod inest ei tristitia, tristis non
est? num forte non pertinet ad animum? quis hoc dixerit?
nimirum ergo memoria quasi uenter est animi, laetitia uero
atque tristitia quasi cibus dulcis et amarus: cum memoriae
conmendantur, quasi traiecta in uentrem recondi illic possunt,
sapere non possunt. ridiculum est haec illis similia putare, nec
tamen sunt omni modo dissimilia.

(22) Sed ecce de memoria profero, cum dico quattuor esse
perturbationes animi, cupiditatem, laetitiam, metum,
tristitiam, et quidquid de his disputare potuero diuidendo
singula per species sui cuiusque generis et definiendo, ibi
inuenio quid dicam atque inde profero, nec tamen ulla earum
perturbatione perturbor, cum eas reminiscendo conmemoro; et
antequam recolerentur a me et retractarentur, ibi erant;
propterea inde per recordationem potuere depromi. forte ergo
sicut de uentre cibus ruminando, sic ista de memoria
recordando proferuntur. cur igitur in ore cogitationis non
sentitur a disputante, hoc est a reminiscente, laetitiae dulcedo
uel amaritudo maestitiae? an in hoc dissimile est, quod non
undique simile est? quis enim talia uolens loqueretur, si
quotiens tristitiam metumue nominamus, totiens maerere uel

| Chapter 14

(21) The same memory contains also the feelings of my mind, not in the way that the mind itself possesses them, when it undergoes them, but quite differently, in the way that the power of memory is related to itself. For, I can remember having experienced joy, yet not be joyful; I recall my past sorrow, without being sorrowful; I recollect that I formerly was in fear, without present fear; and I have remembrance of former desire, without present desire. Sometimes, on the contrary, I reminisce about my departed sorrow with present joy, and my joy with present sorrow.

There is nothing to be wondered at in this, in regard to the body; the mind is one thing, the body another. Thus, if I remember with joy a past pain of the body, that is not so astonishing; however, this is different with the mind, since the mind is memory itself. Thus, when we give something to be memorized, we say: 'See that you keep this in mind'; and when we forget, we say: 'It was not in my mind' and 'It slipped my mind'—for we call the memory itself, mind.

Since this is so, then, how is it that, when I remember with joy my past sorrow, my mind possesses joy and my memory sorrow? And, when the mind is joyful from the fact that joy is present in it, how is it, then, that the memory is not sorrowful from the fact that sorrow is present in it? Does memory, perhaps, not belong to the mind? Who would claim this?

Without doubt, memory is something like a stomach for the mind; so, joy and sorrow are like sweet and bitter food. When they are committed to memory, conveyed down, as it were, into the stomach where they come to be stored, they cannot be tasted. It is ridiculous to consider these things similar, yet they are not entirely dissimilar.

(22) But, look, when I say that there are four passions of the mind, I bring forth from memory desire, joy, fear, and sorrow. Whatever I could say in a discussion about them, by dividing each into the species within the genus of each and by defining them, it is in the memory that I find what to say and from there that I bring it forth. However, I do not suffer any of these passions when I take note of them by remembering. Yet, before they were recalled by me and reviewed, they were there. For that reason, it was possible to draw them out of it through remembrance.

It may be, then, that these are produced from memory, in the process of recall, just as food is from the stomach in the process of rumination. But, why is the sweetness of joy, or the bitterness of sorrow, not perceived in the mouth of cogitation by the man engaged in discussion, that is, the man who is reminiscing? Is this the point of

timere cogeremur? et tamen non ea loqueremur, nisi in
memoria nostra non tantum sonos nominum secundum imagines inpressas a sensibus corporis sed etiam rerum ipsarum
notiones inueniremus, quas nulla ianua carnis accepimus, sed
eas ipse animus per experientiam passionum suarum sentiens
memoriae conmendauit aut ipsa sibi haec etiam non con-
mendata retinuit.

I XV.

(23) Sed utrum per imagines an non, quis facile dixerit?
nomino quippe lapidem, nomino solem, cum res ipsae non
adsunt sensibus meis; in memoria sane mea praesto sunt
imagines earum. nomino dolorem corporis, nec mihi adest,
dum nihil dolet; nisi tamen adesset imago eius in memoria
mea, nescirem quid dicerem, nec eum in disputando a
uoluptate discernerem. nomino salutem corporis, cum saluus
sum corpore; adest mihi res ipsa; uerum tamen nisi et imago
eius esset in memoria mea, nullo modo recordarer, quid huius
nominis significaret sonus, nec aegrotantes agnoscerent,
salute nominata, quid esset dictum, nisi eadem imago ui
memoriae teneretur, quamuis ipsa res abesset a corpore.
nomino numeros, quibus numeramus: en assunt in memoria
mea non imagines eorum, sed ipsi. nomino imaginem solis,
et haec adest in memoria mea; neque enim imaginem
imaginis eius, sed ipsam recolo: ipsa mihi reminiscenti
praesto est. nomino memoriam et agnosco quod nomino. et
ubi agnosco nisi in ipsa memoria? num et ipsa per imaginem
suam sibi adest ac non per se ipsam?

dissimilarity, since they surely are not wholly alike? Who would willingly speak of things of this sort, if every time we mention sorrow or fear we were forced to undergo sorrow or fear? Yet, we would not speak of them unless we found in our memory not only the sounds of their names according to images impressed by the senses of the body, but also the notions of the things themselves which we did not receive through any avenue of the flesh. The mind itself, in sensing, through the experience of its own passions, committed them to memory; or, the memory retained them for itself, even though they were not committed to it.

| Chapter 15

(23) Whether through images or not, who can easily say? In fact, I can name a stone, I can name the sun, while the things themselves are not present to my senses. Of course, their images are at hand in my memory. I can name bodily pain, and it is not present in me when there is no suffering. Yet, unless its image were present in my memory, I would not know what I am talking about, and I would not distinguish it from pleasure, in a discussion. I can name the health of the body, while I am healthy in my body; the thing itself is indeed present in me. Yet, in fact, unless its image were also present in my memory, I would not recall at all what the sound of this name meant. Nor would sick people know what was said, when health is named, unless the same image were kept by the power of memory, although the thing itself were absent from the body.

I can name the numbers by which we count; see, they are in my memory: not their images, but themselves. I can name the image of the sun and it is present in my memory. I do not recall an image of an image, but simply the image; it is present to me when I remember. I can name the memory and I recognize what I am naming. Where do I recognize it unless in memory itself? Now, could it be present to itself through its own image, and not through itself?

▮ XVI.

(24) Quid, cum obliuionem nomino atque itidem agnosco quod nomino? unde agnosco rem, nisi meminissem? non eundem sonum nominis dico, sed rem, quam significat; quam si oblitus essem, quid ille ualeret sonus, agnoscere utique non ualerem. cum memoriam memini, per se ipsam sibi praesto est ipsa memoria; cum uero memini obliuionem, et memoria praesto est et obliuio, memoria, ex qua meminerim, obliuio, quam meminerim. sed quid est obliuio nisi priuatio memoriae? quomodo ergo adest, ut eam meminerim, quando cum adest meminisse non possum? at si quod meminimus memoria retinemus, obliuionem autem nisi meminissemus, nequaquam possimus audito isto nomine rem, quae illo significatur, agnoscere, memoria retinetur obliuio. adest ergo, ne obliuiscamur, quae cum adest, obliuiscimur. an ex hoc intellegitur non se per ipsam inesse memoriae, cum eam meminimus, sed per imaginem suam, quia, si per se ipsam praesto esset obliuio, non ut meminissemus, sed ut obliuisceremur, efficeret? et hoc quis tandem indagabit? quis conprehendet, quomodo sit?

(25) Ego certe, domine, laboro hic et laboro in me ipso: factus sum mihi terra difficultatis et sudoris nimii. neque enim nunc scrutamur plagas caeli aut siderum interualla demetimur uel terrae libramenta quaerimus: ego sum, qui memini, ego animus. non ita mirum, si a me longe est quidquid ego non sum: quid autem propinquius me ipso mihi? et ecce memoriae meae uis non conprehenditur a me, cum ipsum me non dicam praeter illam. quid enim dicturus sum, quando mihi certum est meminisse me obliuionem? an dicturus sum non esse in memoria mea quod memini? an dicturus sum ad hoc inesse obliuionem in memoria mea, ut non obliuiscar? utrumque absurdissimum est. quid illud tertium? quo pacto dicam imaginem obliuionis teneri memoria mea, non ipsam obliuionem, cum eam memini? quo pacto et hoc dicam, quandoquidem cum inprimitur rei cuiusque imago in memoria, prius necesse est, ut adsit res ipsa, unde illa imago possit inprimi? sic enim Carthaginis memini, sic omnium locorum, quibus interfui, sic facies hominum, quas uidi, et ceterorum sensuum nuntiata, sic ipsius corporis salutem siue dolorem: cum praesto essent ista, cepit ab eis imagines memoria, quas

I Chapter 16

(24) Now, when I name oblivion, and likewise recognize what I am naming, what would be the source of my recognition if I did not remember it? I am not talking about the sound of the name, but the thing which it signifies. Now, if I had forgotten this meaning, I should not be able at all to recognize what the sound's function is. Therefore, when I remember my memory, the very memory is present to itself in itself, but, when I remember oblivion, both memory and oblivion are present—memory, as that from which I recall; oblivion, as that which I recall. But, what is oblivion except the privation of memory? How, then, can it be present, so that I may remember it, when I cannot remember while it is present? But, if we keep in memory what we remember, and if, without remembering oblivion, we could not possibly know the meaning of this word when we heard it, then oblivion is retained in memory. Therefore, it is present so that we will not forget, and, when it is present, we do forget.

Or, is one to understand from this that it is not present in memory through itself, when we remember it, but rather through its image—because, if oblivion were present in itself, would not the result be that we would forget, not that we would remember? Now, who will eventually work this out? Who will understand how it is?

(25) Certainly, O Lord, I am working hard on it, and my work is being done on myself; I have become unto myself a soil of difficulty, and of too much sweat. For, we are not now gazing curiously at the sky's expanses, nor are we measuring the distances between the stars, nor are we trying to weigh the earth; I am the one who is remembering, I am the mind. It is not so astonishing if whatever I am not is far distant from me, but what is nearer to me than myself? And, notice, the power of my memory is not understood by me, yet, at the same time, I cannot speak of myself without it. What should I say, when it is a certitude to me that I do remember oblivion? Or, should I say that what I remember is not in my memory? Or, should I say that oblivion is in my memory just for this—that I may not forget? Both are most absurd.

What of a third possibility? On what basis may I say that the image of oblivion is kept in my memory, not oblivion itself, when I do remember it? On what basis, too, may I say this, since, when any image of a thing is impressed on memory, it is first necessary for the thing itself to be present, from which the image can be impressed? For, thus do I remember Carthage; thus, all the places where I have been; thus, the faces of the men I have seen and the things reported by the other senses; thus, the health of the body itself or its pain. When these things were at hand, my memory took the images from

intuerer praesentes et retractarem animo, cum illa et absentia
reminiscerer. si ergo per imaginem suam, non per se ipsam in
memoria tenetur obliuio, ipsa utique aderat, ut eius imago
caperetur. cum autem adesset, quomodo imaginem suam in
memoria conscribebat, quando id etiam, quod iam notatum
inuenit, praesentia sua delet obliuio? et tamen quocumque
modo, licet sit modus iste inconprehensibilis et inexplicabilis,
ipsam obliuionem meminisse me certus sum, qua id quod
meminerimus obruitur.

❙ XVII.

(26) Magna uis est memoriae, nescio quid horrendum, deus
meus, profunda et infinita multiplicitas; et hoc animus est, et
hoc ego ipse sum. quid ergo sum, deus meus? quae natura
sum? uaria, multimoda uita et inmensa uehementer. ecce in
memoriae meae campis et antris et cauernis innumerabilibus
atque innumerabiliter plenis innumerabilium rerum generibus
siue per imagines, sicut omnium corporum, siue per
praesentiam, sicut artium, siue per nescio quas notiones uel
notationes, sicut affectionum animi—quas et cum animus non
patitur, memoria tenet, cum in animo sit quidquid est in
memoria—per haec omnia discurro et uolito hac illac, penetro
etiam quantum possum, et finis nusquam: tanta uis est
memoriae, tanta uitae uis est in homine uiuente mortaliter!
quid igitur agam, tu uera mea uita, deus meus? transibo et
hanc uim meam, quae memoria uocatur, transibo eam, ut
pertendam ad te, dulce lumen. quid dicis mihi? ego ascendens
per animum meum ad te, qui desuper mihi manes, transibo et
istam uim meam, quae memoria uocatur, uolens te attingere,
unde attingi potes, et inhaerere tibi, unde inhaereri tibi potest.
habent enim memoriam et pecora et aues, alioquin non cubilia,
non nidos suos repeterent, non alia multa, quibus assuescunt;
neque enim et assuescere ualerent ullis rebus nisi per memoriam. transibo ergo et memoriam, ut attingam eum, qui
separauit me a quadrupedibus et uolatilibus caeli sapientiorem
me fecit. transibo et memoriam, ut ubi te inueniam, uere bone,
et secura suauitas, ut ubi te inueniam? si praeter memoriam
meam te inuenio, inmemor tui sum. et quomodo iam inueniam
te, si memor non sum tui?

them, which, as being present, I might see directly and review in my mind when I remembered the things in their absence.

If, then, oblivion is held in memory through its image and not through itself, it must certainly have been present itself, in order that its image might be grasped. Now, when it was present, how did it write its image in the memory, when oblivion erases, by its presence, even what it finds already known? Yet, I am certain that I do remember in some manner or other, though this manner be incomprehensible and inexplicable, even oblivion itself, whereby the object we remember is consigned to destruction.

I Chapter 17

(26) Great is the power of memory; its deep and boundless multiplicity is something fearful, O my God! And this is the mind, and I am this myself. What, then, am I, O my God? What is my nature? A life of many aspects and many ways, strikingly immeasurable.

Look into the fields, hollows, and innumerable caverns of my memory, filled beyond number with innumerable kinds of things, either by means of images as in the case of all bodies, or by means of their own presence as in the case of the arts, or by means of some sort of notions or impressions as in the case of the feelings of the mind (which the memory keeps even when the mind is not undergoing them, though whatever is in the memory is in the mind!). I run through all these things, and I flit here and there. I even go as deep as I can, yet there is no limit. So great is the power of memory, so great is the power of life in man who lives mortally!

What shall I do, Thou true Life of mine, O my God? I shall pass over even this power of mine which is called memory; I shall pass over it to reach Thee, sweet Light. What dost Thou say to me? Behold, going up through my mind to Thee, who dwellest above me, I shall even pass over this power of mine which is called memory, desiring to attain Thee where Thou canst be attained, and to cleave to Thee where it is possible to be in contact with Thee.

For, even beasts and birds have memory; otherwise, they could not find their lairs and nests, or the many other things to which they become accustomed. And they could not grow accustomed to any thing, unless through memory. Therefore, I shall even pass over memory to attain Him who has set me apart from the four-footed beasts and made me 'wiser than the fowls of the air.' I shall even pass over memory, so that I may find Thee—where, O truly good and serene Sweetness—where shall I find Thee? But, if I find Thee without memory, I am without remembrance of Thee. And how, indeed, may I find Thee, if I am without remembrance of Thee?

┃ XVIII.

(27) Perdiderat enim mulier drachmam et quaesiuit eam cum
lucerna et, nisi memor eius esset, non inueniret eam. cum enim
esset inuenta, unde sciret, utrum ipsa esset, si memor eius non
esset? multa memini me perdita quaesisse atque inuenisse.
inde istuc scio, quia, cum quaererem aliquid eorum et diceretur
mihi: "num forte hoc est?" "num forte illud?" tamdiu dicebam:
"non est," donec id offerretur quod quaerebam. cuius nisi
memor essem, quidquid illud esset, etiamsi mihi offerretur, non
inuenirem, quia non agnoscerem. et semper ita fit, cum aliquid
perditum quaerimus et inuenimus. uerum tamen si forte
aliquid ab oculis perit, non a memoria, ueluti corpus quodlibet
uisibile, tenetur intus imago eius, et quaeritur, donec reddatur
aspectui. quod cum inuentum fuerit, ex imagine, quae intus
est, recognoscitur. nec inuenisse nos dicimus quod perierat, si
non agnoscimus, nec agnoscere possumus, si non meminimus:
sed hoc perierat quidem oculis, memoria tenebatur.

| Chapter 18

(27) The woman who had lost her drachma and looked for it with a lamp would not have found it, unless she retained some remembrance of it. For, when it had been found, how would she know whether it was the one, if she retained no remembrance of it? I remember many lost things which I have looked for and found. From this, I know that, when I was looking for one of them, and people would say to me: 'Perhaps this is it? Maybe this one?' I would continue to say: 'It is not,' until the thing I was seeking was shown to me. Unless I had some remembrance of it, whatever it was, I should not have found it, even if it were shown to me, for I should not have recognized it. That is always the way it is, when we look for some lost thing and find it. Yet, of course, when by chance something is lost from sight, not from memory—any visible body, for example—its image is retained within, and it is sought until it comes back within view. And, when it is found, it is recognized from the image which is within. We do not say that we have found what we lost, if we do not recognize it, and we cannot recognize it, if we do not remember it. It disappeared, indeed, from before our eyes, but it was retained in memory.

I XIX.

(28) Quid? cum ipsa memoria perdit aliquid, sicut fit, cum obliuiscimur et quaerimus, ut recordemur, ubi tandem quaerimus nisi in ipsa memoria? et ibi si aliud pro alio forte offeratur, respuimus, donec illud occurrat quod quaerimus. et cum occurrit, dicimus: "hoc est"; quod non diceremus, nisi agnosceremus, nec agnosceremus, nisi meminissemus. certe enim obliti fueramus. an non totum exciderat, sed ex parte, quae tenebatur, pars alia quaerebatur, quia sentiebat se memoria non simul uoluere, quod simul solebat, et quasi detruncata consuetudine claudicans reddi quod deerat flagitabat? tamquam si homo notus siue conspiciatur oculis siue cogitetur et nomen eius obliti requiramus, quidquid aliud occurrerit non conectitur, quia non cum illo cogitari consueuit ideoque respuitur, donec illud adsit, ubi simul adsuefacta notitia non inaequaliter adquiescat. et unde adest nisi ex ipsa memoria? nam et cum ab alio conmoniti recognoscimus, inde adest. non enim quasi nouum credimus, sed recordantes adprobamus hoc esse, quod dictum est. si autem penitus aboleatur ex animo, nec admoniti reminiscimur. neque enim omni modo adhuc obliti sumus quod uel oblitos nos esse meminimus. hoc ergo nec amissum quaerere poterimus, quod omnino obliti fuerimus.

| Chapter 19

(28) What? When the memory itself loses something, as happens when we forget and try to remember, pray, where do we look for it, unless in the memory itself? And in it, if one thing is presented in place of another, we reject it until the thing we are looking for turns up. When it does turn up, we say: 'This is it.' We would not say that unless we recognized it, and we would not recognize it unless we remembered. Yet, we certainly had forgotten it.

Or, had it disappeared, not completely, but only in part? And is the other part sought, by means of that which is retained, because the memory felt that its object of consideration was not as complete as usual, and, feeling the defect in a habit which was, as it were, defective in some part, it strove to get back what was missing?

For instance, if a man who is known comes before our eyes or into our thoughts, and we are trying to recall his name, which we have forgotten, then, any other name which occurs fails to be connected, because it has not been customary for our thought of him to go along with it; hence, it is rejected until that name occurs which our customary way of thinking of the man accepts as not inappropriate. And, from what source does it occur, if not from memory itself? For, when we recognize it, on being reminded by someone else, it is from there that it comes. So, we do not accept it as something new, but, in recalling it, we judge that what has been said is the right name. But, if it is entirely wiped out of mind, then we do not remember even when reminded. And, if we even remember that we have forgotten it, then we have not yet completely forgotten. Therefore, we would not be able to look for something that has been lost, if we had altogether forgotten it.

▌ XX.

(29) Quomodo ergo te quaero, domine? cum enim te, deum meum, quaero, uitam beatam quaero. quaeram te, ut uiuat anima mea. uiuit enim corpus meum de anima mea et uiuit anima mea de te. quomodo ergo quaero uitam beatam? quia non est mihi, donec dicam "sat, est illic," ubi oportet ut dicam. quomodo eam quaero, utrum per recordationem, tamquam eam oblitus sim oblitumque me esse adhuc teneam, an per appetitum discendi incognitam, siue quam numquam scierim, siue quam sic oblitus fuerim, ut me nec oblitum esse meminerim? nonne ipsa est beata uita, quam omnes uolunt et omnino qui nolit nemo est? ubi nouerunt eam, quod sic uolunt eam? ubi uiderunt, ut amarent eam? nimirum habemus eam nescio quomodo. et est alius quidam modus, quo quisque cum habet eam, tunc beatus est, et sunt, qui spe beati sunt. inferiore modo isti habent eam quam illi, qui iam re ipsa beati sunt, sed tamen meliores quam illi, qui nec re nec spe beati sunt. qui tamen etiam ipsi nisi aliquo modo haberent eam, non ita uellent beati esse: quod eos uelle certissimum est. nescio quomodo nouerunt eam ideoque habent eam in nescio qua notitia, de qua satago, utrum in memoria sit, quia, si ibi est, iam beati fuimus aliquando—utrum singillatim omnes, an in illo homine, qui primus peccauit, in quo et omnes mortui sumus et de quo omnes cum miseria nati sumus, non quaero nunc, sed quaero, utrum in memoria sit beata uita. neque enim amaremus eam, nisi nossemus. audiuimus nomen hoc et omnes rem, omnes nos adpetere fatemur; non enim solo sono delectamur. nam hoc cum latine audit Graecus, non delectatur, quia ignorat, quid dictum sit; nos autem delectamur, sicut etiam ille, si graece hoc audierit, quoniam res ipsa nec graeca nec latina est, cui adipiscendae Graeci Latinique inhiant ceterarumque linguarum homines. nota est igitur omnibus, qui una uoce si interrogari possent, utrum beati esse uellent, sine ulla dubitatione uelle responderent. quod non fieret, nisi res ipsa, cuius hoc nomen est, eorum memoria teneretur.

| Chapter 20

(29) Now, how do I look for Thee, O Lord? When I look for Thee, my God, I am looking for the happy life. May I seek Thee, so that my soul may live. For, my body has life from my soul, and my soul has life from Thee. How, then, do I seek the happy life? It is not mine, until I can say: 'Enough, there it is.' Here, then, I ought to say how I do look for it, whether through remembrance, as though I had forgotten it and I still retained the fact that I had forgotten, or through a desire to learn it as something unknown, either something I never knew, or which I have so forgotten that I have no remembrance even that I have forgotten it. Surely, the happy life is this: what all men desire and [such that] there is absolutely no one who does not desire it? Where did they know it, this object which they desire in such a way? Where did they see it, to love it so? Certainly, we do possess it, but how I know not.

There is one certain way whereby each man, when he possesses this object, is then happy, and there also are those who are happy in hope. The latter possess it in an inferior way, compared to those who are already really happy, yet they are better off than those others who are happy neither in reality nor in hope. Still, unless this third kind of people possessed it, in some way, they would not desire to be happy; that they have such a desire is most certain. Somehow or other they came to know it, and so they possess it in some kind or other of knowledge. My problem concerning this is whether it may be in the memory; for, if it is there, then we were at one time happy, either all individually, or all in that man who was the first to sin, in whom also we all died, from whom we are all born amidst unhappiness. I do not ask this question now, but I do ask whether the happy life is in the memory.

Now, we would not love it, unless we knew it. We hear this word and we all admit that we seek this thing, for we are not delighted merely by the sound. When a Greek hears this word in Latin, he is not delighted, for he does not know what has been said. Yet, we Latins are delighted, as he is, too, if he hears it in Greek, for the thing itself is neither Greek nor Latin, this thing which Greeks and Latins and men of every tongue yearn to obtain. So, it is known to all men who, if they could be asked whether they desire to be happy, would reply in one voice, without any hesitation, that they do. This would be impossible, unless the thing itself, of which this is the name, were kept in their memory.

I XXI.

(30) Numquid ita, ut memini Carthaginem qui uidi? non; uita enim beata non uidetur oculis, quia non est corpus. numquid sicut meminimus numeros? non; hos enim qui habet in notitia, non adhuc quaerit adipisci, uitam uero beatam habemus in notitia ideoque amamus et tamen adhuc adipisci eam uolumus, ut beati simus. numquid sicut meminimus eloquentiam? non: quamuis et hoc nomine audito recordentur ipsam rem qui etiam nondum sunt eloquentes; multique esse cupiant, unde apparet eam esse in eorum notitia; tamen per corporis sensus alios eloquentes animaduerterunt et delectati sunt et hoc esse desiderant—quamquam nisi ex interiore notitia non delectarentur, neque hoc esse uellent, nisi delectarentur—beatam uero uitam nullo sensu corporis in aliis experimur. numquid sicut meminimus gaudium? fortasse ita. nam gaudium meum etiam tristis memini sicut uitam beatam miser, neque umquam corporis sensu gaudium meum uel uidi uel audiui uel odoratus sum uel gustaui uel tetigi, sed expertus sum in animo meo, quando laetatus sum, et adhaesit eius notitia memoriae meae, ut id reminisci ualeam aliquando cum aspernatione, aliquando cum desiderio, pro earum rerum diuersitate, de quibus me gauisum esse memini. nam et de turpibus gaudio quodam perfusus sum, quod nunc recordans detestor atque exsecror, aliquando de bonis et honestis, quod desiderans recolo, tametsi forte non assunt, et ideo tristis gaudium pristinum recolo.

(31) Ubi ergo et quando expertus sum uitam meam beatam, ut recorder eam et amem et desiderem? nec ego tantum aut cum paucis, sed beati prorsus omnes esse uolumus. quod nisi certa notitia nossemus, non tam certa uoluntate uellemus. sed quid est hoc? quid? si quaeratur a duobus, utrum militare uelint, fieri possit, ut alter eorum uelle se, alter nolle respondeat: si autem ab eis quaeratur, utrum esse beati uelint, uterque se statim sine dubitatione dicat optare, nec ob aliud ille uelit militare, non ob aliud iste nolit, nisi ut beati sint. num forte quoniam alius hinc, alius inde gaudet? ita se omnes beatos esse uelle consonant, quemadmodum consonarent, si hoc interrogarentur, se uelle gaudere atque ipsum gaudium uitam beatam uocant. quod etsi alius hinc, alius illinc assequitur, unum est tamen, quo peruenire omnes nituntur, ut gaudeant.

| Chapter 21

(30) Now, is this the same as the case of the man who, having seen Carthage, remembers it? No! The happy life is not seen with the eyes, since it is not a body.

Is it like the example of our remembering numbers? No! One who possesses these in knowledge does not seek to obtain further, but we possess the happy life in knowledge, and so we love it, yet wish to attain it further so that we may *be* happy.

Is it like the instance where we remember the art of oratory? No! For, though, when this word has been heard, people recall to mind the thing itself, even those who are not yet eloquent—and many do desire to be (whence it is apparent that eloquence exists in their knowledge), but, on the other hand, they have observed through the senses of the body that other people are eloquent and they are delighted and long to be likewise; they would not be delighted except from interior knowledge and they would not desire to be likewise unless they were so delighted. However, we do not have personal experience of the happy life in other people, through any sense of the body.

Is it like the way in which we remember joy? Perhaps so. For, I remember my joy even when sad, just as I do the happy life when I am unhappy, and I have never seen, or heard, or smelled, or tasted, or touched my joy by any sense of the body, but I have experienced it in my mind when I have been joyful. Its knowledge stuck in my memory, so that I am able to remember it, sometimes with contempt, sometimes with longing, depending on the difference between the things from which my joy came, as I remember it. For, I have been imbued with a certain joy arising from shameful things, and, as I now recall this, I feel disgust and curse it; at other times, it arises from good and virtuous things, and I recall it with longing, even though, perhaps, they are no longer available, and therefore I am saddened as I recall my former joy.

(31) Where, then, and when did I experience my happy life that I should now remember, love, and desire it? Not just I alone, or in the company of a few people, but absolutely all people want to be happy. Unless we knew it with certain knowledge, we would not will it with such a certain act of will. But, how is this? If the question be asked of two men whether they wish to serve in the army, it is quite possible that one of them may reply that he wants to, the other that he does not. But, if they are asked whether they wish to be happy, both will say at once and without any hesitation that they do desire it. Nor is there any different reason why one wishes to enter military service and the other does not, than that they wish to be happy. One man,

quae quoniam res est, quam se expertum non esse nemo potest dicere, propterea reperta in memoria recognoscitur, quando beatae uitae nomen auditur.

❙ XXII.

(32) Absit, domine, absit a corde serui tui, qui confitetur tibi, absit, ut quocumque gaudio gaudeam beatum me putem. est enim gaudium, quod non datur inpiis, sed eis, qui te gratis colunt, quorum gaudium tu ipse es. et ipsa est beata uita, gaudere de te, ad te, propter te: ipsa est et non est altera. qui autem aliam putant esse, aliud sectantur gaudium neque ipsum uerum. ab aliqua tamen imagine gaudii uoluntas eorum non auertitur.

perhaps, finds his joy in one thing, another man in another? Even so, they agree that they all wish to be happy, just as they would agree, if asked the question, that they wish to possess joy. This joy they call the happy life. Even though one man attains it here, another there, still it is but one thing which all men strive to reach, so that they may be joyful. Now, since this is a thing which no man can deny experiencing, it is therefore recognized as found in the memory, when the name, happy life, is heard.

I Chapter 22

(32) Far be it, O Lord, far be it from the heart of Thy servant who is confessing to Thee, far be it that I should consider myself happy by virtue of just any joy which I experience. For, there is a joy which is not given to the wicked, but rather to them who serve Thee for Thine own sake; for such people, Thou Thyself art Joy. And this is the happy life, to rejoice unto Thee, from Thee, on account of Thee: this it is and there is none other. They who think that there is another pursue a different joy, and not the true one. Yet, their will is not turned away from some representation of joy.

I XXIII.

(33) Non ergo certum est, quod omnes esse beati uolunt,
quoniam qui non de te gaudere uolunt, quae sola uita beata est,
non utique uitam beatam uolunt? an omnes hoc uolunt, sed
quoniam caro concupiscit aduersus spiritum et spiritus
aduersus carnem, ut non faciant quod uolunt, cadunt in id quod
ualent eoque contenti sunt, quia illud, quod non ualent, non
tantum uolunt, quantum sat est, ut ualeant? nam quaero ab
omnibus, utrum malint de ueritate quam de falsitate gaudere:
tam non dubitant dicere de ueritate se malle, quam non
dubitant dicere beatos esse se uelle. beata quippe uita est
gaudium de ueritate. hoc est enim gaudium de te, qui ueritas
es, deus, inluminatio mea, salus faciei meae, deus meus. hanc
uitam beatam omnes uolunt, hanc uitam, quae sola beata est,
omnes uolunt, gaudium de ueritate omnes uolunt. multos
expertus sum, qui uellent fallere, qui autem falli, neminem. ubi
ergo nouerunt hanc uitam beatam, nisi ubi nouerunt etiam
ueritatem? amant enim et ipsam, quia falli nolunt, et cum
amant beatam uitam, quod non est aliud quam de ueritate
gaudium, utique amant etiam ueritatem, nec amarent, nisi
esset aliqua notitia eius in memoria eorum. cur ergo non de illa
gaudent? cur non beati sunt? quia fortius occupantur in aliis,
quae potius eos faciunt miseros quam illud beatos, quod
tenuiter meminerunt. adhuc enim modicum lumen est in
hominibus; ambulent, ambulent, ne tenebrae conprehendant.

(34) Cur autem ueritas parit odium et inimicus eis factus est
homo tuus uerum praedicans, cum ametur beata uita, quae non
est nisi gaudium de ueritate, nisi quia sic amatur ueritas, ut
quicumque aliud amant, hoc quod amant uelint esse ueritatem,
et quia falli nollent, nolunt conuinci, quod falsi sint? itaque
propter eam rem oderunt ueritatem, quam pro ueritate amant.
amant eam lucentem, oderunt eam redarguentem. quia enim
falli nolunt et fallere uolunt, amant eam, cum se ipsa indicat, et
oderunt eam, cum eos ipsos indicat. inde retribuet eis, ut, qui
se ab ea manifestari nolunt, et eos nolentes manifestet et eis
ipsa non sit manifesta. sic, sic, etiam sic animus humanus,
etiam sic caecus et languidus, turpis atque indecens latere uult,
se autem ut lateat aliquid non uult. contra illi redditur, ut ipse
non lateat ueritatem, ipsum autem ueritas lateat. tamen etiam

| Chapter 23

(33) Is it, then, uncertain that all men wish to be happy, because those who do not wish to find their joy in Thee—and this is the only happy life—do not, in point of fact, desire the happy life? Or, do all desire this, but, because 'the flesh lusts against the spirit, and the spirit against the flesh . . . so that they do not do what they wish, they descend to that of which they are capable and are content with it, for they do not desire that for which they have insufficient capacity, to the extent that their desire would render them capable of it?

Now, I ask all men whether they would prefer to get their joy from truth rather than from falsity? They will hesitate as little to say that they prefer it from truth as they hesitate in saying that they wish to be happy. Indeed, the happy life is joy arising from truth. For, this is the joy coming from Thee, who art the Truth, O God; Thou art 'my light,' the salvation of my countenance, O my God. This happy life all men desire; this life, which alone is happy, all men desire; the joy arising from truth all men desire.

I have been acquainted with many men who wished to deceive, but not one who wished to be deceived. Where, then, did they get their knowledge of this happy life, unless where they got their knowledge of truth, too? For they love the latter, also, since they do not wish to be deceived. And, when they love the happy life, which is nothing other than joy arising from truth, they certainly love truth, also. Nor would they love it, unless some knowledge of it were in their memory.

Why, then, do they not take their joy from it? Why are they not happy? Because they are more keenly concerned with other things which have greater power to make them unhappy than this, which they faintly remember, to make them happy. 'Yet a little while the light is' in men; let them walk, walk, lest darkness overtake them.

(34) But, why does 'truth engender hatred' and Thy man who speaks the truth has become a enemy to them, when a happy life is loved and it is nothing but joy arising from truth? Is it that truth is so loved that, whoever love something else, they wish this object of love to be the truth, and, since they did not want to be deceived, they do not want to be shown that they have been deceived? Therefore, they hate the truth because of the same thing which they love in place of truth. They love truth when it enlightens; they hate it when it reproves. Since they not wish to be deceived, and they do wish to deceive, they love it when it reveals its own self, and they hate it when it reveals themselves. Its retribution upon them stems from this: they who do not wish to be revealed by it, it both reveals against their will and is not itself revealed to them.

sic, dum miser est, ueris mauult gaudere quam falsis. beatus
ergo erit, si nulla interpellante molestia de ipsa, per quam uera
sunt omnia, sola ueritate gaudebit.

| XXIV.

(35) Ecce quantum spatiatus sum in memoria mea quaerens te,
domine, et non te inueni extra eam. neque enim aliquid de te
inueni, quod non meminissem ex quo didici te. nam ex quo
didici te, non sum oblitus tui. ubi enim inueni ueritatem, ibi
inueni deum meum, ipsam ueritatem, quam ex quo didici, non
sum oblitus. itaque ex quo te didici, manes in memoria mea, et
illic te inuenio, cum reminiscor tui et delector in te. hae sunt
sanctae deliciae meae, quas donasti mihi misericordia tua
respiciens paupertatem meam.

Thus, thus, even thus is the human mind, even thus is it blind and weak; it wishes to lie hidden, a foul and unattractive thing, but does not wish anything to be hidden to it. What befalls it is the contrary: it is not hidden before the truth, but the truth is hidden before it. Nevertheless, even while it is in such unhappiness, it prefers to rejoice in true things rather than in false. It will be happy, then, if, with no hindrance interposed, it will come to rejoice in that through which all things are true, in the only Truth.

❙ Chapter 24

(35) See how much I have traveled about in the spaciousness of my memory while looking for Thee, O Lord, and I have not found Thee outside it. Nor have I found anything about Thee which I did not keep in memory, ever since I learned of Thee. For, from the time that I learned of Thee, I did not forget Thee. Now, wherever I found truth, there did I find my God, Truth Itself, and from the time that I learned of the Truth, I have not forgotten. Therefore, from the time that I learned about Thee, Thou dost dwell in my memory, and there do I find Thee when I remember Thee and delight in Thee. These are my holy delights which Thou hast given me in Thy mercy, having regard to my poverty.

I XXV.

(36) Sed ubi manes in memoria mea, domine, ubi illic manes? quale cubile fabricasti tibi? quale sanctuarium aedificasti tibi? tu dedisti hanc dignationem memoriae meae, ut maneas in ea, sed in qua eius parte maneas, hoc considero. transcendi enim partes eius, quas habent et bestiae, cum te recordarer, quia non ibi te inueniebam inter imagines rerum corporalium, et ueni ad partes eius, ubi conmendaui affectiones animi mei, nec illic inueni te. et intraui ad ipsius animi mei sedem, quae illi est in memoria mea—quoniam sui quoque meminit animus—nec ibi tu eras, quia sicut non es imago corporalis nec affectio uiuentis, qualis est, cum laetamur, contristamur, cupimus, metuimus, meminimus, obliuiscimur et quidquid huius modi est, ita nec ipse animus es, quia dominus deus animi tu es, et conmutantur haec omnia, tu autem inconmutabilis manes super omnia et dignatus es habitare in memoria mea ex quo te didici. et quid quaero, quo loco eius habites, quasi uero loca ibi sint? habitas certe in ea, quoniam tui memini ex quo te didici, et in ea inuenio, cum recordor te.

I XXVI.

(37) Ubi ergo te inueni, ut discerem te? neque enim iam eras in memoria mea, priusquam te discerem. ubi ergo te inueni, ut discerem te, nisi in te supra me? et nusquam locus, et recedimus et accedimus, et nusquam locus. ueritas, ubique praesides omnibus consulentibus te simulque respondes omnibus diuersa consulentibus. liquide tu respondes, sed non liquide omnes audiunt. omnes unde uolunt consulunt, sed non semper quod uolunt audiunt. optimus minister tuus est, qui non magis intuetur hoc a te audire quod ipse uoluerit, sed potius hoc uelle quod a te audierit.

| Chapter 25

(36) But, where dost Thou dwell in my memory, O Lord; where dost Thou dwell there? What resting place hast Thou fashioned for Thyself? What sanctuary hast Thou built for Thyself? Thou hast granted this favor to my memory, to dwell in it, but in which part of it Thou dost dwell, this I now consider. When I recalled Thee to mind, I went above those parts of it which the beasts also possess, for I did not find Thee there among the images of bodily things. So, I came to the parts of it in which I keep my mental feelings, but I did not find Thee there. So, I entered into the seat of my very mind, and there is one for it in my memory, since the mind also remembers itself, and Thou wert not there. Because, just as Thou art not a bodily image, nor the feeling of a living being, such as occurs when we are joyful, sorrowful, longing, fearful, mindful, forgetful, or anything else of this kind, so, too, Thou art not the mind itself. For, Thou art the Lord God of the mind, and all these things are mutable, but Thou dwellest as an immutable Being above them all. So, Thou hast deigned to reside in my memory, from the time that I have learned about Thee.

And why do I look for the place in it where Thou dost dwell, as if there really were places in it? What is certain is that Thou dwellest in it, for I remember Thee from the time that I have learned about Thee, and I do find Thee in it when I recall Thee to mind.

| Chapter 26

(37) Where, then, did I find Thee in order to learn about Thee? For, Thou wert not already in my memory before I learned of Thee. Where, then, did I find Thee in order to learn about Thee, unless in Thyself above me? Yet, there is no place. We go backward and we go forward, yet there is no place. O Truth, Thou dost preside over all things, even those which can take counsel with Thee, and Thou dost answer in the same time all who consult Thee, however diverse their questions. Thou dost answer clearly, but all do not hear clearly. All seek counsel concerning what they wish, but they do not always hear what they wish. He serves Thee best who does not so much expect to hear the thing from Thee which he himself desires, but rather to desire what he hears from Thee.

I XXVII.

(38) Sero te amaui, pulchritudo tam antiqua et tam noua, sero te amaui! et ecce intus eras et ego foris et ibi te quaerebam et in ista formosa, quae fecisti, deformis inruebam. mecum eras, et tecum non eram. ea me tenebant longe a te, quae si in te non essent, non essent. uocasti et clamasti et rupisti surditatem meam, coruscasti, splenduisti et fugasti caecitatem meam, fragrasti, et duxi spiritum et anhelo tibi, gustaui et esurio et sitio, tetigisti me, et exarsi in pacem tuam.

I XXVIII.

(39) Cum inhaesero tibi ex omni me, nusquam erit mihi dolor et labor, et uiua erit uita mea tota plena te. nunc autem quoniam quem tu imples, subleuas eum, quoniam tui plenus nondum sum, oneri mihi sum. contendunt laetitiae meae flendae cum laetandis maeroribus, et ex qua parte stet uictoria nescio. ei mihi, domine, miserere mei! contendunt maerores mei mali cum gaudiis bonis, et ex qua parte stet uictoria nescio. ei mihi, domine, miserere mei! ei mihi! ecce uulnera mea non abscondo: medicus es, aeger sum; misericors es, miser sum. numquid non temptatio est uita humana super terram? quis uelit molestias et difficultates? tolerari iubes ea, non amari. nemo quod tolerat amat, etsi tolerare amat. quamuis enim gaudeat se tolerare, mauult tamen non esse quod toleret. prospera in aduersis desidero, aduersa in prosperis timeo. quis inter haec medius locus, ubi non sit humana uita temptatio? uae prosperitatibus saeculi semel et iterum a timore aduer-sitatis et a corruptione laetitiae! uae aduersitatibus saeculi semel et iterum et tertio a desiderio prosperitatis, et quia ipsa aduersitas dura est, et ne frangat tolerantiam. numquid non temptatio est uita humana super terram sine ullo interstitio?

| Chapter 27

(38) Late have I loved Thee, O Beauty so ancient and so new, late have I loved Thee! And behold, Thou wert within and I was without. I was looking for Thee out there, and I threw myself, deformed as I was, upon those well-formed things which Thou hast made. Thou wert with me, yet I was not with Thee. These things held me far from Thee, things which would not have existed had they not been in Thee. Thou didst call and cry out and burst in upon my deafness; Thou didst shine forth and glow and drive away my blindness; Thou didst send forth Thy fragrance, and I drew in my breath, and now I pant for Thee; I have tasted, and now I hunger and thirst; Thou didst touch me, and I was inflamed with desire for Thy peace.

| Chapter 28

(39) When I shall cleave to Thee with all my being, sorrow and toil will no longer exist for me, and my life will be alive, being wholly filled with Thee. At the present time, however, because Thou dost lift up whomever Thou fillest and I am not filled with Thee, I am a burden to myself. My joys, which are to be lamented, struggle against my sorrows, which are cause for joy, and I know not on which side victory may stand.

My evil sorrows struggle with my good joys, and I know not on which side victory may stand. Alas for me! Have mercy on me, O Lord! Alas for me! Behold, I do not hide my wounds: Thou art the Physician, I am a sick man; Thou art merciful, I am a miserable man. Is not 'the life of man upon earth a trial?' Who would want troubles and hardships? Thou dost command that they be endured, not loved. No man loves what he endures, even though he loves to endure. For, though he rejoice that he can endure them, he prefers to have nothing to endure. Amid adversities, I long for successes; amid successes, I fear adversities. What is the middle area between these, where the life of man is not a trial? Woe to the successes of this world, once and again, because of the fear of adversity and the corruption of joy. Woe to the adversities of this world, once, twice and thrice, because of the yearning for success, both because adversity itself is hard and because it may break down endurance! Is not 'the life of man upon earth a trial,' without any interruption?

I XXIX.

(40) Et tota spes mea non nisi in magna misericordia tua. da quod iubes et iube quod uis. imperas nobis continentiam. et cum scirem, ait quidam, quia nemo potest esse continens nisi deus det, et hoc ipsum erat sapientiae, scire cuius esset hoc donum. per continentiam quippe colligimur et redigimur in unum, a quo in multa defluximus. minus enim te amat qui tecum aliquid amat, quod non propter te amat. o amor, qui semper ardes et numquam extingueris, caritas, deus meus, accende me! continentiam iubes: da quod iubes et iube quod uis.

❚ Chapter 29

(40) My whole hope is nowhere but in Thy exceedingly great mercy. Grant what Thou dost command and command what Thou wilt. Thou dost command continence for us. 'And as I knew,' a certain man has said, 'that no one could be continent, except God gave it, this also was a point of wisdom, to know whose gift it was. Through continence, in fact, we are gathered in and returned to the One from whom we have flowed out into the many. For, he loves Thee less who loves something else along with Thee, which he does not love for Thy sake. O Love, who ever burnest and art never extinguished, O Charity, my God, kindle me! Thou dost command continence; grant what Thou dost command and command what Thou wilt.

| XXX.

(41) Iubes certe, ut contineam a concupiscentia carnis et concupiscentia oculorum et ambitione saeculi. iussisti a concubitu,
et de ipso coniugio melius aliquid, quam concessisti, monuisti.
et quoniam dedisti, factum est et antequam dispensator
sacramenti tui fierem. sed adhuc uiuunt in memoria mea, de
qua multa locutus sum, talium rerum imagines, quas ibi
consuetudo mea fixit, et occursantur mihi uigilanti quidem
carentes uiribus, in somnis autem non solum usque ad
delectationem sed etiam usque ad consensionem factumque
simillimum. et tantum ualet imaginis illius inlusio in anima
mea in carne mea, ut dormienti falsa uisa persuadeant quod
uigilanti uera non possunt. numquid tunc ego non sum, domine
deus meus? et tamen tantum interest inter me ipsum et me
ipsum intra momentum, quo hinc ad soporem transeo uel huc
inde transeo! ubi est tunc ratio, qua talibus suggestionibus
resistit uigilans et, si res ipsae ingerantur, inconcussus manet?
numquid clauditur cum oculis? numquid sopitur cum sensibus
corporis? et unde saepe etiam in somnis resistimus nostrique
propositi memores atque in eo castissime permanentes nullum
talibus inlecebris adhibemus adsensum? et tamen tantum
interest, ut, cum aliter accidit, euigilantes ad conscientiae
requiem redeamus ipsaque distantia reperiamus nos non
fecisse, quod tamen in nobis quoquo modo factum esse
doleamus.

(42) Numquid non potens est manus tua, deus omnipotens,
sanare omnes languores animae meae atque abundantiore
gratia tua lasciuos motus etiam mei soporis extinguere?
augebis, domine, magis magisque in me munera tua, ut anima
mea sequatur me ad te concupiscentiae uisco expedita, ut non
sit rebellis sibi atque ut in somnis etiam non solum non
perpetret istas corruptelarum turpitudines per imagines
animales usque ad carnis fluxum, sed ne consentiat quidem.
nam ut nihil tale uel tantulum libeat, quantulum possit nutu
cohiberi etiam in casto dormientis affectu, non tantum in hac
uita, sed etiam in hac aetate, non magnum est omnipotenti, qui
uales facere supra quam petimus et intellegimus. nunc tamen
quid adhuc sim in hoc genere mali mei, dixi bono domino meo

| Chapter 30

(41) Certainly, Thou dost command me to refrain from 'concupiscence of the flesh and concupiscence of the eyes and the pride of this world.' Thou hast commanded [restraint] from concubinage and, in regard to marriage itself, which Thou hast permitted, Thou hast advised something better. Since Thou hast granted it, it has been accomplished, and I reached this state even before becoming a minister of Thy sacrament. But, there still live in my memory, and I have spoken much about it, the images of such things which habit has imprinted therein. When I am awake, they occur to me, though indeed they are not strong, but in sleep it is not merely a question of pleasure; it even goes as far as consent and something very much like the deed. So great is the illusive power of an image over my soul and my flesh that these false things, seen while sleeping, influence me in a manner that real things cannot while I am awake. Am I not myself, at such times, O Lord my God? Nevertheless, there is such a great difference between myself at one moment and myself at another, between the moment when I go to sleep and that when I awaken from it!

Where is reason at such a time, which resists such temptations, when I am awake, and remains firm so that I am unaffected even when real temptations are presented? Is it closed up along with my eyes? Does it go to sleep along with the bodily senses? How is it, then, that we frequently offer resistance during sleep, remembering our good resolutions, most chastely adhering to them, and giving no assent to such allurements? Yet, there is so much difference that, when it happens otherwise, we may return to peace of conscience on waking up, this very difference permitting us to find that it is not we who have done this; we regret, however, that it has been done by us in some way or other.

(42) Is Thy hand, O all-powerful God, not strong enough to heal all the diseases of my soul and to extinguish with Thy more abundant grace these lascivious passions, even during my sleep? Thou wilt increase, O Lord, Thy gifts more and more within me, so that my soul, escaping from the viscous snare of concupiscence, may follow me to Thee, so that it may not be in rebellion against itself, and so that during sleep it will also not only refrain from these debasing acts of turpitude which end in pollution of the flesh as a result of sensual images, but will not even consent to them. For, that such a thing may give no pleasure, or only so slight a pleasure that it can be controlled without difficulty even during the sleep of one who is disposed to be chaste, not only in this life, but even at this stage of life—this is no great feat for an omnipotent Being, 'who art able to

exultans cum tremore in eo, quod donasti mihi, et lugens in eo, quod inconsummatus sum, sperans perfecturum te in me misericordias tuas usque ad pacem plenariam, quam tecum habebunt interiora et exteriora mea, cum absorpta fuerit mors in uictoriam.

accomplish all things in a measure far beyond what we ask or conceive.' Now, however, I have told my good Lord what I am at present in this kind of evil of mine, 'rejoicing unto Him with trembling' for what Thou hast given me; sorrowing for the fact that I am still imperfect; hoping that Thou wilt perfect Thy mercies in me unto the plenitude of peace, which my interior and exterior parts will possess with Thee, when 'death is swallowed up in victory.'

Commentary

This begins an explanation of a text selected from Augustine's *Confessions* (10.1–30) that is pivotal in the development of his philosophic thinking. The first nine books of this work told the story of his life up to the time of his return to North Africa from his years of teaching in Rome and Milan. Like many other Platonists, the young Augustine had hoped to retire with some students and friends in Tagaste, where he could devote his time to the pursuit of wisdom.

But his selection by the Catholic people of Hippo to be ordained their priest under Bishop Valerius gave a new direction to Augustine's life. From the year 391 onward, he was to serve a diocese centering on a busy seaport. Hippo was a cosmopolitan city. Its residents numbered about thirty thousand, representing a variety of faiths—pagans, Jews, and Christians. Perhaps the majority of its Christians were Donatists, members of a schismatic group that had established a sort of African national Church. The Catholic minority lived in an area near the harbor of Hippo Regius. Sometimes their priests, when traveling, were attacked by wandering bands of Donatist thugs called Circumcellions. For a time, the Catholics were not allowed to bring their bread dough to be baked in the shops owned by the Donatists.[1]

Despite having to take full charge of the Catholic diocese with the death of Valerius in 396, Augustine was able to start writing the *Confessions* within a year or so. He may not have come to the tenth book before the year 399/400. When he tells us at the beginning of this book that he is to confess about the present condition of his mind, Augustine is about forty-five years old, a man in full possession of his undoubted talents as a thinker and writer. Much of his philosophy has been established in the treatises written before A.D. 400. But the self-examination offered in book 10 sets the stage for the mature insights of later great works, such as the *Literal*

Commentary on Genesis, The Trinity, The City of God, and most of the *Expositions on the Psalms.* When possible, passages from these later works will be used here to clarify key points in *Confessions* 10. After all, Augustine was a professional rhetorician, trained in the verbal expression of his thoughts and feelings. Much of the time he is his own best commentator.[2]

Our commentary on book 10 will take the structure of short analyses of key thoughts in each chapter, followed by some comment on the philosophical significance of each section. Since the chapter and section numbers are identical in modern editions of the Latin and English, these internal numbers may be used to locate all references to Augustine's writings.

The first pages of book 10 are reminiscent of those at the beginning of the *Confessions,* where he wrote: "To praise Thee is the wish of man who is but a part of Thy creation." This followed a quotation from Psalm 146:5 praising divine power and wisdom. In book 10, Augustine quotes Psalm 50:8, which praises God as the lover of truth. This initiates a profound psychological and philosophical examination of the extent and limits of human understanding and loving.

Analysis 10.1.1: Augustine desires to know more about God by having Him come more intimately into his soul and thus perfect it. God is called "virtue of my soul" (*virtus animae meae*). In Latin, *virtus* means not only a good moral quality but, more broadly, any power. The phrase "go deep into it" (*intra in eam*) recalls the psychological interiorism of his philosophy. The "other things of this life not deserving of tears" (*cetera vero vitae hujus tanto minus flenda*) are temporal goods, such as wealth, health, and earthly successes. The biblical quotation (John 3:21) "he who does the truth comes to the light" (*qui facit eam, venit ad lucem*) stresses the idea that God guides all true judgments.

Comment: This chapter depends on the view that there are three levels of existing beings: God, souls, and bodies, as we have seen earlier (see page 32 above). Just as the soul gives energy to its body, so does God energize souls from above. As Augustine sees the whole of existing reality, the ultimate cause of all functions and movements in created things is their creator (see page 18 above). Augustinian philosophy is theocentric: all things and all events are to be explained by reference to the power of one supreme being.

Think of a modern city, where so many facilities depend on electric power furnished by an electric company. It is useless for a citizen to turn on the lights, push the furnace switch, or try to use the television if the electric power is off. God is to creatures as the source of electricity is to its users. Augustine would not like this feeble comparison, but perhaps it may bring home to us how he saw the utter dependency of his world on God.

Also in this opening text, we have an example of Augustine's use of introspective method (see pages 17–18 above). It is by looking within his own consciousness that he hopes to find out more about supreme wisdom. This theme will be developed throughout book 10. The use of the term "heart" to describe the innermost seat of knowing, willing, and feeling is typical of Augustine's interioristic language. In spite of our knowledge today of the physiological working of the heart as a blood pump, we still offer people our "heartfelt" thanks for a favor.

Analysis 2.2: The first sentence expresses the whole thought of this section; by confessing, Augustine adds nothing to God's knowledge. As he says, "What could be hidden in me from Thee, O Lord, to whose eyes the abyss of human conscience is naked?" (*cujus oculis nuda est abyssus humanae conscientiae, quid occultum esset in me?*). So there must be another reason for Augustine's confessing: it is directed toward his self: "My groaning is a witness that I am displeased with myself" (*gemitus meus testis est displicere me mihi*). His confession is not merely a cognitive expression; it releases his emotional displeasure with himself. Finally, "any right thing" (*recti aliquid*) in his judging of himself is simply a repetition of what God has "previously said to me" (*mihi tu prius dixeris*).

Comment: First of all, we have here a specific instance of the axiom (see pages 27; 39–40 above), "Higher reality may move the lower but the lower cannot move what is higher." What Augustine now admits is that nothing that he knows can cause new knowledge to come to God. What God knows is unchanging truth; no inferior agency can produce a change in divine knowing. This is but another aspect of Augustine's meaning of eternity, which will be explained later.

When Augustine speaks of "the abyss of human conscience" (*abyssus humanae conscientiae*), we should note the double meaning of the Latin *conscientia*. Besides the notion of "conscience" as a function of judging the moral and religious value of a past or proposed action, *conscientia* also has the psychological meaning of "consciousness" or "interior mental awareness." (The Italians say that the translator is always a bit of a traitor, and that may be the case here.) Augustine's Latin means that nothing is hidden to an omniscient God, even within the depths of a person's self-awareness, whether it be of one's bodily actions, one's innermost thoughts and decisions, or one's emotional attitudes. People are, he suggests, an open book to their creator. Augustine has sometimes been accused of being a rigorous intellectualist, but perhaps no philosophical writer has dwelt more upon the role of feelings in a person's inner life.

At the end of the second chapter, Augustine points out that anything he can say about moral rightness (*recti aliquid*) comes to him from God.[3] Notice the complex meaning of "right" (*rectus*); basically it means "straight" (as in geometry, a right line). But it can also refer to that which conforms to standards or laws. Thus the righteous person lives in accord with eternal or natural law. As Augustine uses the word, it has an objective connotation. The right thing (*rectum, justum*) is not some subjective claim that one person may have on another. Rather, it is an extramental relation of conformity between things (*res*). Thus, if *A* trades an old pair of shoes for a day's work by *B,* this deal is right when a reasonable person would see that the two realities in this exchange are equal. This meaning of "right" lies in the background of equity in the legal sense of the term. Such objectivism is an important feature of Augustine's ethics. While his introspective approach to philosophy appears to be very subjective, this does not entail neglect of the real existence of beings outside his mind. Nor does it mean that ethical judgments are mere expressions of one's own views or feelings. For Augustine, there are moral ideals and rules of ethical judgment that transcend the scope of personal whims. He is not a solipsist. He thinks that God has made a world of real things and other persons like himself.

Analysis 3.3–4: As Augustine remarks, readers moved only by idle curiosity about Augustine's youthful misdeeds may not get the full truth from these confessions. But those who love God will understand this: "They whose ears charity doth open unto me, they believe me" (*sed credunt mihi, quorum mihi aures caritas aperit*). It also brings joy to good people when they hear this account of turning away from past evils (*et delectat bonos audire praeterita mala*).

Comment: Augustine realizes that some open-mindedness is required of people who wish to understand his views. Either one has to start from some base of religious belief (as he did), or the benevolent reader must grant that if an ultimate answer to philosophy's problems is sought, then some ultimate supreme cause, and truth, and wisdom, must be considered. We will return to this in the next comment.

Analysis 4.5–6: From such confessions, a person with a "friendly mind" may come to "love in me what Thou dost teach" (*in me fraternus animus quod amandum doces*). In other words, before criticizing any author, the reader should try to grasp the basis, or starting point, from which the writer's thought begins.

In the last part of chapter 6, Augustine repeats that he will tell "not what kind of man I was, but what kind I am" (*non qualis fuerim, sed qualis sum*). This prepares us for the detailed examination of his present state of mind, as he describes it in the coming chapters.

Comment: These four preliminary chapters show the former teacher of rhetoric using a strategy familiar to modern, as well as ancient, orators. This is the attempt to arouse in listeners a mood of benevolence or at least of interest in what is to be said.

Why is Augustine talking about the search for a supreme being, for God? What connection does this have with the philosopher's love of wisdom? Part of his answer to such questions becomes evident in the ensuing chapters of book 10; but a fuller understanding may come from a brief look at some parts of *The Trinity,* which he is starting to write as he finishes the *Confessions.*[4]

In the twelfth book in *The Trinity* (chap. 14) we find one of Augustine's many explanations of the difference between knowledge (*scientia*) and wisdom (*sapientia*). The latter includes the understanding of eternal verities, a great help in the cultivation of moral virtue and consequently in living happily. Then he adds: "But between action, whereby we make good use of temporal things, and the contemplation of eternal things, there is quite a gap; the former is knowledge and the latter belongs to wisdom" (*Distat tamen ab aeternorum contemplatione actio qua bene utimur temporalibus rebus, et illa sapientiae, haec scientiae deputatur*). In other words, the person with a good knowledge of ethical philosophy, for instance, does not necessarily live up to high standards of behavior. Beyond the scope of scientific knowledge, what is required for a truly happy life is a love of the good, a strong inclination of will to put what is known into action. The quality of personal character that combines ordinary knowledge with the love of goodness is human wisdom, as Augustine sees it.

But what does this have to do with all the talk in these opening chapters about searching for God and loving Him? One response to this question is given in the last book in *The Trinity* (15.5, 6), where Augustine reviews what he knows about the triune God in terms of the attributes or names given to the divinity. He studies twelve of them (see 15.5.8): eternal, immortal, incorruptible, immutable, living, wise, powerful, beautiful, just, good, happy, and spiritual (*aeternus, immortalis, incorruptibilis, immutabilis, vivus, sapiens, potens, speciosus, justus, bonus, beatus, spiritus*). These many ways that humans have of looking at God are too much to be grasped at once, Augustine says. Consequently he takes them in groups of three and reduces them to what seems most essential: eternal, wise, and happy. This is a sort of trinity in humanity's limited grasp of the divinity.

Then Augustine asks (15.5.9) whether these three—eternal, wise, and happy—can be further reduced to one unifying attribute. He argues that eternal and happy are included in the quality of being wise. Thus, when we think of the one attribute that is most characteristic of God, we find that it is wisdom. As he states it: "What way of arguing . . . will express how this one thing attributed to God, wisdom, is a Trinity?" (*Quis itaque modus disputandi?*). And since we are thinking about what is essential to God, Augustine adds that "to Him to be is to be wise" (*cui hoc est esse quod sapientem esse*). God's very existence is divine wisdom.

It is noteworthy how many times Augustine quotes in these chapters from Paul's first Epistle to the Corinthians. Clearly he had this part of the New Testament in mind while starting this book. Augustine was well aware of his own debt to Greek philosophy, even though Paul wrote: "While the Jews demand miracles and the Greeks look for wisdom, here we are preaching a crucified Christ" (1 Cor 1:22). Yet Augustine strongly retained the philosophic view that wisdom stands at the peak of the natural moral virtues.

Near the end of book 10.4.6, Augustine addresses God as "Thou omnipotent Being who art with me even before I am with Thee" (*tu omnipotens, qui mecum es et priusquam tecum sim*). To understand this, we must consider his conception of eternity.[5] "Eternal" was listed first among the attributes of God that we have just seen in *The Trinity*.

In the preceding book of the *Confessions* (9.10.24), concluding his account of ascending to a special experience of the divinity with his mother at Ostia, Augustine speaks of this "realm of unfailing abundance in which Thou feedest Israel eternally on the food of truth. There life is wisdom, through which all these things come into being, both those that have been and those which will be" (*per quam fiunt omnia ista, et quae fuerunt et quae futura sunt*). From this it is clear that he considers that God exists eternally.

Perhaps the closest that Augustine comes to a definition of eternity is in *The Trinity* (15.5.7), where he speaks of "the true eternity whereby the immutable God exists without beginning, without end, and consequently not subject to corruption" (*vera aeternitas qua est immutabilis deus sine initio, sine fine, consequenter et incorruptibilis*). As Augustine sees it, God exists in an everlasting present: He has neither past nor future. (More than a century later, Boethius will offer what became the standard definition of eternity in his *Consolation of Philosophy*, 5.6: "*interminabilis vitae tota simul et perfecta possessio,"* that is, the instantaneously whole and perfect possession of unending life.)

The notion of duration in an everlasting present goes well beyond our ordinary understanding, but perhaps an imperfect example may help with it. Suppose you are standing high on a cliff bordering a bend in a river. At your left, some boys are floating down on a raft with the current, but they cannot see what is around the bend. From your exalted position, you can see at the same time that there are rapids ahead, beyond the boys' vision. Your present awareness includes part of the future for the boys. Think of a much higher mind that is able to envision, in an instant, all the past and all the future; there you might have something like what eternity meant to Augustine.

Herodotus tells the story that Thales, the first Greek philosopher of record, was traveling with an Ionian army and, being a competent astronomer, he reckoned that there would be an eclipse of the sun on the day they were to meet the enemy. Messengers were sent to warn the enemy that the gods favored the Greeks and would strike the enemy with darkness unless they surrendered (*History* 1.74). Apparently Thales' knowledge included a larger "present" than that of the enemy. What gives the story some credibility is that modern astronomers have calculated that there was a solar eclipse on 28 May 585 B.C, which could be near the time of Thales. So the "present" of today's astronomers extends to the distant past. In the eternal life of a supreme being, there would be no knowledge of the past or of the future; all would be known now.

It may be well also to note the difference in Augustinian terminology between eternity and immortality. The latter means the characteristic of a living thing that cannot die. It does not mean that an immortal being is necessarily without beginning. Augustine used much of the second book of his *Soliloquies* to explain the immortality of the human soul, in which he firmly believed. But he did not feel that his treatment in that work was adequate. As he reviews it in 426 (*Retr* 1.4.1): "The matter of the immortality of the soul is treated there at length but not completely treated" (*de immortalitate animae diu res agitur et non peragitur*).

Difficulty arises from the fact that Augustine used the term "immortality" in a different sense when discussing the effect of sin upon the soul (*City* 12.4). Thus, a soul that has sinned seriously is called "dead" in the sight of God. This does not mean that a sinner ceases to exist; rather, Augustine thought that all human souls are undying. They live on to a future life of happiness or punishment. In the *Incomplete Work against Julian* (6.30), he acknowledges that there are two meanings of immortality, and the more important meaning is the religious one. In any case, the immortal is not without a beginning, while the eternal has no beginning.

The duration of eternity should also be contrasted with that of time (*tempus*). A long section of the eleventh book (*Conf* 11.10–30) is devoted to a discussion of the nature of time and how it is measured. Augustine has been trying to explain the first verses of Genesis, concerning the creation of the world. Now (11.10) he turns to the people who ask: "What did God do before He made heaven and earth?" For they say: "If God's will that creation should exist is eternal, is creation not also eternal?" His immediate answer is that these questioners do not understand how God acts in eternity; they fail to grasp "the splendor of eternity which stands still forever, and compare this with temporal moments which never stand still and they [fail to] see that it is incomparable" (*splendorem semper stantis aeternitatis et videat esse incomparabilem*). Divine eternity is quite different from the time in which immortal souls exist.

So Augustine must try to explain how time differs from the "everlasting present," eternity. The next chapter (11.12) tells about a man who jokingly informs the questioners that God "was making hell ready for those who pry into these deep questions." But Augustine prefers to give a serious answer by developing an explanation of "before" and "after" in time. His point is that God does not "precede in time the periods of time" (*nec tu tempore tempora praecedis;* see 11.13.16).

The Aristotelian definition of time as "the number of movement in respect to the before and after" (*Physics* 4.11.220a24) is not directly known to Augustine, but he rejects a related physical theory (11.23.29) that "the movements of the sun, moon and stars are times."[6] To this he objects: "If the heavenly bodies stopped moving and a potter's wheel were moving, would there be no time by which we might measure these turnings?" Evidently Augustine is opposed to any explanation that equates time with "the very motion of a body" (*ipsum autem corporis motum tempus esse non audio;* see 11.24.31).

We have seen that the first five books of *On Music* offer a detailed study of the structure of poetic lines and the various rhythms involved in the arrangement of short and long syllables in speech and singing (see page 7 above). The Latin words *tempus / tempora* are used to designate what is called "tempo" in English. Augustine saw that the human mind has the ability to measure such rhythms. He recalls this in the *Confessions* (11.26.33): "Thus we see that the length of a long syllable is measured by the length of a short syllable, and say that it is twice the other. In this way we measure the length of poems by the length of the verses." Thus he is already predisposed by his training in rhetoric and versification to think of time as something measured by the perceiver. His conclusion is: "In thee, O mind of mine, do I measure periods of time" (*tempora metior,* literally, "I measure times," 11.27.36). What he measures is "the present mental disposition which things passing by produce in Thee and which remains after they have passed away" (*affectionem, quam res praetereuntes in te faciunt et, cum illae praeterierint, manet*).

This is a personal and subjective description of the numbering, or measurement, of time. Since the mind (*animus*) is superior to bodies, its awareness of their continuity (*manentia*) is more important than the bodily motions to which the judgment is applied. The verb *manet* in the text just quoted suggests the source of the noun *manentia.* In one of his first letters, to Nebridius (*Epist* 11.3), Augustine says that continuity (*manentiam*) in the existence of all things is an important feature of any nature (*natura*). He uses the verb *manere* to stress the idea of endurance, remaining on from past to future.

As to how the human mind does this measuring of time, he offers this further explanation in the *Confessions* (11.28.37):

> But, how is the future, which does not yet exist, decreased or be eaten up, or how does the past, which is no longer existing, increase, unless because of the fact that three functions occur in the mind (*in animo*) which is doing this? It looks ahead, it attends, and it remembers (*et expectat et attendit et meminit*) in such a way that what it looks forward to passes through what it is attending, into what it is remembering.

We have seen that Augustine calls reason (*ratio*) the gaze of the mind (*mentis aspectus;* see *Soul* 27.58). Now, in *Confessions* 11.28, he indicates the three directions to which the soul may look: to the future its gaze is expectation (*expectatio*); to the fleeting present its gaze is attention (*attentio*); and the looking to the past is recollection (called *memoria praeteriti* in chap. 28, a memory of what has gone before). Psychologically, all three "gazes" are different uses of introspection; the cognitive soul looks within, but in three different ways. There is a lasting quality in what the mind experiences. He now calls it *distentio* (*ecce distentio est vita mea;* see 11.28.39). This is translated as "distraction," for it suggests also a spreading out of present attention.

A noteworthy sentence later in the *Confessions* (12.15.8) sums up these three "visions": "Again it [God's truth] tells me in my interior ear that the expectation of things to come becomes an immediate vision, once these things have come, and the same vision becomes memory, once they pass away."

The notion of turning (*versio*) gives rise to another set of terms Augustine uses to name the willed directing of mental attention to various objects. With God as the greatest object of attention, we are still today accustomed to speaking of conversion (*conversio*), literally a turning to be *with* God. But Augustine also speaks of *aversio*, looking away from God; and *perversio,* turning to apparent "goods" that are really poor substitutes for God. This language provides the theme for a noteworthy book by Jean-Marie Le Blond (*Les Conversions de saint Augustin*) in which the triadic structure of Augustine's *Confessions* is shown to depend on this passage (11.28–29). The first nine books are a looking to his past (*memoria* in the narrow sense of recall). Book 10, a confession of his present condition, which Le Blond calls *contuitus,* attends to what is now in Augustine's mind. And the last three books look to the future, *exspectatio* (so spelled by Le Blond). To some readers it may seem that a commentary on the first lines of Genesis is hardly a way of looking to the future; however, Le Blond and others argue that the incommensurability of eternity and time moves the serious reader of Genesis to look forward to the eventual working out of God's plan for all creatures. Later in this commentary, we will consider how Augustine tried to set up ideals for the future of human society in the *City of God.*

In sum, book 11 details a remarkable explanation of time. Augustine insists that time is some sort of continuity from before to after that is measured in the human mind; he does not mean to deny that all creatures, including bodies, exist and persist in time. So time is a distention, an ongoing process, that is typical of all the beings that God has made. Temporality is the mark of a creature, just as eternity is characteristic of God.[7]

I NOTES

1. Reply to Petilian 2.184; see Bonner, *St. Augustine of Hippo,* 262ff. on the Circumcelliones.

2. In the Skutella-Juergens-Schaub edition of *Confessiones* (1969), divisions of the books are not called "chapters"; the first printed editions introduced the division called "caput."

3. See Bourke, "Moral Illumination," in *Wisdom from St. Augustine,* 106–25.

4. The "Notes Complémentaires" to *De Trinitate* (BA 15:558) place the start in mid-399.

5. Cf. Gilson, *The Christian Philosophy of St. Augustine,* vol. 3, chap. 1.

6. On the possible background of *Conf* 11.23.29–30, see J. F. Callahan, "Basil of Caesarea: A New Source for St. Augustine's Theory of Time," *Harvard Studies in Classical Philology* 63 (1958): 437–54. See also Jean Guitton, *Le temps et l'éternité chez saint Augustin* (Paris: Aubier, 1956).

7. A somewhat different explanation of Augustine's views on time is found in Robert Jordan, "Time and Contingency in St. Augustine," in Markus, ed., *Augustine: A Collection of Critical Essays,* 255–79. Jordan suggests "that it is unrewarding to interpret the eleventh Book as introspective psychology." He is quite right when he states that the references to time in the *City of God* are less subjective than those in the *Confessions.* See also R. Sorabji, *Time, Creation and the Continuum* (London: Oxford University Press, 1983).

In these next three chapters, Augustine turns to God's knowledge of him, to his knowledge of God, and then to his love of God. We may compare these chapters with a passage in the *Soliloquies* (2.1.1), where Augustine simply says: "May I know myself, may I know Thee" (*noverim me, noverim Te*).

Analysis 10.5.7: He says first: "Thou, O Lord, dost judge me" (*Tu enim, domine, dijudicas me*). The Latin *dijudicare* means to "pass judgment" on some object; but it also means "to discern, to see right through something." Since judgment is, for Augustine, a very distinctive climax to understanding,[1] this is an affirmation of the supremacy of divine judgment. It is the function of the superior to judge the inferior (*Free* 2.12.34).

On the other hand, Augustine admits: "I know something about Thee" (*aliquid de te scio*), "that I do not know about myself" (*quod de me nescio*). One such thing that he knows about God, which is not true of himself, is "that Thou canst in no way be affected from without" (*te novi nullo modo posse violari*). This specifies one aspect of divine immutability.

The statement, "I am a wanderer away from Thee" (*peregrinor abs te*) is an echo of the Plotinian commonplace of the soul wandering away from the One, eventually to return to its source. The last point to be noted in chapter 5 is that "what I do know about myself I know by virtue of Thy enlightenment of me" (*quod de me scio, te mihi lucente scio*). This is the first of many references in book 10 to the theory of divine illumination of the human intellect. For the moment, it may suffice to say that Augustine thought that there is a light of the mind which enables people to see the eternal principles (*rationes aeternae*), just as physical light makes bodily objects visible to sense perception.

Comment: Two important concepts appearing in this section are divine immutability and the illuminating of human understanding by God's light. What does Augustine mean when he says that God can in no way be affected from without? He uses the infinitive *violari.* In this context, nonviolation has the meaning of not being subject to the action of any external cause. He is saying that a supreme being is never the object of extrinsic efficient causality. This is essential to the divine attribute of immutability.[2] Earlier in the *Confessions* (7.17.23), Augustine recounted how, as a young man, he came to appreciate the importance of such invulnerability to change:

> I was looking for the source of my approval of the beauty (*pulchritudinem*) of bodies, whether heavenly or earthly, and what enabled me to judge in a sound way concerning mutable things and to say: "This should be this way; that should not." And so, in looking for this source of my judgments, when I did judge in this way, I had discovered the immutable and true eternity of Truth, above my mutable mind.
>
> Thus, by a gradual process, from bodies to the soul that senses through the body, and thence to its interior power to which bodily sensation takes messages about exterior things (and this is as far as brutes can go), and then further to the reasoning power, to which what is taken by the bodily senses is brought for judgment. And this power, also finding itself mutable in me, lifted itself to its understanding (*intelligentiam*) and withdrew the thinking process (*cogitationem*) from the customary level, taking itself away from the customary crowds of phantasms, so that it might discover by what light (*quo lumine*) it was besprinkled when it cried out without any hesitation that the immutable is to be preferred to the mutable.... And, in the flash of a trembling glance, it reached up to that which is (*et pervenit ad id quod est, in ictu trepidantis aspectus*).[3]

This long quotation introduces us to several features of Augustine's psychology and theory of knowledge. It is another of the many passages in which he speaks of the ascent within his consciousness to an experience of the highest reality. Another comparable passage in the *Confessions* (9.10.24) describes an even more impressive mental ascent. This is the famous conversation with his mother at Ostia just before her death. Speaking of the climax of this experience, he says: "There, life is wisdom" (*ibi vita sapientia est*).

Within five years after finishing book 10, Augustine will start his treatise the *Nature of the Good* (1.1) with this explanation involving the notion of immutability:

> The highest good (*summum bonum*), than which there is none superior, is God; and consequently it is an immutable good, and so truly eternal and truly immortal. All other beings have no existence except by Him (*ab illo sunt*) but not out of Him

(*non de illo*). What is out of Him is what He himself is; but the
things made by Him are not what He is. For this reason, if He
alone is immutable, then all that He has made, since made out
of nothing, all such things are mutable.

Thus, divine immutability, the impossibility of any change in
Augustine's God, distinguishes Him from all other beings. Immutability
is one of the supreme attributes of divinity, identical essentially
with eternity, goodness, happiness, and wisdom. Obviously,
Augustine is no patron of process theology.

Another feature of chapter 5 that requires some explanation is
the statement that what I really know about myself, "I know by virtue
of Thy enlightenment of me." Augustine was convinced that true
understanding occurs to a person suddenly and in a flash. It is like
what happens when we are in the dark and then a bright light is
turned on. The invisible becomes visible, at times, to the intellect.[4]

We have already examined some texts on intellectual illumination
from the early writings (see pages 40–41 above). At this point, it
may help to see what Augustine says about this difficult theory in
some works written after the *Confessions*. These will be taken in
chronological order.

In a letter written (circa 409) to Consentius (120.10), we find
this explanation of intellectual light:

> We do not form an image of justice and wisdom or anything
> else like these, rather, we see them differently. We behold
> these invisible qualities by a simple intellectual attention
> (*simplici mentis atque rationis intentione intellecta
> conspicimus*), without any shapes or dimensions in place. . . .
> There is the light itself (*ipsamque lumen*) whereby we discern
> (*discernimus*) all such things, in which is adequate evidence of
> what we believe but do not fully know, of what we grasp in
> knowledge, of what we recall of a bodily shape, what we construct
> in imagination, what bodily sensation grasps, what the
> mind (*animus*) pictures as like a body, what is contemplated by
> understanding (*intelligentia contempletur*) as something certain
> but quite unlike all bodies: this light in which all these
> objects are judged to be different is not, like the glow of the sun
> and other bodily lights, diffused through any place in space. It
> does not illumine our mind with a visible glow; rather it illumines
> invisibly and indescribably, yet to us it is as certain as
> are the things that we intuit with its aid (*quam nobis efficit
> certa quae secundum ipsum cuncta conspicimus*).

This somewhat convoluted text (much of it one long sentence in
Latin) tells us two main things. First, we see or intuit the meanings
of terms such as justice and wisdom. Augustine never called them
universals, as they came to be named after Boethius introduced
them to medieval philosophy in the theory of intellectual abstraction

from sense images. Second, the light of understanding is different from that of the sun, but it illumines ordinary human minds. Near the end of his life, in *Retractations* 1.4.4, Augustine says more bluntly that the explanation why uneducated people, such as the boy in the *Meno,* can answer questions about geometry "is because of the light of eternal reason in which they see these immutable truths" (*lumen rationis aeternae, ubi haec immutabilia vera conspiciunt*). This is Augustine's modification of Plato's story of recollection from a previous life; for Augustine, it is natural to the rational part of the mind to have the aid of an intellectual light.

In the year 413, Augustine sent another famous letter (147, to Paulina), "Seeing God" (*de videndo deo*). In it he explained that direct visions of God are very rare in this life, but that it is possible for people on earth to intuit many higher ideals or meanings without using physical images. And here he lists some of these immutable notions: charity, joy, forbearance, peace, benevolence, goodness, faith, meekness, and continence (*caritas, gaudium, longanimitas, pax, benignitas, bonitas, fides, mansuetudo, continentia*). This gives us some examples of the eternal verities, in addition to the principles of disciplines such as geometry, that are knowable without images but grasped in some special intellectual light.

At about the same time (A.D. 414) Augustine wrote the last book of the *Literal Commentary on Genesis.* In it (12.31.59) he lists several virtues that are understood by means of intellectual illumination: piety, faith, hope, patience. Then he explains:

> But distinct from these objects is the light by which the soul is illumined, in order that it may see and truly understand everything, either in itself or in the light. For the Light is God himself (*nam illud jam ipse Deus est*), whereas the soul is a creature; yet, since it is rational and intellectual, it is made in His image. And when it tries to behold the Light (*cum conatur lumen illud intueri*), it trembles in its weakness and finds itself unable to do so.

This appears to identify the light of the understanding with God Himself. Somewhat the same identification is found in a sentence approving the philosophy of the Platonists: "The light of our minds (*lumen mentium*), whereby all things are to be learned by us, they have stated to be that same God by whom all things were made" (*City* 8.7).

However, most of the passages in which Augustine speaks of the light of the intellect suggest that it is not God Himself, but something that He makes. Usually, when Augustine talks about the light at its source, he uses the term *lux;* when it is received in a medium or reflected, it is usually called *lumen.* But this usage is not invariable.

In the two preceding texts the term employed is *lumen.* One of the most discussed passages on this subject was written some five years later in *The Trinity* (12.15.24). Here again, Augustine is reacting to the story in Plato's *Meno,* for he writes:

> If this had been a recollecting of things previously known, then certainly everyone, or almost everyone, would have been able so to answer when questioned. For not everyone was a geometer in the former life, since geometers are so few among men that scarcely one can be found anymore. But we ought rather to believe (*sed potius credendum est*) that the intellectual mind is so formed in its nature as to see those things, which by the disposition of the Creator are subjoined to things intelligible in a natural order, by a sort of incorporeal light of an unique kind (*sic ista videat in quadam luce sui generis incorporea*).

The Dods translation is used here, for it is quite accurate. However, two things are to be noted in the Latin text. First, even though the word *lux* (*luce*) is found here, the whole text stresses the naturalness of the situation in which intellectual light functions. And second, the phrase *sui generis incorporea* literally means "incorporeal and of its own kind." That seems to imply that the light of the mind, while not bodily, is nevertheless something provided by God to help humans in their natural efforts to understand those principles or truths that do not change.

Later in *The Trinity* (14.15.21), Augustine argues that even wicked people (*impii*) know the basic laws of justice, even though there may be little justice in their souls. It cannot be that they find these rules in their own souls. "Where are these rules written?" he asks, "if not in the book of that light (*lucis*) that is called truth?" This does not tell us anything more about the nature of intellectual light, but it does assure us that this light is available to all people. This view is important to later medieval thinking on natural moral law.

In comments on the opening lines of the Gospel of John from the years 414–17, Augustine quotes (John 1:9), "The Word was the true light that enlightens all men" (*erat lumen verum quod illuminat omnem hominem*). Then he advises: "See this point clearly" (*hoc ergo discernite*), "the light that illumines is one thing, that which is illuminated is another" (*aliud esse lumen quod illuminat, aliud esse quod illuminatur*). And he adds that unless our mind (*mens nostra*) is illumined by the light of truth (*veritatis lumine*), "it will be unable to attain to either wisdom or justice" (*nec ad sapientiam nec ad justitiam poterit pervenire*).

A text in the middle of the *City of God* (10.2) is one of the few places in which Plotinus is named. This too, was written around A.D. 415:

> Plotinus, commenting on Plato, repeatedly and strongly asserts that not even the soul which they believe to be the Soul of

> the world derives its blessedness from any other source than
> we do, namely, from that Light which is distinct from it and
> which created it, and by whose intellectual illumination it
> sends forth the light of understanding (*lumen quod ipsa non
> est, sed a quo creata est, et quo intelligibiliter illuminante
> intelligibiliter lucet*).

A few lines later, Augustine adds that this great Platonist, Plotinus, asserted that the rational soul has no nature superior to it except God; and thus Plotinus is in agreement with John's statements about the light of truth (*consonans Evangelio, ubi legitur. . . . Erat lumen verum . . .*).

Finally, in the *Retractations* (1.4.4), written near the end of his life (A.D. 426), Augustine attempts to simplify the notion of intellectual light. In reference to his *Soliloquies* (2.20.35), where the *Meno* story is criticized, he says: "When unlearned people respond to clever questions about the liberal arts, is it not because there is present in them, insofar as they can grasp it, the light of eternal reason, in which they see these immutable truths" (*quia praesens est eis quantum id capere possunt, lumen rationis aeternae, ubi haec immutabilia conspiciunt*).

However, Augustine's theory of intellectual light is not simple. While it seems to offer an important explanation of how the human intellect understands axioms and conclusions, ideals and values, it is not easy to summarize his many texts on the subject.

He appears to speak about four kinds of light. There is the light that is identical with the substance of God: this cannot be seen directly and naturally by persons living on earth. Then there is the light of the command, "Let there be light" (*fiat lux*) in Genesis 1:3; it is created and seems to include two lights, the incorporeal light of the intellectual soul and the physical light of the sun. Our present concern is with the third kind, the light of human reason.

The so-called Thomistic explanation—that this is the Aristotelian agent intellect which abstracts universals from sense phantasms—has no foundation in Augustine's texts. Yet the light of the mind is some created aid that enables people to make true judgments. It is not the special grace given to a few prophets and especially wise people, for it is naturally available to all. Of course, it is not the physical light of the sun. This "incorporeal light of its own kind" is never clearly explained by Augustine, yet (as I wrote almost fifty years ago[5]), his teaching on spiritual illumination is one of the most characteristic features of his thought.

Analysis 6.8–10: This chapter directs our attention to the loving, rather than the knowing, of God. In Augustinian philosophy, human reason (*ratio hominis*) has a volitional as well as a cognitive function.

So Augustine asserts, "I love Thee, O Lord, not with doubtful but with assured awareness" (*Non dubia, sed certa conscientia, domine, amo te*). Notice how *conscientia* (consciousness) includes what we might call the higher feelings of the human spirit. Looking outside his consciousness, next, he finds that "heaven and earth . . . tell me to love Thee" (*caelum et terra . . . mihi dicunt ut te amem*). This is a recurrent idea in the three sections (8–10) of chapter 6: the beauty of creatures proclaims the beauty of their maker.

Augustine proceeds in section 8 to contrast the attractive features of temporal creatures and things with the eternal attractiveness of God. This is as close as Augustine will get to the analogy between creatures and the Creator. It will be developed eventually into a formal theory of metaphysical analogy in the writings of thirteenth-century thinkers such as Bonaventure and Thomas Aquinas.

Section 9 of this chapter attempts to make precise what it is (*quid est hoc?*) that attracts a person to the love of God. One has to look to something higher than earthly things; they tell one to "look above us" (*quaere super nos*). Augustine criticizes Anaximenes, the pre-Socratic philosopher, for saying that "air" is the key to explaining all things. What Anaximenes actually said was: "Just as our soul, being air, holds us together, so do breath and air encompass the whole world."[6] It is possible that Augustine derived his report on Anaximenes from some secondary source, such as Varro, now nonextant. Again Augustine insists that the beauty of all earthly things suggests that God made them: "Their reply was their beauty" (*responsio eorum species eorum*).

Next, Augustine looks to himself to see what he knows about God. He finds that he is composed of "body and soul" (*ecce corpus et anima in me*). He has had no success in seeking to know more about God through the "messenger rays" (*nuntios radios*) of his eyes, so he must turn within his soul, to the "interior man" (*homo interior*). It is the judge of all that is known through sense perception. Through the help of the "exterior man" (*per exterioris ministerium*), his soul again judges that no earthly being is God.

At the end of section 9, he concludes: "I asked the whole frame of the world concerning my God and it replied to me: 'I am not He but He has made me'" (*interrogavi mundi molem de deo meo, et respondit mihi: 'non ego sum, sed ipse me fecit'*). We will return to this in our following comment.

In section 10, the question is repeated: "Is not this beauty evident to all whose sense perception is intact?" (*Nonne omnibus, quibus integer sensus est, apparet haec species?*). Why do not all people see it? His answer is: "Reason is not placed above the message-carrying senses in them, as a judge" (*non enim praeposita est in eis nuntiantibus sensibus judex ratio*). This concept of "judging reason" also deserves comment.

Again, at the end of section 10, we are told that as the soul gives life to its body, so God confers life on the soul (*deus autem tuus etiam tibi vita est*).

Comment: Since Augustine turns in this chapter to his love of God, we need to consider some of the terms used in his psychology of human affection.[7] At the beginning of section 8, he says, "I love Thee, O Lord" (*amo te, domine*). The noun *amor* is obviously related to the verb *amo*. Almost any inclination of the mind to what appears attractive can be called *amor*. It is the broadest noun that names volitional affection. Will (*voluntas*) is the soul dynamically tending toward any "good," great or small. While will is called a "power" (*vis*) by Augustine, he does not see will as an Aristotelian "faculty." It is the whole soul as active. (He does speak of *facultatem voluntatis* in *The Trinity* 10.11.17, but immediately after that he insists that the three facets of the human soul are one [*tria haec eo sunt unum, quo una vita, una mens, una essentia*]. And next, at 10.11.18, he adds: "I will that I be willing, that I remember, that I understand" [*volo me velle, et meminisse, et intelligere*].)

When Augustine is speaking of the highest and purest love of God and spiritual goods, he uses the noun *caritas* (charity). When he talks about a love that is lower but of approvable objects, he calls it *dilectio*. And when he discusses the lust for low-grade pleasures of the senses, he calls this *cupiditas* or *libido*. However, they are all acts of the soul freely willing, as is brought out in the three books of *Free Choice*. More will be seen about the affective movements of the soul when we come to remembered emotions (*Conf* 10.14.21) and his own temptations on the level of concupiscence (10.30ff.).

The expression "messenger rays of my eyes" (*nuntios radios oculorum meorum*, 10.6.9) requires some explanation. It is to be understood in reference to the active theory of sensation (see 39–40 above). The mind does not passively receive impressions from physical stimuli. Rather, the human mind makes a record within itself of certain changes that it notices in its body. Thus, if my hands are reduced by a piece of ice to a low temperature, then, if I am alert, I produce in my consciousness a perception that is my information about this bodily change. In Augustine's time, apparently there was the popular view that the eyes send forth rays of light to light up objects of sight. Old pictures of saints sometimes showed lines of light issuing from the eyes. Possibly the idea that "like knows like" was at work here.

Much more important in section 8, and later, is the strongly worded claim that all things, celestial or terrestrial, proclaim that they were made by God. Two questions may be asked about this: (1) What is it in these bodily things that Augustine takes to be shouting out that they did not make themselves? and (2) Is he here trying to suggest an argument for the existence of God based on some feature of the physical universe?

What Augustine names as distinctive of all bodies is their *species*. This is one of those complex Latin words that shift meaning when used in English. To us a species is often taken in the biological sense of a class of living things, not as broad as a genus. Or we might use it for any distinctive kind of thing. But in Latin, *species* suggests the outward appearance of a body, particularly to sight. One of Augustine's adjectives for beautiful is *speciosus* (well formed). And that seems to be what he is thinking of when he asks at the start of 6.10: "Is not this beauty (*haec species*) evident to all whose sense perception is intact?"

Perhaps it will help to look at several texts in which Augustine shows his understanding of *species,* while keeping in mind the passage in the *Book of Wisdom* (11:21) which says that God has "arranged all things according to measure, number and weight" (*Omnia in mensura et numero et pondere disposuisti*).[8] While *species* is mentioned only in some of these texts, they all help to understand its meaning. The suggestion in these places is that things that are "specified" are well formed and therefore appealing.

Augustine starts off a passage (*On Genesis against the Manichees* 1.16.26) with the admission: "As a matter of fact, I admit that I don't know why mice and frogs, or flies and worms, were created." Then he says: "I see, however, that all things are beautiful (*pulchra*) according to their types (*in suo genere*). I cannot think of the body and members (*corpus et membra*) of any animal, in which I fail to find that measures and numbers and order contribute to a concordant unity" (*mensuras et numeros et ordinem inveniam ad unitatem concordiae pertinere*).

The above was written in 389, and two years later he returned to this theme in the dialogue *Free Choice* (2.20.54), where he says, "Wherever you see measure and number and order, do not hesitate to ascribe this thing in its entirety to God, its Maker." He explains that these three characteristics combine in the form (*forma*) of a thing, either incompletely or completely. The word *forma* is very close in meaning to *species*. Their adjectival forms, *formosus* and *speciosus,* both mean "beautiful."

At about the same time (390), *On Music* (6.17.56–57) introduces the triad of unity, number, and order as constituents of beauty (*pulchritudo*). Other features, such as equality and likeness (*aequalitas* and *similitudo*), contribute to the perfection of beauty. But the "general beauty" (*species*) that anything possesses con- sists in a unity that arises from the numbered balance of like parts (6.17.58). It is clear that the notion of that which is well formed (*speciosum*) plays a prominent part in Augustine's aes- thetic philosophy.[9]

Contemporary with the *Confessions* is a passage in the treatise *Reply to Faustus* (20.7) where Augustine contrasts the immutability of the Creator with the mutability of creatures. In reference to the immutable will of God, Augustine writes:

> From it comes the beginning of our act of existing (*inde nobis est initium existendi*), the reason of our act of knowing (*ratio cognoscendi*), the law of our act of loving (*lex amandi*). From it comes the nature whereby all irrational animals live, the strength whereby they sense, the motion whereby they desire. From it, too, come to all bodies the measure (*mensura*) enabling them to exist substantially, the number enabling them to live in beauty (*numerus ut ornentur*), the weight enabling them to be well ordered *pondus ut ordinentur*).

Here, instead of ascending to God as Creator from the judgment of various constituents of bodily beauty, Augustine starts with the Creator and descends in his description to the *species,* the well- formed appearance of physical creatures.

Also from the same period (399–405) is a passage in the *Nature of the Good* (3.3) where Augustine outlines the Christian view that all things are good, in contrast to the Manichaean tenet that the universe is divided by a dualism of good and evil beings. To make his point clear, he stresses the principles of mode (*modus*), species (*spe- cies*), and order (*ordo*). He says:

> We Catholic Christians worship a God from Whom come all good things, whether great or small; from Whom is every mode, whether great or small; from Whom is every species, whether great or small; from Whom is every order, great or small. In- deed, the more moderated, specified and ordered all things are (*omnia enim quanto magis moderata, speciosa, ordinata sunt*), the greater are they in goodness. . . . So, these three principles, mode, species and order . . . are like general goods (*tamquam generalia bona sunt*) in the things made by God, either in the spirit or in the body.

From texts such as this, it becomes evident why *species,* in *Confes- sions* 10.6.10, supplies part of Augustine's answer to our first ques- tion: What is it in temporal things that "cries out" that God is their maker? The judgment that they are well formed (*speciosa*) points to a supremely orderly maker.

Two later passages develop this explanation more fully. Book 8 of the *Literal Commentary on Genesis* (25.46 and 26.48) deals with the verse from Book of Wisdom 11:21 saying that God has arranged all things according to measure, number, and weight. The full text is too long to quote here,[10] but it may be summarized as follows. Measure is some sort of principle of action to prevent unalterable and unregulated process; number pertains to the dispositions and powers of the soul, whereby it is properly gathered in from the deformity of foolishness to the form of wisdom (*ad sapientiae formam*); and weight is the quality attracting will and love (*est pondus voluntatis et amoris*) when it becomes evident how much and what weight is to be given to feelings of desire or dislike or of preference and undervaluation.

Then he explains (26.48) how the sources of these principles in the creative mind of God are the *rationes aeternae,* the eternal forms of measure, number, and weight. He advises those who know such principles only as found in bodily things to lift up their mental gaze to the level of higher things. This is the ascent from scientific and temporal knowledge (*scientia*) to wise knowledge (*sapientia*). It is also the justification of Augustine's reliance on introspection.

One last quotation from *The Trinity* (6.10.12) will complete our consideration of this first question by relating these principles of order to the meaning of *species*.

> All these things, therefore, that have been made by the divine creative Art, manifest a certain unity, and form (*species*), and order, in themselves. For each of them is some one thing, as are the natures of bodies and the talents of souls; each is shaped according to a definite form (*aliqua specie*), as are the figures and qualities of bodies and the sciences and arts of souls; and each seeks out or maintains a certain order, as in the weights and arrangements of bodies and the loves and delights of souls.

From this we learn that, besides ideals such as unity and order, there is a supreme *species* (beauty), which Augustine sees as the ultimate source of the well-ordered beauty of both corporeal and incorporeal creatures.

Turning now to our second question: Is Augustine really trying to prove that God exists, on the basis of this survey of the well-ordered character of physical things in the universe? There are experts who answer this in the affirmative. Eugène Portalié had no hesitation in writing that Augustine "mentioned all the classic proofs for the existence of God."[11] And as good an interpreter as A. Solignac, commenting on *Confessions* 10.6.9–10, speaks of it as "the Augustinian proof of God."[12] Of course, Charles Boyer (who always interpreted Augustine in the light of Thomism) found a variety of proofs in Augustine.[13] But there are other interpreters who are more cautious on this point. J.-M. Le Blond, for instance, remarks that Augustine's concern in passages such as those in book 10, where he writes about bodies "crying out" that God is their maker, is not occupied with some speculative consideration of the *origin* of things but rather with the practical appreciation of the low-grade *value* of bodies.[14]

It should be remembered that Augustine was not writing for non-Christians or unbelievers in theism. His contemporary audience was 99 percent theistic. Augustine was trying to show that basic items of Catholic faith were not irrational. Of course, he utilized many parts of Platonic philosophy to do this. Like later thinkers in the Middle Ages, Augustine's intent was incorporated into the slogan, "faith seeking understanding."[15] For this reason, it is not proper to take Augustine's rhetorically persuasive statements about the existence of God being evident to all people as if they were on the same philosophical level as the famous "Five Ways" of Thomas Aquinas or the argument from design offered by William Paley. Most of the people for whom Augustine wrote believed that God was ever-present in their daily experiences.[16]

The argument that is most characteristic of Augustine's philosophical thinking about God's existence is Platonic in character. It is found in the early dialogue *Free Choice* (2.2ff.). There he argues that human beings know some truths, such as the principles of geometry, that are eternally true. Reason acknowledges that such truths are eternal and immutable, and that reason sees itself as lower than the source of these truths, and that there must be something higher than human reason. This being which is eternal and immutable is God (*Free* 2.6.14). Most of the subsequent chapters (2.7–15) develop this argument to the conclusion (15.39) that there exists a being superior to human minds and that this being is God.[17] The reasoning depends on Augustine's principle of subordination in judgment: "The judge is always better than the thing judged" (*nulli autem dubium est eum qui judicat, eo de quo judicat esse meliorem;* see *Free* 2.5.12).

If this is to be called a philosophical reasoning to the existence of God, it must be remembered that it began with Evodius' statement (*Free* 5.11) that they were seeking to answer the question: "How can it be made obvious to the understanding, that God exists, even though it is to be believed most tenaciously and firmly?"

There are similar arguments from the lower forms of living things through the rational life of humans to a higher source of all life, God. These are frequent in the *Expositions of the Psalms* (*Exp Ps* 41.5–10; 36.2, 12; 99.5). In one such *Exposition* (73.25), he actually addresses the argument from different stages of life to the unbeliever (*infidelis*). Several early works also present variations of this argument from life in lower things to a supreme life (*Morals of the Catholic Church* 5.7; and *True Religion* 11.21).

Later in the *Confessions* (11.4.6), Augustine repeats that heaven and earth "cry out that they have been made." Their beautiful appearance (*pulchra sunt enim*) shows that God made them (*tu ergo, domine, fecisti ea, qui pulcher es*), for He is Beauty. And near the end of the *Confessions,* under the influence of Exodus 3:14 (I am who am, *sum qui sum,* in Augustine's Bible), he concludes that with divine help we can see that God "does not merely exist 'in some way,'" but that He *is* absolutely (*sed est est*).

Analysis 7.11: Still another ascent of the soul is briefly presented here (*per ipsam animam meam ascendam ad illum*). Now he is inquiring as to *what* God is as an object of love (*quid ergo amo*). His search rises from considering the "life-force" that animates his body through the powers of sensation, and he will transcend his own life (*transibo et istam vim meam*).

Comment: This brief chapter does not answer its question. We are not told here *what* it is that attracts his soul so that it comes to love God. From the preceding chapters we know that Augustine has a number of supreme attributes for God. He is eternal, omnipotent, beautiful, a just judge, and the maker of all things in the universe. But the answer to which Augustine comes, after lengthy introspective analysis of "memory" in the ensuing chapters, is never an exhaustive description of God's essential nature. Like the One of Plotinus and the divinity of many medieval mystics, the God of Augustinian thought transcends all efforts at complete description. As we saw in the immediately preceding chapter (6.8), the words and thoughts to describe God are not available to us. Divine beauty is not the same as the attractive qualities of sense objects; yet God, as an object of human love, is "something like a light, a voice, an odor, a food, an embrace." To advance further in this introspective search, Augustine must next try to find God in the depths of his conscious mind.

I NOTES

1. On judgment in Augustine's theory of knowledge, see Gilson, *The Christian Philosophy of St. Augustine,* part 2, chap. 5.

2. Cf. Bernard Cooke, "The Mutability-Immutability Principle in St. Augustine's Metaphysics," *The Modern Schoolman* 23 (1946): 175–93; 24 (1946): 37–49.

3. This passage from *Conf* 7.17.23 is modified from my version in FOC, 21:187. The punctuation in recent Latin editions (see Gibb-Montgomery, 192) has been changed; the comma after *id* has been placed after *est*.

4. For a selection of the Latin texts on divine illumination, see L. W. Keeler, S. *Augustini doctrina de cognitione: Textus selectus* (Rome: Universitas Gregoriana, 1934), 53–63.

5. See Bourke, *Augustine's Quest of Wisdom,* 216–17.

6. The Anaximenes fragment is in H. Diels and W. Kranz, eds., *Die Fragmente der Vorsokratiker* (Berlin: Weidmann, 1956), 12a10; the English version is in K. Freeman, trans. and ed., *Ancilla to the Pre-Socratic Philosophers* (Oxford: Blackwell, 1948).

7. See Hélène Pétré, *Caritas: Etude sur le vocabulaire latin de la charité chrétienne* (Louvain: Institut Supérieur de Philosophie, 1948).

8. These texts based on Book of Wisdom 11:21 may be read in Latin and English in my *Augustine's View of Reality,* texts 6, 7, 16, 19, and 27.

9. See chap. 2, "The Constituents of the Aesthetic Object," in E. Chapman, *Saint Augustine's Philosophy of Beauty* (New York: Sheed & Ward, 1939). Also useful is K. Svoboda, *L'esthétique de saint Augustin et ses sources* (Brno-Paris: Les Belles Lettres, 1933).

10. For this portion of *De Genesi ad litteram* 8.25–26, see the Latin and English in Bourke, *Augustine's View of Reality,* 68–74.

11. Portalié, *A Guide to the Thought of St. Augustine,* 125; *Conf* 10.6.9 is definitely called a "proof."

12. Solignac, "Notes Complémentaires," 556–57: "La preuve augustinienne de Dieu."

13. Boyer, *L'idée de vérité dans la philosophie de saint Augustin,* 65ff.

14. J.-M. Le Blond, *Les conversions de saint Augustin* (Paris: Aubier, 1950), 174.

15. As Evodius says, "What we believe, we desire also to know and to understand" (*Free* 2.2). See 21–22 above, on "Believing and Understanding."

16. This is the central theme of S. J. Grabowski, *The All-Present God: A Study in S. Augustine* (St. Louis, Mo.: Herder, 1954).

17. Book 2, *De libero arbitrio,* with its argument pointing to the existence of immutable truth, was excellently translated in R. McKeon, *Selections from Medieval Philosophers* (New York: Scribners, 1929), 1:27–58. This section is obviously the source of Anselm's famous argument in the *Proslogion.*

This begins Augustine's profound study of memory (*memoria*), a term that covers much more than the remembrance of things past. Memory is a feature of the soul that extends far beyond the consciousness of retained or present experiences, to projections into the future, and to some aspects of the subconscious mind.[1]

Analysis 10.8–10.12.15: Augustine turns from his discussion of the soul's capacity to sense various qualities of bodies and says: "I shall also pass above this power of my nature" (*Transibo ergo et istam naturae meae,* 8.12). This is another step in his ascent toward God, his Maker (*ascendens ad eum, qui fecit me*). "I come," he adds, "into the fields and broad palaces of memory" (*venio in campos et lata praetoria memoriae*). Forced to use spatial terms for this aspect of his soul, he finds "treasures of innumerable images" (*thesauri innumerabilium imaginum*). "There is stored away whatever we cogitate" (*ibi reconditum est, quidquid etiam cogitamus*).

With almost breathless amazement, Augustine describes the contents held in the storehouse of his memory. He can find almost anything there, even things "which forgetfulness has not yet engrossed and buried" (*quod nondum absorbuit et sepelivit oblivio*). This mention of oblivion (which will come up later) is typical of Platonic discussions of memory (see *Philebus* 33e, where Plato calls oblivion the "exit of memory"). In fact, the Greek word for recollection (*anamnesis*) means literally "not forgetting." All efforts to find a thing remembered are under control of the will: "I can request that whatever I wish (*quidquid volo*) be brought forward."

The next section (8.13) tells us that memory keeps all its contents "distinct and classified" (*distincta generatimque servata*). The various colors seen through the eyes, for instance, are not confused with the objects of hearing, or with odors, flavors, or tactile experiences. Yet Augustine stresses the "vastness of the containing memory and its indescribably hidden and mysterious chasms" (*grandis memoriae recessus et nescio qui secreti atque ineffabiles sinus ejus*). Again, he emphasizes the importance of voluntary control of any search within the memory: "I can remember at will the other things that have been taken in and piled up through the other senses" (*ita cetera quae per sensus ceteros ingesta atque congesta sunt, recordor prout libet*).

Then Augustine dwells on the inwardness of all these contents and activities: "I do this inside, in the immense palace of my memory" (*Intus haec ago, in aula ingenti memoriae meae*, 8.14). We are witnessing here his psychological interiorism at work. He even finds himself within his memory. "In it, I even encounter myself" (*Ibi mihi et ipse occurro*). He can think of "when and where I did something, and how I felt when I did it" (*quando et ubi egerim, cum agerem, affectus fuerim*).

But, in spite of the vast size of this power of memory, Augustine does not think that he ever fully understands himself: "I myself do not grasp all that I am" (*nec ego ipse capio totum quod sum*, 8.15). He is astonished at the many unanswered questions about his own identity. "A mighty wonder rises before me . . . astonishment seizes me" (*super hoc oboritur admiratio . . . stupor adprehendit me*). Then comes a much-quoted lyrical passage: "Yet, men go to admire the mountains' peaks, giant waves in the sea, the broad courses of rivers, the vast sweep of the ocean, and the circuits of the stars—and they leave themselves behind" (*et relinquunt se ipsos*). Continuing, he points out some of the things that he has not seen—the Atlantic Ocean is an example of an object for which he has a memory picture, but which he has never visited. But these are all objects represented by images obtained either directly through the bodily senses or constructed from other images retained in memory.

Comment: One notices in the preceding analysis that there is a tendency to quote almost every sentence in Augustine's opening remarks on memory. Both his language and his thought are very dense in structure, and each phrase seems to be important. This treatise on memory is the reason for selecting this part of the *Confessions* for our examination. Although both Plato and Plotinus have contributed something to the Augustinian description of memory, when compared with what Augustine offers in this and the ensuing chapters, their accounts are much less striking than Augustine's. A good deal of what he writes is original, marked with the character of his own personality and talent for self-examination.[2]

One important commentator, R. J. O'Connell, emphasizes Augustine's debt to Plotinus here.[3] He sees this part of the *Confessions* as a Christian restatement of the "fall of the soul" from a previous existence in the Plotinian One. What is remembered, according to O'Connell, is frequently derived from experiences and retained images of an earlier life. Now, it is correct that Augustine could not explain to his own satisfaction the origin of the soul of each individual person. It is also true that Augustine did not know whether to accept or reject the ancient concept of a World-Soul.[4] But in spite of this lack of decisiveness, particularly in his earliest writings, on these two points, I think that Augustine had certainly rejected the notion of the preexistence of the individual human soul in another body well before the time of writing the *Confessions*.

As early as the dialogue *The Teacher* (11.38), which was written at Tagaste in 389, we find him explaining:

> As for all the generalities (*de universis*) that we understand, not from someone speaking outside (*foris*) but inside (*intus*), when we consult the truth presiding over the mind itself, perhaps when we have been urged (*admoniti*) by words to make such consultation: now He who is consulted teaches, He who is called Christ, dwelling in the interior man. That is the immutable Power of God (*Dei Virtus*) and the ever-eternal Wisdom (*sempiterna Sapientia*), which in fact every rational soul consults (*quam quidem omnis rationalis anima consulit*).

What we have here is the early theory of divine illumination of the intellect supplanting the doctrine of the *Meno*.

In the next section of *The Teacher* (12.39), he does admit his ignorance of how some sensory images get into our memory (*imagines in memoriae penetralibus rerum ante sensarum quaedam documenta gestemus*). But when it is a question of understanding the objects of reason (12.40), *The Teacher* says that "we intuit them by their presence in that inner light of truth, by which the inner man, as it is called, is enlightened and brought to perfect fruition" (*ea quidem loquimur quae praesentia contuemur in illa interiore luce veritatis, qua ipse qui dicitur homo interior illustretur et fruitur*). So, as far as the understanding of axioms and general truths is concerned, Augustine has abandoned reminiscence from a previous life ten years before book 10 of the *Confessions*.[5]

Years later, in *The Trinity* (11.7.11–11.11.18), the role of memory in the production of intellectual judgments is more fully described by Augustine when he writes about the various psychological "trinities" that remotely resemble the divine Trinity. Just as there is a triad to be found in the act of sensing some aspect of bodily things, so he finds a sort of "trinity" within the mind (*in alia trinitate interiore,* 7.11). This interior trinity is conceived (*concepta est*) after the mind records various images in memory. What he calls the *acies animi,* the cutting edge of the mind, actively works on the various

species in the images preserved in memory and produces in cogitation upon these images another *species* (a unified form for understanding), which is also kept in memory. This is a sort of offspring
(*quasi proles*) of which the *acies animi* is the parent. The language in
section 7.11 is suggestive of something like biological conception. As
Solignac comments in explaining the function of the *acies animi* in
this text: "This is essentially a psychological event in which the *acies*
is active; it is the act in which consciousness grasps the world:
memory is merely the condition that makes it possible."[6]

Following this in *The Trinity,* there is a description of a sort of
constructive operation in the mind. Since the *acies animi* is presented with countless sense images (*innumerabilia*) that follow each
other in succession, the perspicacity of the mind (*acies animi*) must
unify these contents of memory so that several can be grasped in one
look (*uno aspectu contueri*). This is as close as Augustine will come to
a theory of intellectual abstraction (11.8.12). After further consideration (11.11.18) in *The Trinity,* Augustine relates his explanation to
the triad of number, measure, and weight.

Quite important in chapter 8 of the *Confessions* is the description of the ascent of the soul by steps (*gradus*) toward God. This is
not a matter of going backward to some previous life; it is a voluntary effort to rise above the concerns of the body and the facts of
sense perception. The upward movement of the soul toward the
highest wisdom is described in more than ten passages in Augustine's
writings.[7]

We have seen (see pages 38–39 above) that the *Magnitude of the
Soul* (27.53) finds seven grades of psychic energy. From the lowest to
the highest, they are: *animation* of the body; *sensation; artistic skill*
(*ars*); *discernment* of the good (*virtus*); *stabilization* within the soul
(*tranquillitas*); *fixation* on truth; and *contemplation* of the highest
truth.

On Genesis against the Manichaeans (1.25.43) offers seven allegorical stages of development in the soul: reception of the light of
faith; release of the soul from passions; vision of higher truths; acting in fraternal service to others; submission of the soul to reason
and justice; and resting in the hope of perpetual peace. These are
pictured as seven "days" of psychic growth.

True Religion (30.54; 31.57; 32.59; 39.72; 55.108; and 55.113)
presents seven cognitive stages: immutable law (*lex*) is seen above
reason; God (*Deus*) is the source of this law; unity in bodies (*unitas*)
is known as a vestige of immaterial unity; eternal values, such as
wisdom, beauty, and goodness, are seen as transcending the soul;
spiritual remedies, such as reflection in charity, are discerned as

cures for sensuality and pride; true religion is distinguished from the world of lower things; and, finally, religion binds the soul to the divine Truth.

The *Commentary on the Lord's Sermon on the Mount* (1.13; 2.4–9) describes seven steps up to perfect happiness (*beatitudo*): fear, meekness, sorrow, hunger for goodness, mercy, purity of heart as preparation for the vision of God, peace making, and resting in the perfection of peace. Here Augustine is using the Beatitudes listed in the sermon in combination with the Gifts of the Holy Spirit.

Christian Doctrine (2.7.9–11) also discusses the Gifts of the Holy Spirit as stages in the soul's approach to perfection. Fear converts it to the knowledge of God's will; piety brings respect for the Scriptures; knowledge turns one's love toward God; fortitude grounds delight in eternal goods; mercy cleanses evil thoughts and induces love of neighbor; cleanliness of heart leads to the vision of Truth; and, finally, wisdom brings full enjoyment of eternal peace.

All the foregoing texts fall in the decade preceding the *Confessions,* in which book 7 (17.23) offers a description of an experience in which there are also seven steps upward (numbers added here bring this out):

> And so, step by step (*gradatim*) from [1] bodies, to [2] the soul which senses through the body, and thence to its [3] interior power to which the senses report about external things, . . . further to [4] the reasoning power . . . which lifted itself to [5] its understanding (*ad intelligentiam*) . . . whence it discovered [6] the Immutable Itself (*ipsum incommutabile*) . . . and in the flash of a trembling glance [7] it reached up to That Which Is (*et pervenit ad id quod est, in ictu trepidantis aspectus*).

This passage may be compared with the famous vision at Ostia (*Conf* 9.10), where Augustine and Monica shared an ascent to the point at which "we reached out and, with the speed of thought, touched the Eternal Wisdom abiding above all things" (*et rapida cogitatione attingimus aeternam sapientiam super omnia manentem*). Notice how, in many of these texts, wisdom names the peak of the ascent.

Letter 147 ("On Seeing God," to Paulina) was written about a dozen years after the *Confessions*. It distinguishes three levels of "vision" (1.3ff.): of bodily things through external sensation, of objects cogitated in terms of images, and of imageless intellectual "seeing" of eternal truths, such as the meanings of life, will, cogitation, memory, intelligence, knowledge, and faith (sect. 4). In the remainder of this letter, Augustine continues to advise the Lady Paulina that, while several Old Testament prophets are recorded as seeing God in a special way, it is well to remember that ordinary people will have to wait until the future life for the blessed vision of God.

Somewhat the same gradation of three "seeings" (*visiones*) is found in the *Literal Commentary on Genesis* (12.2.15). Augustine takes the example of reading or hearing the commandment, "Thou shalt love thy neighbor as thyself," and comments:

> We experience three kinds of vision here: one through the eyes, by which we see the letters; a second through the spirit (*per spiritum hominis*), by which we think (*cogitatur*) of our neighbor, nearby or distant; and a third through an intuition of the mind, by which we see and understand love itself (*per contuitum mentis, quo ipsa dilectio intellecta conspicitur*).

This was written in the year 414. Besides describing three levels of vision through which the soul may rise to see eternal truths, the text clearly uses words for the top grade that suggest a direct intuiting of things like love (*dilectio*), meanings that are available to all who really understand this commandment.

The Trinity, written at about the same time (412–16), speaks of how "we tried [back in book 8] to raise the aim of the mind (*erigere temptavimus mentis intentionem*) to understand that most excellent and immutable Nature, which is not our own mind" (*ad intellegendam illam praestantissimam naturam quod nostra mens non est*, 15.6.10).

In *The Trinity* 8.3.4, we find a survey of many objects of love. These are all "goods." He talks about the good earth, a good estate or house, good air, good food, good health, and so on. Then he mentions some goods that are less concrete, the mind of a friend, the sweetness of agreement, the confidence of love. After listing other examples of goods, Augustine concludes:

> This thing is good and so is that, but take away this and that and look at good itself (*et vide ipsum bonum*), if you can. Thus will you see God: not Good by a good that is other than Himself but the Good of all good (*non alio bono bonum, sed bonum omnis boni*). . . . So, God is to be loved, not as this and that good but the good itself. For the good that must be sought by the soul is not something to which it is to fly up in judging (*supervolitet judicando*) but, rather, that to which it must cleave in loving (*cui haereat amando*) and what is this except God? Not a good mind, or a good angel, or a good heaven, but a good good (*sed bonum bonum*).

There is a sort of ascent in loving here, but it can no longer be numbered. Augustine says, after a few lines more, that we could not judge among all such goods whether one was better than the other "unless there were impressed on us a conception of the good itself" (*nisi esset nobis impressa notio ipsius boni*), so that "according to it we might both approve some things as good, and prefer one good to another." What we have here, then, is not a number of steps but the suggestion that there is an ordered evaluation of imperfect goods leading up to a highest standard of goodness, whereby lower goods may be ranked.

Toward the end of his life, when he was reacting against the teachings of Pelagius, Augustine emphasized one's need for divine grace, some special help from God, in order to live a good and meritorious life.[8] Augustine's views on such grace are not within the scope of philosophy; they are important in theology. The writings of this period indicate that he was now thinking not so much of the soul's ascent to higher wisdom as of the descent of God's power in merciful aid to humans.

However, in the last book of the *City of God* (22.24.3), where he is speaking of God's blessings on mankind, he ties in the concept of supreme wisdom with the attainment of an ultimate Good:

> In regard to the human soul (*anima*), God infused into it a mind (*mens*), in which reason and understanding (*ratio, intelligentia*) lie as it were asleep during infancy, but in the course of years it awakens into a life that involves learning and education, skill in grasping truth (*perceptio veritatis*) and loving the good (*amor boni*). This capacity flows into that wisdom and virtue which enables the soul to fight (with the arms of prudence, fortitude, temperance and justice) against error and waywardness, and other inborn weaknesses, and to conquer them with a desire to reach the supreme and immutable Good (*desiderium summi boni*).

Here again we have seven steps in the soul's ascent to the *summum bonum:* animation, consciousness, intuition of truth, love of the good, wisdom, moral virtue, and desire for the highest good. This part of the *City of God* may have been written as late as the year 426. It is the last in this series of psychological analyses.

In the final paragraph of book 10 (8.15), Augustine advises his readers to pay more attention to the contents of memory than to mountain peaks and sea-waves; one should not take this rhetorical outburst as counseling complete neglect of the physical world and its wonders. Unlike Plotinus, who was contemptuous of all material things, Augustine was convinced that all things in existence are good and valuable, in one way or another. Throughout the treatise *The Nature of the Good* and in the mature *Literal Commentary on Genesis,* we find Augustine vigorously opposed to any suggestion that bodily things are evil in nature. Book 3 of the *Confessions* records his youthful failure to understand "that evil is but the privation of the good, even to the extent that evil does not exist at all" (*quia non noveram malum non esse nisi privationem boni usque ad quod omnino non est,* 7.12). The *Enchiridion* (3.11) puts this succinctly: "What does evil mean, other than the privation of the good?" (*Quid est autem aliud quod malum dicitur, nisi privatio boni?*).

Evil is always some sort of disorder. Everything in existence is subject to three formal determinants: number, measure, and weight (*numerus, mensura* or *modus*, and *pondus*). This triad was suggested to Augustine by the biblical statement (Book of Wisdom 11:21) that God "ordered all things in measure and number and weight." Many texts throughout Augustine's writings, passages in which he speculated philosophically on the way that creatures were organized, stemmed from this triad. We have seen one such text, in *The Trinity* (10.11.18), where, on the level of psychic existence, memory is said to function according to these three principles. It is easy to see measure providing order in one's thinking and feeling. Number, he says, helps to bring the many contents of memory into understandable unity. The word "weight" (*pondus*) applies not only to the tendency of bodies to seek their own level but also to the inclinations of conscious spirits to be attracted to their appropriate goods. So, in *Confessions* 4.14.22, Augustine asks: "Where are these weights (*pondera*), inclining to different and opposed loves, distributed in one soul?"

But it is in the world of bodies that Augustine most frequently finds these organizing factors at work. In the *Literal Commentary on Genesis* (4.3.7–4.4.9), there is a fuller discussion of how measure, number, and weight order all creatures:

> It is a great feat, granted to few, to rise above all things that can be measured, so as to see the measure that is without measure; to go beyond all that may be numbered, to see number without number; to surpass all that can be weighed, and see weight without weight. For this meaning cannot be thought in terms of these principles as observed in stones only, and in pieces of wood and bulky things like that, or in bodily things of whatever size, either on earth or in the heavens. Measure is some sort of principle of action, to prevent an unalterable and unregulated process (*Est enim mensura aliquid agendi, ne sit irrevocabilis et immoderata progressio*). Number pertains to the dispositions and powers of the soul, whereby it is properly gathered in from the deformity of foolishness (*insipientia*) to the form of wisdom (*sapientia*). And weight applies to will and love, when it becomes evident how much and what weight is to be given to feelings of desire or dislike, or of preference and undervaluation (*et est pondus voluntatis et amoris, ubi apparet quanti quidque in appetendo, fugiendo, praeponendo, postponendoque pendatur*).

So, while Augustine stresses the importance of these supreme standards of numbering, moderating, and motivating all things, he is not inclined to neglect entirely the principles that bring order to the lowest things in the world. Several texts name "order" (*ordo*) among these principles (*On Genesis against the Manichaeans*

1.16.26; *Free Choice* 2.20.54; *True Religion* 7.13; *On Music* 6.17.56–57). But he never lets us forget that God is the source of all such regulation. From the Creator "come to all bodies the measure enabling them to exist substantially, the number enabling them to live in beauty, the weight enabling them to be well ordered" (*Reply to Faustus* 20.7).

Nor is Augustine blind to the marvels of nature that were part of the popular "science" of his day (*City* 21.4–5): how the "salamander lives in fire"; how some well-known mountains in Sicily "have been continually on fire from the remotest antiquity"; how the flesh of the peacock keeps "for thirty days and more" without corrupting; how chaff has the power to freeze "snow buried under it" but also has "such power to warm that it ripens green fruit." Fire, he points out, "blackens everything it burns, though itself bright" but, on the contrary, fire bakes stones and turns them white. Charcoal has wonderful properties: "no moisture rots it, nor any time causes it to decay." Lime has surprising qualities: when burned, it becomes white, and it can turn other things white, but doused with water, lime becomes "a hidden store of fire." That is why it is called "quick lime" (*propter quod eam calcem vivam loquimur*). Diamonds have marvelous properties: they cannot be changed "either by iron or fire." The only thing that can affect them is goat's blood. The lodestone has a strange ability to attract iron: it can make iron rings stick together to form a chain without being interlinked. Visiting a bishop friend, Severus of Milevis, Augustine was entertained by such a magnet, which was "held under a silver plate on which he placed a bit of iron, then as he moved his hand with the magnet underneath, the iron on the plate was moved backwards and forwards, following the movement of the magnet below." The salt of Agrigentum in Sicily, "when thrown into the fire, becomes fluid as if it were in water, but in water it crackles as if it were on fire." In Arcadia there is a stone called asbestos, "because once lit it cannot be put out."

One biography of Augustine, written by Hugh Pope, devotes a whole chapter to nature and is entitled "St. Augustine and the World of Nature." It gives many other details that show Augustine's fascination with cosmic curiosities. Of course, he never lost an opportunity to point out that all such wonderful things and events simply manifest the omnipotence of the Creator.

Since this commentary is being written on the eve of the five-hundredth anniversary of Columbus's voyage to America, it may not be amiss to note the role that Augustine played in that event. The biography of Columbus written by his son, Fernando, tells of the many objections by learned contemporaries to Columbus's plan to sail west from Spain to India. At one point, Fernando says, "in chapter 9 of Book XXI of the *City of God* the Saint denies the existence of the Antipodes and holds it impossible to pass from one hemisphere to the other."[9]

The passage mentioned by Fernando is in book 16, not 21, but what Augustine wrote was hardly encouraging to explorers. He said that the stories told about people on the other side of the earth are but fables (*fabulantur*). The spherical shape of the earth is a conjecture of astronomers. There is no known evidence of the existence of land on the other side of the earth or of people down under (*Antipodes*). Moreover, it is "quite absurd (*nimisque absurdum est*) to suggest that men have been able to sail down below, over the vast extent of the ocean" (*ut dicatur aliquos homines ex hac in illam partem, Oceani trajecta, navigare ac pervenire potuisse*).

So Fernando Colombo was not mistaken in his reference to the *City of God*. Augustine's knowledge of geography was that of other educated men of his time. Preaching on the Psalms (*Exp Ps* 71.8; 95.13), Augustine advised his listeners not to be concerned about the shape of the earth (*figure hujus mundi*), but he spoke of it many times as an orb or globe (*orbis terrae*). In a famous letter (199.3), written in 418/19, when there was a widespread scare among people that the world was coming to an end, Augustine advised that when it is time for the end of the world, "the Gospel will have been proclaimed in the whole globe (*in universo orbe*), as a witness to all people, and then the end will come."

Actually, Augustine's world comprised but three continents: Africa, Europe, and Asia. The *City of God* (16.17) attests to this:

> These continents are not equal in size. Continental Asia stretches far to the south, to the east, and to the north; Europe to the north and west; Africa to the west and south. Thus, Europe and Africa together take up one half of the world and Asia the other. Africa is divided from Europe by the great oceanic gulf whose waters bathe both shores.

Several books in the *City of God* (5.21; 7.32; 8.9; and 10.32) name the peoples inhabiting these regions. There are many groups of Africans (Augustine himself was probably a Berber)—Romans, Assyrians, Persians, Hebrews, and people of Libya, Egypt, India, Chaldaea, Scythia, Gaul, and Spain.

Certainly Augustine, despite his concentration on God and the human soul, was not without interest in the material world about him. As Othmar Perler has shown in his informative study of Augustine's travels, the bishop of Hippo made more than fifty land journeys in Africa, apart from his dangerous sea voyage to Rome.[10]

Analysis 9.16–12.19: These chapters focus on the theory of imageless thought. Many examples are now considered. "Here, also,

are all those things which have been grasped from the liberal disciplines" (*omnia quae de doctrinis liberalibus percepta*). These are the
matters taught in the seven liberal arts, on which Augustine's early
education centered. He adds concerning their rules, definitions, arguments, and conclusions: "Nor do I carry the images of these, but
the things themselves" (*nec eorum imagines, sed res ipsas gero*). He
does not deny that there may be images associated with such reasonings, say for example the meaning of "equality," but his point is
that there is no true image of what this sort of term signifies.

In section 10.17, Augustine speaks of three kinds of questions:
"Whether a thing is? What it is? What kind it is? (*an sit, quid sit,
quale sit*). These were probably well known in the schools at that
time. The spoken questions are recorded by images in the mind and
held by memory, but the meanings of the questions and their answers are not images (*et in memoria recondidi non imagines earum*).
Augustine admits that he cannot now fully explain how such general ideas come to his memory: "From what source and by what
route did these things enter into my memory? I do not know how"
(*unde et qua haec intraverunt in memoriam meam? nescio
quomodo*). As we have seen in the previous comment, some interpreters take this expression of partial ignorance as an indication of a
lingering fascination with the Platonic theory of reminiscence.

However, section 11.18 does offer a positive explanation of how
at least some of these imageless insights are produced. He says: "We
find that to learn things of this kind . . . is nothing else than, by cogitation, to make a kind of collation" (*invenimus nihil esse aliud
discere ista . . . cogitando quasi colligere*). This is a collecting of the
"haphazard and unarranged contents of memory" (*quae passim
etque indisposita memoria continebant*). This is an anticipation of
the description of concept formation that we have just seen in *The
Trinity* (11.7–11).

In the last half of 11.18, Augustine returned to the problem of
forgetting things previously known. "If I cease to recall them to mind
for even a short period of time, they are again submerged" (*si
modestis temporum intervallis recolere desivero, ita rursus
demerguntur*). This is an acute observation of what is still true of our
everyday experiences: to remember something, it is wise to think
about it frequently. This is particularly the case with complicated
reasonings. How many of us who have passed geometry tests with
flying colors can recall key theorems after a few years unless we
have been teaching or using the science of geometry regularly? It is
at this point, at the end of 11.18, that Augustine volunteers the etymology of *cogitare* and *cogito* and underlines the suggestion that
conclusions in academic disciplines, if forgotten, must be rethought

by again gathering together the facts and images on which they were found previously to depend.

That he is, indeed, thinking about mathematical examples becomes clear from the beginning of the next chapter. "Memory contains the reasons and innumerable laws of numbers and dimensions" (*continet memoria numerorum dimensionumque rationes et leges innumerabiles,* 12.19). We do not know the extent of Augustine's education in mathematics. There is a part of the *Magnitude of the Soul* (8.13–11.19) where he and Evodius discuss some of the properties of figures in elementary geometry: lines, angles, equality and inequality, rectangles, intersections of internal angles, the point as center of a circle, and so on. Simple diagrams are incorporated into the text. Thus there is no doubt that Augustine's schooling was not exclusively literary. However, there are also many examples in his works of a sort of fascination with the allegorical and mystical explanations of various numbers. These are often fanciful, more a matter of numerology in the pejorative sense than of scientific number theory. An example is found in book 4 of *The Trinity* (chaps. 4–6), where the number six is given many marvelous properties.[11]

Again to call attention to his claim that some thoughts are imageless, Augustine points to the fact that words that signify mathematical concepts and reasonings are different in Greek and Latin (*aliae sunt, nam illi aliter graece, aliter latine sonant,* 12.19). "They are known by whoever recognizes them interiorly, without cogitation about any body whatever" (*novit eas quisquis sine ulla cogitatione qualiscumque corporis intus agnovit eas*). These *rationes* of numbers "really exist" (*ideo valde sunt*), he insists.

Comment: Just how these meanings and laws of numeration "really exist" requires some further explanation. Involved is Augustine's teaching on the *rationes aeternae,* the eternal principles of all beings and all understanding. From our discussion in Chapter Three above (see pages 33–34), it may be recalled that he took over Plato's theory of ideal forms and placed them in the creative mind of God (*ars Dei*). These *rationes* are the divine archetypes making up God's plan for all things created. Besides the Platonic background for this theory of eternal reasons, there was biblical evidence for Augustine's teaching. In particular, he stressed the statement in Genesis 1:31 that God looked upon what He had created and saw "that it was good." To Augustine this meant that God judged all creatures to be in accord with their divine ideas, that is, with the *rationes aeternae.* These exemplars are not only the patterns for all "classes" of things that exist; they are also the models for every individual created being. God's omniscience requires that every human person, for instance, be known in the divine wisdom. Although humans think of the divine ideas as plural, this is due to the imperfection of human intellect; they are really one in God.

It may help with this teaching to think of the mathematical meaning of "ratio" in English. The ratio of two to four is an easily understood relation in the order of quantity. The ratio of two to five is not quite so understandable, but it still has a definite meaning and use. The ratio of the diameter to the circumference of a circle is even less understandable; mathematicians call it irrational, but it has a useful meaning named by the Greek letter *pi.* All these relations are *rationes* for Augustine. Equality is a ratio that extends beyond mathematics. When we say that all people are born equal, in some sense we are expressing what Augustine calls an imageless thought or ratio. The relation of parent to child, of citizen to country, and so on, are all seen as intelligible meanings.

What is more difficult for readers of Augustine to grasp is his insistence that the *rationes aeternae,* the eternal exemplars in the mind of God, are more real existents than the creatures patterned on them. This means that a person, say Harry Truman, exists in two ways. Truman lived on earth for a given number of years, but he also exists eternally as an idea in the Creator. Augustine thought that this is the case with all individual creatures. It is also true of other "meanings," such as the principles of mathematics, science, philosophy, virtues, and reasonable laws. Augustine took quite seriously the claim that what is "really real" is present in the divine mind. This gives greater meaning to Augustine's view that all things came initially from the One Creator and that they are all, in one sense or another, to return to their origins in the eternal *rationes.* [12]

I NOTES

1. Gilson, *The Christian Philosophy of St. Augustine,* part 1, chap. 3, relates memory to the subconscious. See also John Mourant, *Saint Augustine on Memory* (Villanova, Pa.: Villanova University Press, 1980). On memory and introspection in Plato, see Charles L. Griswold, Jr., *Self-Knowledge in Plato's Phaedrus* (New Haven, Conn.: Yale University Press, 1986).

2. The Gibb-Montgomery footnote to 10.8.12 stresses this originality.

3. See R. J. O'Connell, *St. Augustine's Confessions: The Odyssey of Soul* (Cambridge, Mass.: Harvard University Press, 1969), 122–34.

4. In "The Problem of a World-Soul" (in *Wisdom from St. Augustine,* 78–90), I have reviewed his comments on the idea of a cosmic soul. He did not completely reject it.

5. This is the judgment of F. J. Thonnard, "Notes Complémentaires" to *De magistro,* BA, 6:475–76.

155 I Memory and Its Wonders

6. Solignac says: "C'est cette *acies*, phénomène psychologique essentiellement actif, qui est proprement l'acte de prise de conscience du monde; la mémoire en est seulement la condition de possibilité" ("Notes Complémentaires," BA, 14:559).

7. For a fuller study see Bourke, "Augustine of Hippo: The Approach of the Soul to God," in *The Spirituality of Western Christendom,* ed. E. R. Elder, 1–12; 189–91 (Kalamazoo, Mich.: Cistercian Publications, Inc., 1976).

8. *The Grace of Christ and Original Sin* 1.43.46–47; *Enchiridion* 30–32, 107. These works are from the years 418 to 421.

9. Fernando Colombo, *The Life of the Admiral Christopher Columbus by His Son,* trans. Benjamin Keen (Westport, Conn.: Greenwood Press, 1978), 39.

10. Perler, *Les Voyages de saint Augustin,* 119–406 describes about fifty documented trips taken by Augustine; some additional ones are uncertain.

11. On Augustine's interest in numerology, see A. Schmitt, "Mathematik und Zahlenmystik," in *Aurelius Augustinus,* edited by M. Grabmann and J. Mausbach, 353–66 (Cologne: Aschendorff, 1930). Some examples are found in my *Augustine's Quest of Wisdom,* 32, 207, and 231.

12. Cf. L. F. Jansen, "The Divine Ideas in the Writings of St. Augustine," *The Modern Schoolman* 22 (1945): 117–31.

In this chapter, we shall examine a portion of book 10 in which previously discussed topics are reemphasized and a number of new questions are introduced.

Analysis 10.13.20: At the end of 12.19, Augustine spoke rather defiantly about a critic who ridiculed him for thinking that there are imageless objects of recollection. "I shall pity him for laughing at me" (*rideat me ista dicentem, qui non eos videt, et ego doleam ridentem me*), he says. So he begins chapter 13 with the claim, "I hold all these things in memory, and I also remember the way I learned them" (*haec omnia memoria teneo et quomodo didicerim memoria teneo*). The manner (*quomodo*) of learning is a mental activity exclusively and has no direct image.

Immediately this brings up an additional instance of another notion that is imageless: falsity or error. Of the criticisms brought against him that he considers false, Augustine insists that "the fact that I remember them is not false" (*tamen ea meminisse me non est falsum*). In the next sentence, he contrasts truths and errors. "I distinguish between those truths and these errors which are said in opposition" (*et discrevisse me inter illa vera et haec falsa*). Note that this relation of truth to error is another example of a ratio. Opposition is a valuable logical aid to judgment.

The last important point comes at the end of this brief chapter (13.20) and concerns reflexive thinking: "I remember that I remembered" (*meminisse me memini*). At first glance, this may seem a platitude, but it is another useful example of thinking that has reached well beyond any initial images from the outer world.

Comment: Augustine's suggestion that one can remember the mental act of learning without any present imagery shows that the spectre of Plato's *Meno* still hovers over him. What is still bothering

Augustine is the notion that some of the things in our memory are carried over from having been learned in a previous life. Of course, one would have to have learned such things initially without recollection in one's first life. That is why Augustine keeps returning to the explanation of learning that he had outlined in *The Teacher*. There must be some occasion when the human mind first understands the rules and judgments of mathematics, for instance. But he feels that there are many other examples of such objects, apart from the immutable truths of numbering. One such object would be the act of recalling the first learning of an important rule. He claims that he can remember "how" (*quomodo*) he learned such things. Augustine expects his readers to agree that this sort of reflection is purely mental. At the end of chapter 13, he offers another example of reflexive recall: he remembers that he remembered something previously. Here again, it is difficult to find an image of such activity.

To my knowledge, Augustine does not advert to the fact that most words which humans use are derived primarily from sense perceptions. Indeed, it is difficult to find any verbal signs that have not come from the experience of physical objects and actions. In spite of his interiorism, Augustine cannot seem to avoid words that are physical in origin, as these chapters show. Thus, in chapter 2, he speaks of the "abyss" of human consciousness. In 6.8, we saw him use words such as "light, voice, odor, food and embrace" in reference to our experience of God. In 7.11, we find him talking about the "head" of his soul; in 8.12, we hear about the "face" of remembrance and the "hand" of one's heart. Indeed, the continual use of "heart" for the seat of feeling in the soul is a prime instance of this transfer from the material order to the immaterial. When we come to the descriptions of memory, we encounter terms such as "recess" (8.13), "chasms" (8.13, 14), "palace" and "storehouse" (8.14), and the "hand" of memory (11.18). Perhaps the most astonishing is Augustine's talk (14.21, 22) about memory as the "stomach" of the soul and of recall as a sort of regurgitation.

No doubt Augustine was aware of the metaphorical quality of psychological language, but he remained fully convinced that we have mental experiences that are quite independent of sensory images.

Augustine's remarks in chapter 13 about the opposition of error to truth call for some explanation.[1] Human error, for Augustine, is a willed act of approving or accepting one thing in place of another (*error namque est pro alio alterius approbatio;* see *Trin* 9.11.16). In the dialogue *On Music* (6.11.32), he commented that the greatest error (*summus error*) is to take imaginative fictions (*phantasmata*) for realities that are actually known (*pro cognitis*). Or, as L. W. Keeler concluded in his Latin comment on a passage in Augustine's *Literal Commentary on Genesis* (12.25): "The typical case of error occurs when we assent to sense images, as if they were real things or accurate representations of things" (*Error ut ita dicam typicus, is est quo assentimur imaginibus sensibilibus, quasi ipsae essent res vel res accurate representarent*).[2]

Augustine carefully distinguishes error from ignorance. The latter is a lack of any sort of knowledge, but it is not usually a willful privation. This is well stated in the *Enchiridion* (17):

> Although we ought to avoid error with the greatest possible care, not only in great but even in little things, and although we cannot err except through ignorance, it does not follow, that, if a man is ignorant of a thing, he must forthwith fall into error. That is rather the fate of the man who thinks he knows what he does not know. For he accepts what is false as if it were true, and that is the essence of error (*pro vero quippe approbat falsum, quod est erroris proprium*).[3]

Later in book 10 (23.33), Augustine will claim that to prefer falsity to truth is as bad as to will to be unhappy rather than happy. This tendency to attribute the assent given to errors to an act of willing persists in modern philosophy with René Descartes' statement that "it is this wrong use of freedom of will in which is found the privation that constitutes the form of error."[4] There is little evidence that Descartes knew the writings of Augustine, but we do know that he was friendly with people such as Antoine Arnauld and Cardinal de Bérulle, who were well acquainted with Augustinian philosophy.[5]

Analysis 14.21–22: In this chapter, we encounter some entirely different objects in Augustine's memory: feelings or emotions (*affectiones, passiones, perturbationes*). "The same memory contains also the feelings of my mind" (*affectiones quoque animi mei eadem memoria continet*). Note that there are not two kinds of memory in Augustine's psychology (such as sensory and intellectual memory in later Scholastic philosophy), nor are there two levels of affective power (sense appetite and will as intellectual appetite). For Augustine, all affective reactions are acts of the soul as willing.[6]

Yet Augustine carefully points out that the first human experience of an emotion, say the feeling of sorrow at the death of a friend, is quite different from the later remembrance of that emotion. As he puts it here (14.21): "I can recall my past sorrow, without being sorrowful" (*tristitiam meam praeteritam recordor non tristis*). He even says that sometimes "I reminisce about my departed sorrow with present joy, and my joy with present sorrow."

The four basic emotions of classical Stoic thought are mentioned here (14.21, 22): sensual desire or lust (*cupiditas*), joy (*laetitia*), fear (*metum*), and sorrow (*tristitia*). These and all other affective disturbances (*perturbationes*) are suffered by the mind (*ipso animus, cum patitur eas*); they are also called "passions of the soul." This terminology continues in Cartesian philosophy. Moreover, "the mind is memory itself" (*animus sit etiam ipsa memoria*, 14.21).

In both sections of chapter 14 (21 and 22), we read that "memory is something like a stomach for the mind" (*memoria quasi venter est animi*). All sorts of previous experiences, cognitive, volitive, and emotive, can be brought up again, "as food is from the stomach in the process of rumination" (*sicut de ventre cibus ruminando, sic ista de memoria recordando proferuntur*, 14.22). He even speaks of the "mouth of cogitation" (*in ore cogitationis*) at this same place.

Finally, in chapter 14, Augustine insists that "we found in our memory not only the sounds of their names according to images . . . but also the notions of the things themselves" (*in memoria nostra non tantum sonos nominum secundum imagines . . . sed etiam rerum ipsarum notiones inveniremus*). Here it would not be wrong to translate *notiones* as the "meanings" of stored experiences.

Comment: Clearly, Augustine's treatment of feelings as "disturbances" suffered by the soul is strongly influenced by his early studies of Cicero.[7] Through this source, Augustine learned that at least some of the Greek and Latin Stoics thought that the wise person should be entirely without feelings, in the sensual meaning of the term. The condition of *apatheia* characterized the Stoic sage. Augustine comments on this in the *City of God* (9.4):

> Among the philosophers there are two opinions about these mental emotions (*animi motibus*), which the Greeks call *pathē*, while some of our own writers, such as Cicero, call them perturbations (*perturbationes*), some say affections (*affectiones*), and others, to render the Greek word more accurately, say passions (*passiones*). Some say that even the wise man is subject to these perturbations, though moderated and controlled by reason, which imposes laws upon them, and so restrains them within necessary bounds. This is the opinion of the Platonists and Aristotle; for Aristotle was Plato's disciple and founder of the Peripatetic school.[8] But others, as the Stoics, are of the opinion that the wise man is not subject to these perturbations. But Cicero, in his book *De finibus* (*On Ends*), shows that the Stoics are here at variance with the Platonists and Peripatetics rather in words than in reality (*verbis magis quam rebus*); for the Stoics decline to apply the terms "goods" (*bona*) to external and bodily "advantages" (*commoda*), because they reckon that the only good is virtue, the art of living well, and this exists only in the mind. The other philosophers, again, use the simple

and customary phraseology, and do not scruple to call these
things goods, though in comparison with virtue, which guides
our life, they are little and of small esteem.

Here Augustine is his own best commentator, for this text from
the *City of God,* though written later, certainly does not go beyond
information that he had gathered as a schoolboy from Cicero and
Seneca. Actually, the distinction between *bona* (as moral goods) and
commoda (as things appropriate for any use) is a commonplace in
classical literature. Seneca explained it (*Letter* 87, near the end) as
follows: "The *commodum* is that which is more useful than harmful;
the *bonum sincerum* (truly good) ought to be harmless in every way."
Thus, a house, for example, is a utility good (*commodum*), even if
designed to become a house of ill repute, for it is suitable or useful for
its purpose.

Parallel to Augustine's distinction between utility goods
(means) and goods in themselves (ends) is the difference between
the will-act of use (*uti*) and that of enjoyment (*frui*). This is a key to
much of Augustine's ethics and to his psychology of loving.[9] Later
medieval moral theology[10] and both utilitarian and teleological
trends in modern ethics owe something to Augustine's meditations
on the difference between the ethical significance of ends and
means. The *uti-frui* theme runs through Augustine's writings in all
periods. We will consider them chronologically.

The *Eighty-three Various Questions* (A.D. 388–95) explains the
distinction between use and enjoyment by contrasting the objects of
these will-acts. The language that Augustine uses here (question 30)
becomes standard in later centuries: what he simply calls *bonum* in
the *City of God* (9.4 and above) is the *honestum* (good-in-itself) in
question 30. And the *commodum* is called *bonum utile* (useful good
or means) in this question. Here is his early explanation:

> Just as there is a difference between a good-in-itself
> (*honestum*) and a useful good (*utile*), so also is there between
> enjoying (*fruendum*) and using (*utendum*). Although one might
> try to show by subtle argument that every good-in-itself is use-
> ful, and that every useful good is a good-in-itself, nevertheless
> it is more correct and in keeping with good usage to say that
> *honestum* means what ought to be sought for its own sake
> (*propter se ipsum*), while *utile* designates that which is desired
> because it is directed to something else. This is the distinction
> in our present explanation, keeping in mind of course that the
> good-in-itself and the useful good are in no way mutually exclu-
> sive. Sometimes our critics think of this in an inexperienced
> and unsophisticated way (*imperite ac vulgariter*) but we say we
> enjoy (*frui*) that from which we take pleasure (*voluptas*) and we
> use (*uti*) that which we refer to an object from which pleasure is

taken. Thus every instance of human perversion (we could also say vice) consists in willing to use the objects of enjoyment (*fruendis uti velle*) or in willing to enjoy the objects of use (*atque utendis frui*). So, all good order (*omnis ordinatio*), in other words all virtue, requires that the objects of joy be enjoyed (*fruendis frui*) and those of use be used (*et utendis uti*). That is, goods-in-themselves (*honestis*) are to be enjoyed, while useful means (*utilibus*) are to be used.

This explanation is further refined in a work of the same early period, *Christian Doctrine* (1.3). Possibly a year or so after question 30, quoted above, Augustine describes three sorts of will-acts directed toward three kinds of object. One sort of reality is to be enjoyed (*fruendum est*); a second sort of thing is to be used (*utendum est*); and then he names a third class of objects that one both enjoys and uses (*aliae quae fruuntur et utuntur*). What he seems to think is that certain objectives, say getting a good job, are looked forward to as desirable ends-in-themselves, but, when achieved, they turn out to be merely means to some further objective, such as raising a family. Some modern critics of Augustine,[11] under the influence of Kant's dictum that human beings should never be treated as means, have objected to this third category of will-objects. But Augustine did not suggest that other people could be regarded properly as means to another good. His position on the love of other persons is made very clear in *The Trinity* (9.8.13), where he says:

> Since every creature is either equal or inferior to us, the inferior is to be used for God (*ad Deum*) but the equal is to be enjoyed in God (*in Deo*). Just as you ought to take joy in yourself, not focusing on self but on Him who made you, so also should it be in regard to the other person that you love as you do yourself (*sic etiam illo quem diligis tanquam te ipsum*).

Kant would not have objected to this. All that Augustine intended to say in the passage from *Christian Doctrine* is that certain proximate ends, at first desired as goods-in-themselves (*bona honesta*), eventually are recognized as means to higher goods. Of course, Augustine thought that the only perfect good-in-itself is God.

A letter (140.3–4) sent to Honoratus in 412 shows how moderate Augustine's view was:

> Truly there is in man a rational soul, but which way he turns the use of reason by his will makes a difference: whether to the goods of his external and lower nature, or to the goods of his interior and higher nature; that is, whether his enjoyment is corporeal and temporal (*utrum ut fruatur corpore et tempore*), or divine and eternal. . . . The rational soul can, then, make good use (*bene uti*) of temporal and corporeal pleasure (*felicitas*), provided it does not give itself up entirely to created

things and thereby abandon the Creator, who has enriched it
with the overflowing abundance of His own goodness.[12]

Here we find a mature Augustine expressing tolerance for the enjoyment of lesser goods provided that they be kept on their proper level
by the ethical person.

Finally, the *City of God* (11.25) offers a very simple exposition of
what Augustine thought about use and enjoyment. His example of
the use of money is still interesting today:

> Nor am I unaware that, properly speaking, fruition is appropri-
> ate for a person concerned with enjoyment (*fructus fruendi*),
> while use pertains to the person engaged in employment (*usus
> utentis sit*). There seems to be this difference, that we speak of
> an object being enjoyed (*ea re frui*) when it gives us delight
> (*delectat*) for its own value and not because it is a means to ob-
> tain something else; but a thing is used when we desire it for
> the sake of something further. Consequently we should use
> temporal things in such a way that we may deserve to enjoy
> (*frui*) eternal goods. Not like perverse people who wish to enjoy
> money (*qui frui volunt nummo*) but to use God (*uti autem Deo*):
> they do not spend money for God's sake but cultivate God for
> money's sake. Nevertheless, in more customary usage, we both
> use the fruits of enjoyment and enjoy the objects of use
> (*verumtamen eo loquendi modo quem plus obtinuit consuetudo,
> et fructibus utimur et usibus fruimur*).

This is Augustine's usual way of answering critics who find his ethics rigid and too otherworldly. He merely asks his readers to remember that there is a rational order among all goods; some are lower,
others are higher.

Later in the *City of God* (14.6), after discussing the four Stoic
passions of the soul, Augustine remarks that the character of the
human will is what is important; because, if the will is wrong, these
motions of the soul will be wrong, but if it is right, they will be not
merely blameless but even praiseworthy (*si perverse [voluntas] est,
perversos habebit hos motus, si autem recta est, non solum
inculpabiles, verum etiam laudabiles erunt*). And so, for Augustine,
because of his psychology of willing, not only is one morally responsible for one's uncontrolled actions but also for immoderate feelings.
(Kant was not the first deontologist!)

Augustine mentions two occasions on which he gave way to excesses of sorrow and later felt guilt. As a young man teaching in
Tagaste, Augustine had a close friendship with another youth.
When this young friend died, Augustine allowed himself to feel too
much sorrow (*Conf* 4.4.7–9). Years later, when his mother died at
Ostia (*Conf* 9.12.29), "a huge wave of sorrow flooded [his] heart." His
account gives the impression that his initial grief at Monica's death

was excessive. But he still talks (*Conf* 10.14.22) of the "bitterness of sorrow" (*amaritudo maestitiae*).

Analysis 15.23: At the beginning of this section comes the admission that it is not easy to distinguish imageless recall from the recollection of things that are represented by images, such as a stone or the sun. But the recalling of a previous feeling of actual pain is even more difficult to handle. As he says, "I can name bodily pain and it is not present in me, when there is no suffering" (*nomino dolorem corporis, nec mihi adest, dum nihil dolet*). He thinks that he must have an image of such physical sufferings retained in memory, otherwise "I would not know what I am talking about" (*nullo modo recordarer, quid hujus nominis significat sonus*). The same seems to be the case with the recall of bodily health: there must be some image of it, even though it is difficult to picture. For "sick people know what was said, when health is named." It is an admirable feature of Augustine's thought that he is ready to admit his failure to answer many philosophical questions.

Returning to the presence of numbers in memory, Augustine insists: "They are present in my memory, not their images but themselves" (*ea adsunt in memoria mea non imagines eorum, sed ipsi*). He adds two other puzzling examples: he does not recall an image of an image but simply the image" (*neque enim imaginem imaginis eius, sed ipsam recolo*). Next he names "memory" itself, wondering whether it could be "present to itself through its own image, and not through itself" (*et ipsa [memoria] per imaginem suam sibi adest ac non per se ipsam?*). There are limits to Augustine's ability to explain self-knowledge.

Comment: The discussion of bodily pain as a feeling is quite interesting because, like hunger and thirst, pain is suffered through some disorder in the material constitution of a person; but it is felt, or recorded, as a *notio* (an item of knowledge) by the soul. With such an explanation of bodily suffering, Augustine will obviously have difficulty in describing how the pain is remembered. This cannot be a simple case of the actual pain being undergone again. Rather, he appears to think that the recall of a given pain, say a toothache, involves a cognitive act rather than another instance of suffering.

We have an example of this in the previous book of the *Confessions* (9.4.12), where Augustine describes a toothache suffered some fourteen years earlier at Cassiciacum. Writing about this now, Augustine is not suffering the bodily pain, yet he recalls it very clearly:

> Thou didst torment me at that time with a toothache (*dolore dentium*). When it became so bad that I could not talk, the notion

> arose in my heart to urge all my friends who were there to pray for me to Thee, the God of every manner of good health. . . . As soon as we had bent our knees with a prayerful disposition, the pain fled (*fugit dolor ille*). . . . I had never had such an experience from the beginning of my life (*nihil enim tale ab ineunte aetate expertus fueram*).

Even though Augustine cannot quite explain how he recalled this painful experience, the very fact that he asks questions about its presence in memory is of psychological value.

The next example, of the sick person who is able to recall good health after this condition has left the body, is an even greater problem for Augustine. Obviously the reality of good health is no longer present in the sick person. If he says that it is remembered through an image of good health, then one might well wonder what such an image would be like. Certainly Augustine's continual stress on the unity of the human psyche made him recoil from a strong differentiation between the cognitive and the affective abilities.

So Augustine returns to the two clear examples of different objects of memory: numbers themselves, not their images, are stored in memory; while physical things, such as the sun, are retained as images after the initial perception and not in themselves. But a third type of recollected object continues to puzzle Augustine. There does not seem to be an image of an image (*neque enim imaginem imaginis*). Indeed, it would seem to be without profit to duplicate images in such a series. The other puzzling example, of memory remembering itself, is equally difficult to explain. Yet Augustine is quite right in saying that awareness of one's own identity seems to require such self-examination.

If those questions appear to be excessively complex, then they at least prepare us for the next chapter, which brings up the problem of remembering that one has forgotten something.

I NOTES

1. For Augustine's treatment of error, the best study is Leo W. Keeler, "St. Augustine on the Problem of Error," *Thought* 8 (1933): 410ff.; reprinted in Keeler, *The Problem of Error from Plato to Kant* (Rome: Pontificia Universitas Gregoriana, 1934).

2. Keeler's Latin comment on *De Genesi ad litteram,* 12.25, is in his Sancti Augustini, *Doctrina de cognitione,* 77.

3. The full text of Dod's version of *Enchiridion,* chap. 17, may be found in *TEA,* 41–42. See also *Enchiridion* 20 and *Contra Academicos* 3.14.32 for an earlier view of error.

4. Descartes, *Meditations* 4; the English version is from A. D. Lindsay, ed., *A Discourse on Method* (London, Toronto, New York: Dutton, 1924), 117. Spinoza severely criticized the Cartesian emphasis on will in accounting for error; see James Collins, *A History of Modern Philosophy* (Milwaukee, Wis.: Bruce, 1954), 208.

5. Cf. F. Copleston, *A History of Philosophy* (New York: Doubleday Image Books, 1963), 4:112.

6. *Concerning the Two Souls* (*De duabus animabus contra Manichaeos*) 10.14: "Will (*voluntas*) is the movement of the mind (*animi motus*), under no compulsion, either not to lose, or to acquire, something" (*Definitur itaque isto modo, Voluntas est enimi motus, cogente nullo, ad aliquid vel non amittendum, vel adipiscendum*).

7. See Cicero's *Tusculan Disputations*, 4–11; and his *De finibus*, 3.10.35.

8. This is one of the few instances where Augustine mentions Aristotle by name.

9. See J. Mausbach, *Die Ethik des heiligen Augustinus*, 1:168–221, 264–71. For a critical treatment, see Thomas Deman, *Le traitement scientifique de la morale chrétienne selon s. Augustin* (Montreal: Institut d'Etudes Médiévales, 1957), 9–12; and Bourke, *Joy in Augustine's Ethics*, 30–49.

10. Peter Lombard's *Four Books of Sentences* (*Libri 4 Sententiarum*), a compendium of the views of the Church Fathers, was used as a textbook in theology from the early thirteenth century; the *uti-frui* teaching of Augustine begins book 1.

11. See John Burnaby, "Augustine of Hippo and Augustinian Ethics," in *Dictionary of Christian Ethics*, ed. J. Macquarrie (Philadelphia: Westminster Press, 1967), 23, where he cites Karl Holl, "Augustins innere Entwicklung," *Abhandlungen der preussischen Akademie der Wissenschaften*, Philos.-hist. Klasse, 1923, 1–51, for denouncing Augustine because he thought one could use other people as means. Cf. Hannah Arendt, *Der Liebensbegriff bei Augustins* (Berlin: J. Springer, 1925), 68–71, where this same Kantian criticism is evident.

12. The translation of *Epist* 140.3–4, by Sister Wilfrid Parsons (FOC, 20:59–60), is somewhat modified here.

CHAPTER
N I N E | **Oblivion and Transcendence**

The next four chapters (16–19) introduce a number of problems having to do with forgetting and with the possibility of transcending ordinary experience in consciousness and rising to a union with
perfect divine wisdom. Some of Augustine's queries here have been
called abstruse,[1] but he admits that sometimes one becomes a mystery to oneself.[2]

Analysis 10.16.24: "When I name oblivion, and likewise recognize
what I am naming, what would be the source of my recognition, if I
did not remember it?" (*Cum oblivionem nomino atque itidem
agnosco quod nomino, unde agnosceram nisi meminissem?*). Is Augustine asking how one can remember forgetting something? Is
there an important distinction to be made between using a name
correctly and knowing its full meaning? In our comment we will see
that there are different ways of not knowing something.

To some extent, Augustine does explore this difficulty when he
remarks next, "If I had forgotten this meaning, I should not be able
at all to recognize what the sound's function is" (*quam si oblitus
essem, quid ille valeret sonus, agnoscere utique non valerem*). This
might be true of total amnesia in reference to a given meaning. Thus
a person might be unable to define the meaning of "mass," as used in
physics, and yet be able to spell the word correctly.

Another difficulty is presented when Augustine points out
that "when I remember my memory, the very memory is present
to itself" (*cum memoriam memini, per se ipsam sibi praesto est
ipsa memoria*). Of course, there is a difference between recalling
the meaning of "memory" in general and the act or content of a given
case of remembering (say, recalling one's mother's middle name).
This individual instance of recalling or forgetting would not erase
the use of memory in regard to other matters. Nor would forgetting
one thing entail the absence of all awareness of memory.

Ambiguity also appears with the next statement: "When I remember oblivion, both memory and oblivion are present" (*cum vero memini oblivionem, et memoria praesto est et oblivio*). Again, it is not clear in this sentence whether the terms "oblivion" and "memory" are to be understood in a general or a particular sense. Augustine was not an expert in classical logic; he did not make use of the term *universale* for the meaning of a genus or species. Boethius introduced the problem of universals to Latin philosophy, using the term "universal," later. Of course, the nature of general terms is known to Augustine. But his difficulty is repeated in the question: "But what is oblivion except the privation of memory?" (*sed quid est oblivio nisi privatio memoriae?*). As suggested earlier, total privation of recall (amnesia in the complete sense) would be required before all memory acts became impossible.

These and other questions in section 24 are not trivial; they serve to alert the reader to the bases of Augustine's admission that he does not understand forgetfulness: "Who will understand what it is?" (*quis comprehendet quomodo sit?*). Even modern psychology may not have all the answers to questions about the subconscious mind.

Comment: Latin as a language for philosophical discussion lacked the precision that Boethius (a logician) gave it in the century after Augustine. The Greeks had a word for "forgetting" (*amnesis*), and to speak of recollecting they used the term "*anamnesis*"; it means not-forgetting, or remembering. This may not have been the actual etymology of *anamnesis* (which is also used in English), but, from at least the time of Plato, philosophical discussions of recollection often included its contrast with oblivion. In some cases, forgetting and remembering are contradictories, and in other instances they are not. One may forget one item of knowledge and yet be quite mindful of other previously acquired bits of information.

From Augustine's examination of three kinds of forgetting, early in his career (*Soliloquies* 2.20.34), we know that he was aware of at least that many sorts of oblivion. First, you may have forgotten something (say, how to demonstrate a conclusion in geometry), and friends may say: Is it this, or that? You may reject their suggestions and still not recall what you once knew. Second, if someone tells you that you smiled a few days after you were born, you would not dare deny this, provided your informant is a reliable witness. Without any memory of this event in infancy, you might still believe that it is so. And third, Augustine suggests that you may encounter something and remember that you have seen it before, but you cannot remember where or when or how it was known. So the young Augustine knew that there are many ways of not remembering something.

In a following section of the *Soliloquies* (35), Augustine notes that it is possible that some knowledge that we have forgotten may be dug out of our mental depths, from some previous experience (*siquidem illas sine dubio in se oblivione obrutas eruunt discendo, et quodammodo refodiunt*). In the version by C. C. Starbuck, this convoluted sentence reads: "Such are those who are well instructed in the liberal arts; since they by learning disinter them, buried in oblivion, doubtless, within themselves."[3] Augustine is thinking of Plato's *Meno* and the theory of reminiscence. This comment in the *Soliloquies* was written a decade before the *Confessions*. Whether Augustine had totally rejected the theory of reminiscence by the year 396 is still debated. But it is quite clear that Augustine the bishop cannot accept the notion that an individual human soul could be associated with two different bodies in successive lives.

At this point, we should note that Augustine has a rather special meaning for the term "ignorance" (*ignorantia*). He does not usually equate ignorance with the simple fact of not knowing something. Instead, even in his early philosophical period, *ignorantia* is considered a failure to know something that one was free to know. In this sense ignorance is blameworthy, and sins committed as a result of ignorance cannot be excused. The third book of *Free Choice* (3.18.51–52) speaks of "acts performed as a result of ignorance which are not approved and so judged to merit punishment" (*per ignorantiam facta quaedam improbantur, et corrigenda judicantur,* sect. 51). He finds this usage of the term in several places in Scripture. Augustine regards such culpable ignorance as the result of previous sin. In later life, Augustine's anti-Pelagian writings, such as the *Grace of Christ and Original Sin* (A.D. 418) and *Grace and Free Choice* (426–27), reinforce this special meaning of ignorance.[4] A passage in *The Trinity* (10.5.7) suggests that much of the soul's ignorance of itself is due to lust: "For it does many things as a result of foul desire, as if forgetful of itself" (*Multa enim per cupiditatem parvam, tanquam sui sit oblita*).

In view of this background, it is not surprising that Augustine makes no use of the concept of a mere privation of knowledge when he is discussing these problems centering on forgetfulness. He does say: "What is oblivion except the privation of memory?" but, instead of exploring this further, he proceeds to a paradox stemming from an oversimplified play on words, saying that oblivion is "present so that we will not forget, and when it is present, we do forget." The need to remember the meaning of one word, oblivion, does not result in total amnesia.

Analysis 16.25: "I am working hard on it, and my work is being done on myself" (*laboro hic et laboro in me ipso*). This could have been translated "in myself." It is another example of Augustine's awareness that he is using introspection. So that we cannot miss his point, he adds that we are not considering "the sky's expanses," or "the distances between the stars," or the weight of the earth. These problems of physical science are set aside. He repeats: "I am the one remembering, I am the mind" (*ego sum qui memini, ego animus*). Augustine continually identifies himself with his immaterial part. This emphasis will continue into the next chapter (17.26).

Confessing next (16.25) that "the power of my memory is not understood by me" (*memoriae meae vis non comprehenditur a me*), he concludes, "I cannot speak of myself without it" (*cum ipsum non me dicam praeter illam*). His reason for this conclusion stems from his idea that psychic life is an ongoing process, and so awareness of one's personal identity as an individual requires continued recollection of one's past experiences and one's expectations of future mental events.

The question of forgetfulness is not dropped. Again Augustine asks a series of questions about oblivion, leading to this query: "On what basis may I say that the image of oblivion is kept in my memory?" He uses the phrase *quo pacto,* that is, by what convention, or force of popular agreement, are we led to think that there is forgetfulness in a person's memory? It is clear, as he says next, that a place—Carthage, for example—which has been visited remains in memory by its image. But oblivion is not like this example: "How did it write its image in the memory, when oblivion erases by its very presence?" (*quomodo imaginem suam in memoria conscribebat, quando . . . praesentia sua delet oblivio?*). Terms that are negative or privative puzzle Augustine because he can hardly convince himself that he can "see" their meanings.

Comment: As a trained rhetorician, Augustine knew the value of repetition. This chapter emphasizes the fact that we remember some notions that have no exact physical images. It glosses over the observation that we may have a partial memory of something, with some forgetting of associated details, and yet we may retain good recall of other items of knowledge or feeling. For example, one may remember that a friend's birthday falls in June and yet forget the precise day of the month or the friend's present address. Augustine makes little use here of the role of opposition in giving meaning to somewhat empty contraries. Thus "zero" can hardly be understood unless it is contrasted to other numbers. Similarly, oblivion derives its meaning, without an image, from its opposite, which is memory.

One feature of Augustine's psychology that makes these paradoxes and problems vital to him is his idea that memory, or any other capacity of soul (*vis animae*), is identical with the *whole* soul.

With this view, it makes some sense to wonder how a person can retain any psychic continuity or identity when a loss of memory is suffered. Augustine's very difficulty here serves to emphasize the point that when he speaks of "powers" (*vires*) of the soul, he is not thinking of distinct faculties.

Analysis 17.26: We have seen that in Augustine's early writings he said that only two beings were the objects of his search for wisdom: God and his own soul. So, right at the start of this chapter, he asks about the latter. "What, then am I? . . . What is my nature? A life of many aspects" (*Quid ergo sum? . . . Quae natura mea? varia, multimoda vita . . .*). In the comment to follow, we will look at some of his answers to this key question not only in the *Confessions* but elsewhere.

The second important thing in chapter 17 is Augustine's decision to go beyond his fascinating memory in order to approach the other great object of his interest, God. "I shall pass over even this power of mine which is called memory . . . to reach Thee, sweet Light" (*transibo et hanc vim meam, quae memoria vocatur . . . ut pertendam ad te, dulce lumen*). This is one of Augustine's many efforts to transcend ordinary experience and ordinary objects of study. He calls the divine light "sweet" and speaks in the next sentence of "contact" with God (*inhaerere tibi*), terms often used by later Latin mystics. But Augustine seems to be working here on the level of natural effort to approach the supreme Good: "O truly good and serene Sweetness" (*vere bona et secura suavitas*). Again, he wonders how he can discover God unless he already knows something about Him: "But, if I find Thee without memory . . . how, indeed, may I find Thee?" (*si praeter memoriam meam te invenio . . . et quomodo jam inveniam te?*).

A sentence or two before this, Augustine pointed out that "even beasts and birds have memory" (*habent enim memoriam et pecora et aves*); and he quoted Scripture (Job 35:11), saying that God has made him "wiser than the fowls of the air." Here we have Scripture combined with philosophy. The belief that God conveys wisdom on humanity is an indication that, for Augustine, the ultimate source of wisdom is God.

Comment: At this point, we will try to assemble some of the things that Augustine has written in answer to the question: What is my nature? First of all, let us see what the young Augustine considered human nature to be. Back when he was writing the *Morals of the Catholic Church* (A.D. 387–89), Augustine first asked: What is man? (4.6). Of course, it is generally agreed, he says, that we are "composed of soul and body" (*ex anima et corpore nos esse compositos*).

But is a human being only the body or only the soul? Earlier in this work (1.27.52), he had defined a human as "a soul using a body" (*anima utens corpore*). Yet Augustine admits that neither is exclusively called human in ordinary usage. But are we going to say that perhaps the body is the servant of the soul, or that it is ruled by the soul, or that the soul is related to its body as a rider to a horse (a Platonic comparison)? This is hard to determine, but the early Augustine is sure that the soul is the greatest good of the body (*summum bonum corporis,* 4.7). Here his reason for identifying a human being with the soul is primarily because, when it is a question of morals (*cum de moribus agitur*), we give the role of instructor to the soul, not to the body (4.8).

Many years later, in the last book of *The Trinity* (15.7.11), he quotes the ancient definition of a human being, "a rational animal" (*animal rationale*), or more analytically, "a rational substance constituted from soul and body" (*homo est substantia rationalis constans ex anima et corpore*). The mature Augustine avoids the notion that a person includes two substances.

Midway in time between the foregoing two works is the *Confessions,* where he still tends to identify a human being with the soul. As Henry Chadwick remarks, "The Platonic tradition made him want to define the essence of man in terms which almost omitted the physical nature of the creature."[5]

The further question, then, is: What is the rational soul or mind (*animus*)? If we take the term "psychology" in its original etymological meaning (*psyche* and *logos*), as "a rational account of the psyche," then the answer to this question would have to be a treatise on Augustinian psychology. All that can be attempted here is a brief description of the human soul as Augustine saw it.[6] Much of our information is found in the three books of *Free Choice* and, for the mature period, the last seven books of *The Trinity* (9–15) are basic.

Probably the first thing that Augustine would say, if asked the above question now, is that the human soul is the "life" of the body. As such, it is not enough to say that it is simply the entelechy, or orderly arrangement, of the parts of the living body. Rather, the soul is an immaterial nature or "substance sharing in rationality and suitable for the ruling of the body" (*mihi videtur esse substantia quaedam rationis particeps, regendo corpori accommodata*; see *Magnitude of the Soul* 13.22). There is little doubt that the early Augustine considered that a person was a composite of two substances, the body being material and limited in time and space, the soul immaterial and subject only to changes in time.[7] The soul is not a thin gas or anything corporeal, for if it were a body, it would not be able to grasp incorporeal concepts (*nam profecto quia corpus non est, neque aliter incorporea ulla cernere valeret,* 14.23). Besides this function of understanding eternal truths (such as the propositions of geometry), the soul vivifies its body and produces sense perceptions, as we have seen in the *Confessions* (10.7.11). Its higher capacities, mind (*mens*), memory (*memoria*), and will (*voluntas*) are not accidents (in the Aristotelian sense), but each is identical with the whole soul as understanding, retaining experiences, and acting in any dynamic way.[8]

Freedom to decide and act upon one's decision (*liberum arbitrium*) is another distinctive property of the human soul, proved from consideration of the fact that humans perform both good and bad actions (sins), as the dialogue *Free Choice* shows (1.11.21; 3.18.50). This personal liberty is governed from outside the soul by laws, divine and human, and from within the soul by the use of reason (*Free* 1.6.14). Another kind of human freedom, which we might call "eminent liberty" (*libertas*), is conferred on a person by divine grace. It frees one from the inclination to sin and enables one to perform good works that merit salvation. (Such eminent liberty is a theological concept, mentioned here so that philosophers will not confuse it with freedom of choice.)

Since Augustine regarded human life on earth as a short journey from birth to a future existence after bodily death,[9] what he thinks about the start and ending of this terrestrial trip is an essential feature of his philosophy of the human being. In other words, we need to look at his views on how the soul of each person begins to exist and what its expectations of future life are.

When Augustine speaks of his need for some previous memory of God in order to be able to discover Him (17.26), he is not necessarily attempting to revive the Platonic myth of metempsychosis. It is possible that he did think, at times, that the individual soul pre-existed without a body and may have had some cognitive experiences before its life on earth. This statement depends on Augustine's speculations on the origin of the individual human soul. It was a problem that appeared in many of his writings, before and after the *Confessions*.

In the first book of *Free Choice* (1.12.24), Augustine reacted to Evodius' assumption that humans were born without any wisdom. It is a great question (*magna quaestio*), Augustine says, whether the soul had another life before its association with its body (*utrum ante consortium hujus corporis alia quadam vita vixerit anima*). He is not talking about the soul migrating from an earlier body to a later one; we shall see that Augustine was speculating about a previous incorporeal existence of the soul. The third book of *Free Choice* (3.20–21, 56–59) returns to this and describes four opinions on how the soul originates: (1) it may be propagated from one first soul; (2) it may be created by God as a new soul for each birth; (3) it may have been created at the beginning of time, stored up "in another place" (*alicubi*) without a body and then sent by God at the appropriate time to join its body; or (4) this created and previously existing soul may spontaneously (*sponte*) come to its body. Of these four views, none may be boldly approved (*nullam temere affirmare oportebit,* 31.59).

Throughout his writings, these same four opinions recur (*Literal Commentary on Genesis* 1.10; *Letter* 143, 164, 166; *On the Soul and Its Origin* 1.2; *Reply to Julian* 5.17; *Retractations* 1.1.3). Augustine is never able to find in Scripture or in philosophy a ground for approving only one of them. In a very late work (*Incomplete Reply to Julian* 2.168), he frankly admits: "I have to confess that I do not know" (*me nescire confiteor*).[10]

The reader might well ask, What made Augustine hesitate in dealing with this problem? The answer depends in great part on two items in his religious beliefs. From Genesis he learned that God created *all things* in the first six days. No new creatures are made during the later course of time. On the other hand, Augustine firmly believed that all humans are descended from Adam and Eve, and that all their descendants are stained by the original sin of these first parents. So Augustine had to think that each person's soul was made in the beginning by God. Moreover, each person in some way inherits the imperfection of original sin, presumably through parental descent; not even philosophical wisdom could rescue him from this impasse.

In any case, it is not surprising that in the tenth book of the *Confessions,* Augustine continues to assume that some prior knowledge of God is present in small children. (One thinks of William Wordsworth's poem "Intimations of Immortality from Recollections of Early Childhood," but there the source is Plato rather than Augustine.) Such knowledge is not necessarily innate; the theory of divine illumination of the mind makes it possible for one to become conscious of certain truths at any point in life.[11]

Augustine was convinced that it is more important to know where one is going than where one started one's life journey. So the question of the human soul's immortality is an essential part of his view of human nature. Here he has no doubts: the soul can never die. Many of the writings before the *Confessions* offer proofs of immortality that are more or less dependent on Platonic psychology. Thus the *Soliloquies* (2.13.23) will argue that the soul is the subject in which immutable knowledge of truth resides, and so the soul itself must endure forever without substantial change. In the same text, we find a very simple argument proposed by "the great philosophers" (*a magnis philosophis*) to the effect that the human soul is life itself and it can never be subject to its contradictory, which is death (*rem quae quocumque venerit, vitam praestat, mortem in se admittere non posse*).

These and a number of similar arguments are presented in the early work *Immortality of the Soul* (see 9.16; 11.18; and 12.19 for examples). But since Augustine practically rejected this work as "hardly intelligible" (*intentionem meam vixque intelligatur a me ipso, Retr* 1.5), we will not detail its arguments here.

In *Letter* 143.7 (A.D. 411–12), while discussing his hesitation in *Free Choice* about the origin of the human soul, Augustine remarks that "I have no doubt either that the soul is immortal—not in the same sense that God is immortal." Within a few years, *The Trinity* (13.4.7–8.11) offers a quite different argument in favor of immortality. He starts with a study of the meaning of beatitude or happiness (*beatitudo,* sometimes *felicitas*). He reviews the opinions of philosophers such as Epicurus (on pleasure), Zeno the Stoic (on virtue), and Cicero (who criticized both and said that one is less unhappy in failing to satisfy one's wishes than in securing something that should not be desired). But Augustine concludes that these philosophers described the happy life in accord with their own wishes (7.10), so he did not find in ancient philosophy a satisfactory reason for accepting immortality. Instead, Augustine turned in this section of *The Trinity* (13.8.11) to the claim that all people will to be happy (*cum ergo beati esse omnes homines velint*) as a basis for philosophical reasoning in favor of immortality. He thinks it obvious that satisfactory happiness for all persons is not possible in this life, so there must be an everlasting future life in which to satisfy this natural desire for happiness.

Since this matter of natural desire is taken up in the next chapters of book 10, we will leave further consideration of it for later comments.

Analysis 18.27: In this brief chapter, Augustine returns to the problem of partial memory of something. The biblical story of the woman who has lost a coin is used as an example. She "would not have found it, unless she retained some remembrance of it" (*nisi memor ejus esset, non inveniret eam*). Helpers may say: "Perhaps this is it? Maybe this one?" (*num forte hoc est? num forte illud?*), and she cannot answer unless she has some memory of it. This is not really a good example, as we will show in our comment.

Then Augustine tries to redeem the example by adding: "When by chance something is lost from sight, not from memory . . . its image is retained within, and it is sought until it comes back within view" (*si forte aliquid ab oculis perit, non a memoria . . . tenetur intus imago ejus, et quaeritur, donec reddatur aspectui).* This is of some help with the problem, but the case of a lost physical object requires more precision on the difference between the image of the object and the image of the place in which it was lost.

Comment: If Augustine is attempting here to get the reader to realize the complexity of memory contents, then he is successful. But if he thinks he is dealing with Plato's problem in the *Meno* (79–80d), then his example is not helpful. Socrates and Meno were talking about whether it is possible to know part of a virtue without knowing its whole nature. Finally, when Socrates proposes an investigation of what virtue really is, Meno says: "And how will you enquire, Socrates, into what you do not know? What will you put forth as the subject of enquiry? And if you find what you want, how will you ever know that this is the thing which you did not know?"[12]

Now of course, Augustine did not have Plato's *Dialogues* in front of him when composing the *Confessions,* but he knew from Cicero, and possibly other Latin sources, what the *Meno* problem was. It did not confront the difficulty of a lost physical object but rather the problem of teaching and learning something entirely new. Augustine had faced this question in *The Teacher,* where he suggested that a teacher cannot put new knowledge into the mind of a student. Teaching requires the use of signs, often auditory and visual. Such signs must have meanings already somewhat understood by the student, or they are useless (*The Teacher* 10.33). As Augustine puts it: "When a sign is given to me, if it finds me ignorant of what the sign signifies, then it can teach me nothing" (*cum enim mihi signum datur, si nescientem me invenit cujus rei signum sit, docere me nihil potest*). His own example of this, for his son Adeodatus, is the Latin word *saraballae*, used in the Old Testament translation (Daniel 3:94) about the young men in the fiery furnace. Augustine's Latin text read: "*et saraballae eorum non sunt immutatae*" (and their *saraballae* were not affected [by the fire]). This is an excellent example for Augustine's purpose in *The Teacher.* One can repeat *saraballae* over and over to a student, but if the student does not know its meaning, it will say nothing. Indeed, the student has no memory of what this term means. (Actually, *saraballae* has been taken to signify "head-dresses," as apparently Augustine understood the word, but other meanings have been given this little-used word, such as "hair of the head, cloak, or even sandals."[13]) What Augustine overlooks, both in *The Teacher* and the *Confessions* 10, is that the teacher, and often the student, may use other signs that are understood, and also demonstrations of other things and actions, to get at the meaning of an unfamiliar term.

The example of a lost coin is unfortunate, since any coin of the same appearance that is found would be satisfactory. It is not usually the precise image of the coin that has gone into oblivion but rather the image of the place, or other conditions under which the object was lost, that is not remembered.

Analysis 19.28: Some progress is made in this chapter because Augustine now focuses on what would seem to be different levels in memory. Thus he tentatively points to cases where items are retained in memory, but the mind (*mens*) is not aware of them. So he speaks of "when the memory itself loses something" (*cum ipsa memoria perdit aliquid*). As Augustine observes, there are times when we cannot recall something (say, where we have left a book); various possibilities are reviewed and rejected until we come to the right answer (we may have left it at a friend's house). Of this sort of thing, Augustine comments: "Yet, we certainly had forgotten it" (*certe enim obliti fueramus*).

Next he considers the possibility of partial forgetting, which, of course, involves partial memory. "Or, had it disappeared, not completely but only in part?" (*an non totum exciderat, sed ex parte?*). Here Augustine uses the example of forgetting a well-known person's name. It could be that we remember a first name and cannot think of the family name. Or we know something about the person (say, she taught us in third grade), but the whole name eludes us. Various names may be reviewed and rejected as not fitting. Then the proper one comes to mind because it fits "our customary way of thinking" (*cum illo cogitari consuevit*). Here Augustine comes close to the role of mental "habits" or customary dispositions. But he does not develop this promising theme.

Toward the end of this chapter, he nearly introduces the modern concept of the subconscious mind. If a name, for example, "is entirely wiped out of mind, then we do not remember, even when reminded of it" (*si autem penitus aboleatur ex animo, nec admoniti reminiscimur*). He is almost saying that memory retention takes place on two levels: below conscious awareness and in full awareness.

Comment: This section of the examination of memory comes close to, or reaches, several precisions. It becomes clear that there are two kinds of forgetting: one in which something previously experienced seems totally lost, for it never comes back to remembrance; the other is the case of something—a person's name, for example—that does not immediately come to mind but is retained without awareness until something "reminds" us of the right name. Some modern psychologists try to explain this sort of thing by speaking of a subconscious level of mind. At the very least, we can conclude that Augustine paved the way for the entry of such a theory.

Another feature that is striking here and in earlier sections of book 10 is Augustine's awareness of "customary ways of thinking," or mental habits. After reading, as a youth, the *Categories* of Aristotle in Latin (*Conf* 4.16), he says, "I read it by myself and understood it." However, one wonders how much he retained of this not very demanding little work. One of the accidental categories described by Aristotle is quality. One type of quality is habit (*hexis*). Aristotle explained it as a permanent disposition, particularly of the mind. Thus a geometer is a person who has acquired a special quality or skill in thinking about a subject, a habit that nongeometers lack. Later Greek and Latin commentators on Aristotle make much philosophical use of the role of habit formation. Thomas Aquinas, for instance, uses *habitus* to explain intellectual memory and the acquisition of virtue. But Augustine does not relate the category of quality to his account of memory.

Another important omission in this part of the *Confessions* is the lack of attention to what we call "rote" memory. This system of implanting something in memory is often oral and auditory; it frequently uses some sort of rhyme or jingle as a mnemonic device. When first reacting against the Donatists, Augustine wrote a chant entitled *Psalmus contra partem Donati* (*Jingle against the Donatist Sect*) to enable unlearned people to distinguish the Donatists from traditional Catholics. Surely in his early classes in Latin grammar, he was taught how to remember the prepositions that take an accusative object: "*ad, ante, con, in, inter-ob, post, prae, sub, super.*" But he does not mention this sort of acquired memory here in book 10. In spite of Augustine's dedication to oral communication, his memory imagery seems to lie mainly in the visual rather than the auditory area. When he speaks of "images," it appears that little pictures of things are retained and are uppermost in his mind.

| NOTES

1. See Solignac's remark where he calls the problems centering on oblivion "excessively subtle" (*Les Confessions,* BA 14:563). As the footnotes in the Gibb-Montgomery *Confessions,* 291–94, indicate, there is some ambiguity in Augustine's use of the term *oblivio.*

2. Cf. O'Connell, *St. Augustine's Confessions,* 125–27.

3. *Basic Writings of St. Augustine,* ed. Oates (New York: Random House, 1948), 1:296.

4. Readers interested in Augustine's anti-Pelagian writings, and especially his criticism of Caelestius, might consult Bonner, *St. Augustine of Hippo,* chap. 9.

5. Henry Chadwick, *Augustine* (Oxford: Oxford University Press, 1986), 115.

6. There is no complete general account of Augustine's psychology in English. Nor is it easy to find a good book in other languages. The old work by M. Ferraz, *De la psychologie de saint Augustin* (Paris: Durand, 1862) is still cited but inadequate. Of course, there are many studies of particular problems in this field. Most helpful is Pegis, "The Mind of St. Augustine."

7. Mourant, *Introduction to the Philosophy of St. Augustine,* 14, correctly observes: "Such a view maintains the necessity of a union between two created substances, body and soul. . . . As a philosophical explanation of the relationship between body and soul it still leaves much to be desired, but Augustine provides no further solution." See also Bourke, "The Body-Soul Relation in the Early Augustine."

8. For how willing works, see *Conf* 8.8–10.24. Bourke, *Will in Western Thought* (New York: Sheed & Ward, 1964) treats this in chap. 5, and contrasts this dynamic-power view of will with other views. *City* 14.6 offers a mature treatment of willing.

9. Perler, *Les voyages de saint Augustin,* 383–89, describes death as Augustine's last journey.

10. Thonnard accurately summarizes Augustine's views on the soul's origin in "Notes Complémentaires," BA 6:539–41.

11. As Joseph Owens clearly explains in his study of the light of the mind according to Augustine: "It means that to have knowledge of a thing, no matter what the thing may be, is to behold it as it exists eternally in the divine Word. Sense cognition is required, but only to alert us to look at the thing as it is present in the divine intellect that enlightens every human knower." See Owens's textual exposition of *De magistro* 40, entitled "Deo Intus Pandente," *The Modern Schoolman* 69 (1992).

12. The *Meno* 8d quotation is from Ben Jowett's classic version, *The Dialogues of Plato* (New York: Random House, 1937), 1:359–60. The Gibb-Montgomery *Confessions* prints the Greek text of *Meno* 8d, 294, n. 9.

13. See the "Note" by Thonnard (BA 6:486–87) on the Augustinian use of *saraballae.* For Augustine's general theory of signs, consult R. A. Markus, "St. Augustine on Signs"; and B. D. Jackson, "The Theory of Signs in St. Augustine."

CHAPTER
T E N | **Happiness and Immortality**

Throughout chapters 20 to 23, Augustine tries to convince his readers that the "happy life" (*beata vita*) for humans is really the life of "blessedness" (*beatitudo*). That is to say, he sees no possibility of true human self-perfection apart from God. In this context, Augustinian philosophy is obviously theocentric. It will not work without a supreme being who presides over all events in the universe. But he is also convinced that complete happiness cannot be achieved by people in an earthly life, so he argues that the universal desire for happiness shows that the human soul must not die with the death of the body. Only in an unending future life can one's highest aspirations be fulfilled. Our comments will indicate that Augustine had this way of looking at things even in his earliest writings.

Analysis 10.20.29: "When I look for Thee, my God, I am looking for the happy life" (*cum enim te, deum meum, quaero, vitam beatam quaero*). Augustine is asserting this identification of the happy life with God, but he does not presuppose immediate or complete agreement at this point. He proceeds to a number of insights that are intended to ground his assertion.

First Augustine goes back to the proposition that he has mentioned before: "My body has life from my soul, and my soul has life from Thee" (*vivit enim corpus meum de anima mea et vivit anima mea de te*). Thus body is related to its soul as this soul is related to God. Next he asks: "How, then, do I seek the happy life?" (*quomodo ergo quaero vitam beatam?*). Do I look forward to it (1) "through remembrance" (*per recordationem*) "of something experienced but now forgotten?" Or (2) do I look for it "through desire to learn it as something unknown?" (*per appetitum discendi incognitum?*). To attempt an answer, Augustine appeals next to the commonplace of ancient ethics, the universal desire for a happy life. "Surely the happy life is this: what all men desire" (*nonne ipsa est beata vita, quam omnes volunt*). But he is not sure how people know enough about the meaning of happiness to be able to desire it so universally.

Another complexity is introduced when he observes: "There is one certain way whereby each man, when he possesses this object, is then happy, and there are also those who are happy in hope" (*et est alius quidam modus, quo quisque cum habet eam, tunc beatus est, et sunt qui spe beati sunt*). Augustine sees that one can be joyful either in the actual having of something or in the anticipation of such possession. Anticipation is not as good as the reality of acquisition, but it is better than the state of a third class of people, those who desire happiness but have never possessed it and never hope for it (*illi qui nec re nec spe beati sunt*). Even this third group must have some knowledge of happiness, and that knowledge would have to remain in their memory. To deal with this, he suggests that perhaps all people share some memory of the first happiness experienced by Adam, "that man who was the first person to sin, in whom we all died, from whom we were all born amidst unhappiness" (*an in illo homine, qui primus peccavit, in quo et omnes mortui sumus et de quo omnes cum miseria nati sumus*).

He insists that we cannot love what we do not know (*neque amaremus eam, nisi nossemus*). It is not the word that names happiness (which name, of course, varies in Greek, Latin, and other languages) but the meaning of happy life itself that must be kept in memory (*eorum memoria teneretur*).

Comment: Chapter 20 is not Augustine's first discussion of the universal desire for happiness and its implications. The very first dialogue that he completed was the *Happy Life* (*De beata vita*). It records a three-day conversation held at Cassiciacum (the country villa in northern Italy) on the occasion of his birthday, 19 November 386. Present with Augustine were his mother; his brother, Navigius; his pupils Trygetius and Licentius; Augustine's son, Adeodatus; and two poorly educated relatives named Lastidianus and Rusticus. Not yet a baptized Christian, Augustine dedicated the *Happy Life* to a Christian gentleman, Manlius Theodorus, who had befriended Augustine in Milan and belonged to the group that studied Neoplatonic philosophy in that city.

In the polished peroration, the *Happy Life* describes the seagoing voyage to the port of philosophy (chaps. 1–5). There are, Augustine says, three classes of seafarers on the way to philosophical wisdom. Some, having reached the full use of reason, sail on with little effort, and their example encourages others to make the journey. A second group goes too far, perhaps they are blown off course, but eventually they wake up in port. The third class of travelers falls between the first two; they are tossed about but "remember, even amidst the waves, the great sweetness of home" (*jactati tamen quaedam signa respiciunt et suae dulcissimae patriae, quamvis in ipsis fluctibus recordantur;* see chap. 2). All these people may eventually find the happy life. Augustine admits to Theodorus that he has had his troubles making this trip, but he is still underway and now sure that the happy life could well be termed a "gift of God."[1]

Early in the dialogue (chap. 10), the speakers all agree that they wish to be happy. Augustine asks, "We wish to be happy, do we not?" And he notes: "They agreed, with one voice" (*beatos esse nos volumus, inquam; vix hoc effuderam, occurrerunt una voce consentientes*). At the end of this discussion, it was decided that "to be happy simply means to lack nothing, and that is to be wise" (*ergo beatum esse nihil est aliud quam non egere, hoc est esse sapientem;* see the summary chap. 33).

But also in these autumnal weeks at Cassiciacum, they discussed the skepticism of the later Platonic Academy, and this discussion is recorded in the dialogue *Answer to the Academics.* Here we find an informative review of Augustine's ideas on the relation of wisdom (*sapientia*) to the happy life. Three definitions of wisdom come under discussion. (1) Wisdom is the right way of life (*sapientiam rectam viam vitae esse,* 1.5.13); (2) wisdom is the right way that leads to truth (*sapientia est via recta, quae ad veritatem ducat,* sect. 14); and (3) the famous classical definition: "Wisdom is the knowledge of divine and human things" (*sapientiam esse rerum humanorum divinarumque scientiam,* 6.16).[2]

Later in the criticism of Academic skepticism, Augustine and his friends agree that "the knowledge of human affairs consists in the science of prudence, the beauty of temperance, the strength of fortitude, and the sanctity of justice" (*Illa est humanarum rerum scientia, qua novit lumen prudentiae, temperantiae decus, fortitudinis robur, justitiae sanctitatem,* 1.7.20). They sharply distinguish such useful knowledge of earthly affairs from that part of wisdom which is concerned with divine truths (1.8.22). In a summary of the Stoic view, they conclude: "Human wisdom is the search for truth, on which, because of mental tranquillity, the happy life depends" (9.24).

At the start of the second book of *Answer to the Academics* (2.1.1), this youthful group agrees that full wisdom can only be secured with God's help (*tum in primis auxilium omni devotione ac pietate implorandum est*). This marks the beginning of what came to be known later as Christian philosophy.[3]

Thus, long before he wrote the *Confessions,* Augustine was fully convinced that God is not only wisdom in its perfect reality but also is identical with the ideal happy life. How human minds retain some faint knowledge of this important insight in memory remains a puzzle for the mature Augustine. But now he introduces the suggestion that human minds may inherit from Adam some recollection of the initial happiness enjoyed by the first man before he sinned. Apparently Augustine is thinking that, just as later generations are handed on something of Adam's original sin, so also they may inherit some echo of the original happiness in the Garden of Eden. Rather casually Augustine suggests that "we were at one time happy, either all individually, or all in that man who was the first to sin" (20.29).

In any case, irrespective of the language that people speak, there is universal acceptance of happiness (*beatitudo* or *felicitas*) as the supreme object of human aspiration. Something in the area of knowledge of perfect bliss must be present in the memories of all human beings. We will see later (at 23.33) that this way of thinking leads Augustine to a sort of demonstration of the rationality of belief in God's existence, based on the conclusion that only a highest Good (*summum bonum*) could satisfy this universal desire for eventual felicity.

Analysis 21.30–22.32: Granting that all people must keep some experience of happiness in memory, Augustine now asks a series of questions about whether this remembrance "is like" recollecting other experiences. First, "Is this the same as the case of the man who, having seen Carthage, remembers it?" (*ut memini Carthaginem qui vidi?*). No, it is not like that, for the happy life is not seen with the bodily eyes; it is not corporeal. Second, "Is it like the case of our remembering numbers?" (*numquid sicut meminimus numeros?*). No, our recalling the meanings of mathematical truths does not imply any future expectations, but knowing about happiness does look to future possession of it. Third, is it like "remembering the art of oratory" (*numquid sicut meminimus eloquentiam?*). No, we have sense experiences of the eloquence of other people, but we do not so experience happiness in others. Fourth, "Is it like the way in which we remember joy?" (*numquid sicut meminimus gaudium?*). "Perhaps so," he says (*fortasse ita*). Since the feeling of joy is closely connected with the experience of happiness, Augustine is inclined to see a close analogy here. But as we saw earlier (10.14.21), the recall of feelings such as joy is a very complex matter: we can recall an earlier joy with present sadness, just as one can remember the happy life and still be unhappy. So, it seems that opposites can be retained and mentally experienced at the same time. Despite the resemblance between the memory of happiness and that of joy, the analogy does not solve Augustine's problem.

Continuing in 21.31, he now asks bluntly: "Where, then, and when did I experience my happy life, that I should now remember, love, and desire it?" (*Ubi ergo et quando expertus sum vitam meam beatam, ut recordor eam et amem et desiderem?*). Obviously Augustine does not consider his earlier suggestion that we inherit from Adam some knowledge of happiness to be completely convincing. He reiterates his position: "Absolutely all people want to be happy" (*sed beati prorsus omnes esse volumus*). Only knowledge that has certainty can stimulate such certainty in willing. He realizes that different individuals may enjoy different objects but insists that only one ultimate objective, happy life, is what "all men strive to reach" (*unum est tamen, quo pervenire omnes nituntur*).

Apparently Augustine is preparing the reader for the next chapter (22.32), where he leaves no doubt unresolved about the identity of the source of true joy. He now confidently asserts that God exists as pure joy.[4] "Thou Thyself art Joy. And this is the happy life, to rejoice unto Thee . . . and there is none other" (*gaudium tu ipse es. et ipsa est beata vita, gaudere de te . . . et non est altera*). People who pursue a different joy are not exceptions to this conclusion: "Their will is not turned away from some representation of joy" (*ab aliqua tamen imagine gaudii voluntas eorum non avertitur*). In spite of the forthright character of this assertion, Augustine still has problems with the way in which happiness is present in memory, for he now speaks of a representation or image (*imagine*) of joy, where previously he had insisted that happiness is remembered in itself and not through an image.

Comment: These two chapters (21 and 22) find Augustine clearly stating that he identifies God with both joy and the happy life. Of course, the happy life for the individual human person is an enjoyable state of existence, a perfected but finite human condition, and this subjective state is not identical with God. What Augustine means is that without God the human person cannot achieve final happiness. He practically says this when he adds that the happy life is "to rejoice unto Thee, from Thee, on account of Thee" (*gaudere de te, ad te, propter te;* see 22.32). So his point is not that one becomes God, when happy, but that the human person is totally dependent on God for eventual bliss.

Analysis 23.33: Here Augustine wonders whether he has been wrong in so strongly asserting the universal desire for human

happiness. "Is it, then, uncertain that all men wish to be happy, because those who do not wish to find their joy in Thee . . . do not, in
point of fact, desire the happy life?" (*non ergo certum est, quod omnes
esse beati volunt?*).

To settle this doubt, Augustine turns to the broad appeal of
truth. He asks all people "whether they would prefer to get their joy
from truth rather than from falsity?" (*utrum malint de veritate
quam de falsitate gaudere*). To answer this, he first quotes Scripture,
then he proceeds to a philosophical argument. He has known "many
men who wished to deceive, but not one who wished to be deceived"
(*multos expertus sum, qui vellent fallere, qui autem falli, neminem*).
Since no one really desires to be tricked into error, it must be the
case that all people love truth. And in loving what is true, they are
loving joy arising from truth. Thus, "they certainly love truth" (*utique amant etiam veritatem*), and there must be "some knowledge of
it . . . in their memory" (*nec amarent, nisi esset aliqua notitia ejus in
memoria eorum*). Augustine wonders why some people do not understand this. "Is it because they are more keenly concerned with other
things?" (*quia fortius occupantur in aliis*). Perhaps it is because
"they faintly remember" (*quod tenuiter meminerunt*) not quite
enough of the truth to make them happy.

Comment: In the background of this appeal to the love of truth is a
passage in *Free Choice* (2.14.38–2.15.39) that some interpreters
take as a rational proof of God's existence, based on the awareness of
a Truth above people's minds:[5]

> But this beauty of truth and wisdom, so persistent in the will to
> enjoy it, does not discourage all comers though they are im-
> peded by the throngs of listeners. . . . For those who turn to it,
> away from the whole world, those who love it find it available
> to all, everlasting for all . . . no one passes judgment on it, and
> no one makes good judgments without it (2.14.38).

This means, Augustine concludes, that it is clear to our minds
(*manifestum est mentibus nostris*) that there is, without doubt,
something greater than our minds (*sine dubitatione esse potiorem*).
So he proceeds to show that this supreme being must be God. He
reminds Evodius that they had agreed that, if it could be shown that
there is some being greater than human minds, then that, or whatever is more excellent than it, must be God (*si autem aliquid est
excellentius, ille potius Deus est*). In any case, God must exist.

To this Evodius responds: "I accept these things. . . . I concede it
to be not only good but the supreme good and the maker of happiness" (*quod non solum bonum, sed etiam summum bonum, et
beatificum esse concedo*). This text from *Free Choice* was written sev-

eral years before book 10 of the *Confessions*. It helps us to understand Augustine's confidence that all people look forward to some guarantee of future happiness.

Even back in the first book of *Free Choice* (1.14.30), Augustine had asked why, if all people will to achieve a happy life, it is that some people never attain it. His answer, then, was that there is a difference between wishing for happiness and "living rightly" (*recte scilicet vivere*). People with good will, he explains (1.14.30–1.15.31), strive to obey two types of laws: eternal and temporal. The morally good person obeys both divine and human laws willingly. But the eternal law commands one to turn away from temporal things and, thus purified, to convert to eternal things (*Jubet igitur aeterna lex avertere amorem a temporalibus, et eum mundatum convertere ad aeterna*, 1.15.32).

At the end of 10.23.33, Augustine adds, concerning those who are unhappy: "Yet a little while the light is in men; let them walk, walk, lest darkness overtake them" (*adhuc enim modicum lumen est in hominibus; ambulent, ambulent, ne tenebras comprehendant*). Augustine is not a pessimist. He encourages even those who are not presently happy to persevere in their journey through life on earth and to cooperate with whatever understanding they have of the right way to live.

Analysis 23.34: In the preceding section, Augustine has argued that all people must agree that happiness cannot be found in errors but only in what is true. Now he asks: "Why does truth engender hatred?" (*Cur autem veritas parit odium?*). This is part of a line from the classical Roman writer Terence, who said: "Fawning flattery (*obsequium*) makes friends, the truth gives rise to hatred" (*odium parit*). This wry remark stimulates Augustine to reflect on the nature of deception. He is sure that people never desire to be deceived, and "since they did not want to be deceived, they do not want to be shown that they have been deceived" (*quia enim falli nolunt . . . et oderunt eam, cum eos ipsos indicat*). Deception starts from the desire to lead others into error. In the following comment, the role of this bad will-act in the actions of a liar will be explained.

Section 34 ends with a gloomy comment on those who wish to conceal the truth about their inner dispositions: "Even thus is the human mind, even thus is it blind and weak; it wishes to lie hidden, a foul and unattractive thing, but does not wish anything to be hidden to it" (*se autem ut lateat aliquid non vult*). This is one of the times that Augustine speaks bitterly about the person who disagrees with him. But even such a mind, "if with no hindrance interposed, will come to rejoice in that through which all things are true, in the only Truth" (*si nulla interpellante molestia de ipsa per quam vera sunt omnia, sole veritate gaudebit*). There is no doubt that he is here identifying truth with God.

Comment: At the end of these chapters stressing the universal desire for happiness and its implications, we might take a look at a more popular treatment in a sermon that Augustine preached a few years later (possibly in 403) on the thirty-second Psalm (*Exp Ps* 32, *Enarratio* 3.15–16).[6] Verse 12 of this famous psalm (33 in some modern versions) reads: "Happy the nation whose God is Yahweh." Augustine is delighted with this and the preceding psalm, in both of which joy is celebrated. He asks his audience in the church of St. Cyprian: "But what is this? 'Blessed is the nation?' Who would not rouse himself at hearing this? All men love happiness (*amant enim omnes beatitudinem*) and therefore men are perverse in wanting to be wicked without being unhappy." Then he proceeds to assure his audience that even wicked people crave happiness. People steal to achieve the pleasure that is false happiness. Unfortunately, many persons opt for the wrong means to assure them of a good life. Wealth, fine homes, many servants, these are "fleeting and perishable." All such things are inferior to human souls. "Gold and silver and other material things that you long to obtain are of less value than yourself." What you should really seek, he advises his hearers, is something in your mind (*in animo est quod quaeris*). But there is a greater good for you to seek out that is of better worth than your soul (*Jam ergo superest, ut quaeras quid sit melius quam animus tuus.*). What will that be, except your God? (*Quid erit obsecro, nisi Deus tuus?*).

This is the theme that the goods of the body (such as beauty and health), of the soul (knowledge and virtue), and of society (fame and political power) are all inferior to the one supreme and ultimate Good. Subjectively, it is joy in the vision and love of God; but objectively it is God Himself. This is a reasoning that is expanded in later centuries by Boethius and Thomas Aquinas.[7]

As a matter of fact, Augustine returns to this theme in the nineteenth book of the *City of God* (19.1–4). There he notes in the first chapter that "philosophers have expressed a great variety of divergent opinions regarding ultimate goods and evils, and they have eagerly canvassed this question, in order, if possible, to discover what makes a man happy." He mentions that Varro (in his now nonextant work *On Philosophy*) reviewed 288 opinions on what the ultimate good might be. Here Augustine again examines corporeal, psychic, and social goods, and in chapter 4 he briefly outlines what he thinks about the highest good. Beyond the four great virtues known to classical philosophy—prudence, fortitude, temperance, and justice—he sees higher virtues—faith, charity, and hope. It is hope that Augustine emphasizes: "As, therefore, we are saved by hope, so are we made happy by hope" (*sicut ergo spe salvi, ita spe beati facti sumus*).

Another key issue arising in this part of the *Confessions* (23.33) stems from Augustine's talk about "many men who wished to deceive, but not one who wished to be deceived." This is related to the extensive treatment that he gave to the problem of telling lies. He wrote two works dealing with lies: the first, *On Lying (De mendacio)* dates from the early months of 395; and the second, *Against Lying (Contra mendacium)*, was written twenty-five years later, in 420.

We can dispose of the second work quickly, although it covers many points treated in the earlier one. *Against Lying* is of less philosophical interest than *On Lying,* for it is mainly concerned with a religious problem. In 420 a Spanish priest named Consentius asked for Augustine's approval of using lies to combat the Priscillianist heresy. Augustine answers that all lies are morally objectionable and cannot be approved, even if they are used to obtain a good end. As he puts it bluntly to the Spanish cleric (*Against Lying* 3.4), "There are many kinds of lies and we ought to detest them all completely" (*Mendaciorum genera multa sunt quae omnia universaliter odisse debemus*). He does relent sufficiently to admit that "it is important to consider, first of all, for what reason, for what end, and with what intention, something is done" (*interest quidem plurimum qua causa, quo fine, qua intentione, quid fiat*, 7.18). However, he immediately closes off the questioning: "But acts that are obviously sinful are not to be done, whatever the good reason achieved, or the apparent good end or intention" (*sed ea quae constat esse peccata, nullo bonae causae obtentu, nullo quasi bono fine, nulla velut bona intentione, facienda sunt*). In effect, Augustine says that a good end does not justify a bad means. Note that the term "*intentio*" is used here but not in the early treatise *On Lying.*

The youthful work is much more tentative, and philosophical, in character. However, *On Lying* ends by judging that all lies are somewhat immoral. Since many of his examples are taken from the Bible, Augustine concludes (*On Lying* 21.46): "It becomes clear from all this discussion that the evidence from Scripture advises nothing else than never, under any circumstances, to tell a lie" (*Elucet itaque discussis omnibus, nihil aliud illa testimonia Scripturarum monere nisi nunquam esse omnino mentiendum*). The details of Augustine's examination of many apparent reasons for excusing lies are too involved for summary here.[8] However, we may note a few key points that illustrate the keen mind of Augustine as a moralist. First, he excludes jokes from consideration; they are not lies (ibid. 2.2). Then he distinguishes belief from opinion (3.3). Not every person who utters a false statement is lying, he explains, for it may be his belief or opinion that his utterance is true. "Sometimes the believer feels that he lacks knowledge of what he believes, yet he has no doubt about this item of belief" (*aliquando ille qui credit sentit se ignorare quod credit quamvis de re quam se ignorare novit omnino non dubitet*). On the other hand, "the person who has an opinion thinks that he knows something of which he is ignorant" (*qui autem opinatur putat se scire quod nescit*). In either case, "whoever enunciates something, even if it be false, that he accepts in his mind, by belief or opinion, does not lie" (*Quisquis autem hoc enuntiat quod vel creditum animo vel opinatum tenet, etiamsi falsum sit, non mentitur*).

Continuing, Augustine offers a preliminary definition of a lie: "The person lies who holds something in his mind and expresses something different in words or other signs" (*ille mentitur qui aliud habet in animo et aliud verbis vel quibuslibet significationibus enuntiat*, 3.3). Notice that this definition says nothing about the intention of the speaker. A second definition follows immediately: ". . . but if a lie is nothing but the expression of something with a will to deceive . . ." (*si autem mendacium non est nisi cum aliquid enuntiatur voluntate fallendi . . .*). Here the act of willing is equivalent to what is called "intention" in the later treatise. Augustine sees that what is intended has a great deal to do with the seriousness of a lie. He goes through a long examination of the malice of various falsehoods (14.25–20.41). In a summary (21.42), eight levels of seriousness are distinguished. In decreasing order of malice, they are: (1) The greatest evil is lying in order to induce someone to accept the Christian faith. (This is why Augustine is very severe in answering Consentius later.) Then the less serious lies are: (2) lying to harm one's neighbor; (3) lying for the pleasure of deception; (4) lying to help one person by harming another; (5) lying to help a person without harming anyone; (6) lying to improve the morals or social relations of one's associates; (7) lying to save someone's life; and (8) lying to save a person from sexual defilement. Many examples that Augustine introduces in these eight categories of lying become standard cases in applied ethics throughout later centuries. Readers of Kant will recognize the seventh.

Near the end of section 34, Augustine comments on the imperfection of our understanding: the human mind (*animus humanus*) is "blind and weak" (*caecus et languidus*). This point is reinforced in the *Confessions* (10.30), where Augustine examines some of his own moral defects. Aristotle has an important discussion of moral weakness (*akrasia*) in his *Nicomachean Ethics* (7.1–10.1145a15–1152a35), where he relates this human condition to lack of knowledge, imprudence, faulty opinions, and base sensuality. However, Augustine makes no use of this Aristotelian analysis. Evidently any acquaintance that Augustine had with the ethics of Aristotle is indirect and much diluted.

Actually, Augustine had a religious belief—that, of course, was never shared by Aristotle—in the reality of original sin.[9] Briefly, Augustine taught that the descendants of Adam inherit, from his first fall into sin, a predisposition to concupiscence and some deficiencies in practical understanding. For Augustine, this general fault in humanity is not simply a matter of religious credence. A passage in the *City of God* (22.22.1) backs up this view with a sort of historical and sociological survey of the human condition:

> That the whole human race has been condemned in its first origin (*Nam quod ad primam originem pertinet omnem mortalium progeniem fuisse damnatam*), this life itself, if life it is to be called, bears witness by the host of cruel ills with which it is filled. Is not this proved by the profound and dreadful ignorance which produces all the errors that enfold the children of Adam, and from which no man can be delivered without toil, pain, and fear?

Augustine continues with a long list of the wicked things that all humans are prone to do. He speaks of quarrels, lawsuits, wars, treasons, angers, hatreds, thefts, robbery, murders, parricides, insolence, fornications, incests, unnatural acts too shameful to mention, blasphemies, plots, falsehoods, plunderings, and a dozen other evildoings. In conclusion, this famous text (which has been the source of later lamentations about "the human condition") observes: "These are indeed the crimes of wicked men, yet they spring from that root of error and misplaced love that is born with every son of Adam."

Passages such as this have given rise to charges of moral pessimism in Augustine's thought. But he thinks that there are remedies for this brutish condition; some are supernatural, such as the help from divine grace; and others are quite human and natural, such as the control of laws and good instruction from wise leaders and teachers. As he adds to the above dirge: "But because God does not wholly desert those whom He condemns . . . the human race is restrained by law and instruction."

Only a little later in the *City of God* (22.24.3), Augustine shows his fundamental optimism about one's prospects for happiness. Humans start life with a mind endowed with reason and understanding, but in the infant they are asleep (*animae humanae mentem dedit, ubi ratio et intelligentia in infante sopita est quodam modo*). As the child develops, learning and education make the mind skilled in grasping truth and loving what is good (*habilis perceptioni veritatis et amoris boni*). This skill is perfected by good habits of wisdom and the other virtues, enabling a person to conquer weakness and vicious tendencies prudently, forcefully, temperately, and justly (*prudenter, fortiter, temperanter, et juste*). Thus the desire of nothing but the good succeeds in bringing one to the highest and unfailing Good. Even when this supreme Good is not reached (*quod etsi non faciat*), human nature still retains a capacity for good so exalted that this rational work of divine omnipotence exceeds our ability to describe or even think of it (*ipsa talium bonorum capacitas in natura rationali divinitus instituta quantum sit boni quam mirabile opus omnipotentis, quis competenter effatur aut cogitat?*).[10]

These are not the words of a moral pessimist. They express the attitude of a man who is really optimistic about the eventual well-being of the human species. In this sense, Augustine, with his emphasis on happiness shown here in the *Confessions,* may well be classified as an ethical eudaemonist.[11]

I NOTES

1. The name *Theodorus* means "gift of God," as does *Adeodatus,* given to Augustine's son.

2. Cf. Cicero, *De officiis* 2.5; *Tusculan Disputations* 4.57.

3. See the remarks of Pegis, "The Mind of St. Augustine," 3–12. Pegis studied under Etienne Gilson, one of the most prominent advocates of Christian philosophy in the twentieth century. A good selection of his writings on Augustine and this subject is printed in *A Gilson Reader,* ed. A. C. Pegis (Garden City, N.Y.: Doubleday, 1957), 169–276.

4. Bourke, *Joy in Augustine's Ethics* rebuts the Jansenist charge that Augustine's ethics is pessimistic.

5. This argument for the existence of God in *De libero arbitrio* 2.38–39 will develop into the famous proof offered by Anselm of Canterbury in the twelfth century.

6. For a translation of this *Enarratio* in Ps. 32 (modern 33), see ACW, 30:130–33; and *TEA,* 151–53.

7. See Boethius, *Consolation of Philosophy,* trans. H. F. Stewart and E. K. Rand (New York: Loeb Series, 1926), bk. 3, 224–97; and Thomas Aquinas, *Summa contra Gentiles,* 3.25–37; in English, *On the Truth of the Catholic Faith: Summa contra Gentiles,* trans. V. J. Bourke (Notre Dame, Ind.: Notre Dame University Press, 1975), 3:97–127.

8. The treatise *De mendacio* is critically edited in CSEL 41:413–66; and well translated in FOC, vol. 16.

9. Readers interested in details of Augustine's teaching on original sin might consult the Latin texts selected by Franciscus Moriones in his *Enchiridion Theologicum S Augustini* (Madrid: Biblioteca de Autores Cristianos, 1961), 255–73. For a short English explanation, see Portalié, *A Guide to the Thought of St. Augustine,* 204–13.

10. The Dods translation of *City* 22.24.3 has been modified here.

11. In his "Note Complémentaire" on this portion of book 10, Solignac (BA, 14:369) observes that it is quite proper to call Augustine's ethics a eudaemonism (in that it approves the pursuit of personal well-being), but his view does not reduce to the satisfaction of pleasure, or to the mere perfection of human society.

Augustine continues in chapters 24 through 27 to ask many questions about his search for the highest wisdom, but now he is less tentative in suggesting some answers to his queries. It is through the attribute of divine truth that he finds the best ground for his assertions.

Analysis 10.24.35: All that he knows about God is kept in memory: "Nor have I found anything about Thee which I did not keep in memory, ever since I learned of Thee" (*neque enim aliquid de te inveni, quod non meminissem ex quo didici te*). All this questioning and mulling over possible answers is an exercise of the power to cogitate.

"For, from the time that I learned of Thee, I did not forget Thee" (*nam ex quo didici te, non sum oblitus tui*). This was the constant message accompanying Augustine's self-accusations in the first nine books of the *Confessions:* he never ceased to believe in God. As he admits (*Conf* 6.5.8), "I always believed that Thou dost exist" (*semper tamen credidi et esse te*). But in mid-life he has come to greater appreciation of the importance of eternal truths. "Now, wherever I found truth, there did I find my God, Truth Itself" (*ubi enim inveni veritatem, ibi deum meum, ipsam veritatem*).

So God is really there in Augustine's consciousness, and this presence is the source of his greatest joy. "Thou dost dwell in my memory, and there do I find Thee, when I remember Thee and delight in Thee" (*manes in memoria mea, et illic te invenio, cum reminiscor tui et delector in te*). The verb *manere* (*manes*) means to continue in existence, to abide or dwell, as used here and frequently in the next chapter. Our comment will attempt to show its special significance.

Comment: In the Middle Ages and Renaissance, many thinkers will continue to insist with Augustine that truth is not only a conformity of understanding with reality (*adaequatio intellectus et rei*) but that in its highest manifestation truth is a real being, God. Philosophers such as Anselm of Canterbury and Duns Scotus will argue that truth is not merely the concern of epistemology; for them, and indeed for all Scholastic writers on philosophy or theology, there is a metaphysical truth that serves as the ground for right judgments. Despite his admiration for Aristotelian philosophy (in which ontological truth is not prominent), Thomas Aquinas is no exception to this insistence on the existing reality of supreme truth. The *Summa contra Gentiles* (1.60.2) puts this concisely: "Truth is a certain perfection of understanding or of intellectual operation. . . . But the understanding of God is His substance. . . . It remains, therefore that the divine substance is truth itself."[1]

From Augustine's opening sentence in chapter 24, we encounter the strong conviction that the only way that God (and so, supreme wisdom) is to be found properly is from inside human consciousness. As he says, "I have not found Thee outside it" (*non te inveni extra eam*). Later (chapter 26) we will see him asserting that God must eventually be discovered above the soul (*supra me*), but he continues to say that the approach to God is through introspection.

This brings us to the central idea in chapter 25, which later Christian writers will call the "indwelling" of God in the human soul. Some thinkers call it the "inbeing" of the Creator in all parts of creation.[2] This is not pantheism, for Augustine does not think that God is identical with the universe, nor that He exists only in the universe. But the divine immanence in the human spirit is to be understood in terms of what we have already seen in connection with the complex meaning of presence (*praesentia*) in Chapter Five above. One being can be present to another in time and/or in space. Of course, in speaking of God, Augustine must take these terms in an analogous sense. God's presence is not restricted to time and place. The point is that Augustine thinks that God is always *with* His creatures, whatever their time or place may be, and he also thinks that God is *inside* people's minds. He operates inwardly in the human soul, cooperating with its good use of freedom and guiding the exercise of intellectual judgment.[3]

In addition to this concept of divine presence, there is his view of continuous existence (*manentia*). Note its relation to the English word "immanence." Several times in chapters 24 and 25, we will find Augustine saying of God, "Thou dost *dwell* in my memory" (*manes in memoria mea*). The Latin verb *manere* means to endure, to continue to exist, to abide. It not only means to last through time but also to persist in the eternal present (*praesens*) that is the divine mode of existence. We have seen how in the early works, especially in the first book of *On Order,* the concept of *ordo* (order) plays a special role. It designates not only spatial symmetry but more particularly the ongoing regularity in which every being inclines and moves toward its natural end. In the order that God builds into human nature, there is the continuing presence of divine guidance. From the human point of view, this is a feature of human experience in the course of time; from God's point of view (which, despite Spinoza, we cannot fully grasp), this divine *manentia* is an eternal present, above the past and future of time.

The last noteworthy point in chapter 24 is the remark that God's presence, as truth in the mind, brings joy to humanity. "These are my holy delights (*sanctae deliciae*) which Thou hast given me in Thy mercy." One of the things that Augustine never found in ancient philosophy was the idea of mercy tempering justice. That is a Christian idea and is very reassuring to Augustine.

Analysis 25.36: Now Augustine tries to push this investigation of divine indwelling in the soul to a more detailed definiteness. "But where dost Thou dwell there?" He even asks whether God has made a "holy place" (*sanctuarium*) in the human soul and "in which part of it Thou dost dwell" (*in qua parte maneas*). It is not the part of memory that irrational animals (*bestiae*) share with humans, for "I did not find Thee among the images of bodily things" (*quia non ibi te inveniebam inter imagines rerum corporalium*). Augustine found it difficult to direct the attention of his listeners or readers away from bodies to the world of immaterial existents.

Next he considers whether God is present through one's retained emotions. "I came to the parts of it in which I keep my mental feelings, but I did not find Thee there" (*et veni ad partes ejus, ubi commendavi affectiones animi mei, nec illic inveni te*). These are not feelings through the body—of hunger or thirst, for example—but emotive responses, such as love or fear. He now sees no reason to identify them with God's presence. Finally, he talks about "the seat of my very mind" (*ipsius animi sedem*). It is where the mind is present to, and remembers, itself. He says, "There is one [a seat] for it [the mind] in my memory, since the mind also remembers itself" (*quae illi est in memoria mea—quoniam sui quoque meminit animus*). We might expect him to say that God is there, but he denies that: "Thou wert not there" (*nec ibi tu eras*). His reason for this denial is, "Thou art not the mind itself" (*nec ipse animus es*).

Augustine returns to the contrast between mutability and immutability, saying, "All these things are mutable, but Thou dwellest as an immutable Being above them all" (*et commutantur haec omnia, tu autem incommutabilis maneas super omnia*). Through divine condescension, "Thou hast deigned to reside in my memory" (*et dignatus es habitare in memoria mea*).

The chapter closes with the question: "Why do I look for the place in it [memory] where Thou dost dwell, as if there really were places in it?" (*et quid quaero, quo loco ejus habites, quasi vero loca ibi sint?*). His conclusion is definite; he does find God in his memory "when I recall Thee to mind" (*et in ea invenio, cum recordor te*).

Comment: Augustine asks three main questions concerning the manner of God's presence to the human soul: Is it where he keeps the images of bodies; is it with his higher emotions; or is it where memory reflects upon or directly intuits itself? To all these questions, he answers negatively. None of the three places he suggests seems a suitable "residence" for God. He has two chief reasons for such rejections. First, all three possibilities are mutable, ever changing, whereas God is an immutable being. Second, there are no places (*loca*) in the human soul, for it is not bodily. So these questions only serve to show the folly of attempting to think of God by using bodily imagery.

At the end of chapter 25, Augustine expresses the conviction that he finds God present within his memory. God is there ever since he first learned about Him. This conviction as to the divine presence is another reason for Augustine's devotion to self-examination. Introspection brings surprising results, as he will explain later in *The Trinity* (15.9.16):

> Let no one wonder, then, that we strive to see Thee in any way at all, even in that manner of seeing that is granted to us in this life, namely, through a glass, in an enigma. For we would not hear of an enigma in this text if sight were easy. And this is a yet greater enigma, that we do not see what we cannot but see. For who does not see his own thought? (*Quis enim non videt cogitationem suam?*). And yet, who does see his own thought, I do not say with the eye of the flesh, but with the inner sight itself (*sed ipso interiore conspectu*)? Who does not see it, and who does see it? Since thought is a kind of sight of the mind (*Quandoquidem cogitatio visio est animi quaedam*), whether those things are present that are seen also by the bodily eyes, or are perceived by other senses; or whether they are not present but their likenesses are discerned by thought; or whether neither of these is the case, but things are thought of that are neither bodily nor likenesses of bodily things, as the virtues and vices; or as indeed, thought itself is thought of (*sicut ipsa denique cogitatio cogitatur*); or whether it be those things that are the subjects of instruction and of the liberal sciences; or whether the higher causes and reasons (*rationes*)

themselves of all these things in their immutable nature are thought of (*sive istorum omnium causae superiores atque rationes in natura immutabili cogitentur*); or whether it be evil even, and vain, and false things that we are thinking of, with either unconsenting perception, or with erroneous consent (*vel non consentiente sensu, vel errante consensu*).

This long and complicated passage shows that even the mature Augustine is still puzzled by human knowledge of thought objects that are neither corporeal nor the images of bodies. But the general concepts given here in *The Trinity* text illustrate the sort of meanings that are eternal and above all change. Augustine comes close to a description of universals, without actually using that word.

Analysis 26.37: The opening lines here repeat Augustine's frustration at trying to locate God's presence in his soul. He says twice that "there is no place (*nusquam locus*) within the human soul." God is to be discovered originally "in Thyself above me" (*in te supra me*). However, this leads to a new and very important observation: "O Truth, Thou dost preside over all things, even those which can take counsel with Thee" (*veritas, ubique praesides omnibus consulentibus te*). Creatures who can look to God for advice and guidance are rational persons, human beings. Unlike beasts, plants, and nonliving bodies, which are divinely regulated by built-in, natural inclinations, humans are able to seek out God's rules of orderly life. They are free to obey or disobey divine laws. God in His providence comes into an intimate and special contact with humanity. We will examine this in the following comment.

The last sentence in this chapter underlines Augustine's point about seeking divine advice: "All seek counsel concerning what they wish but they do not always hear what they wish" (*omnes unde volunt consulunt, sed non semper quod volunt audiunt*). He now explains that a person should not expect to hear what humans desire but rather desire what God says.

Comment: In his several commentaries on Genesis, Augustine distinguishes two moments in divine creation: There is the period of the first six days, in which God founded (*condidit*) all creatures; and there is the subsequent course of time, in which God presides over the development, the ongoing order, of all things (*Gen Lit* 4.8.15–4.12.23). Providence is the divine overseeing of all existence. From our earthly viewpoint, it operates in the second moment of creation.

Years before he began to write the *Confessions*, Augustine offered (in *Free Choice* 2.17.45) an explanation of the need for God's providence. He noted that it is generally agreed that all things are governed by providence (*comprehenditur omnia providentia gubernari*), which he may have known from the early Stoic "Hymn to Zeus." Even before he became a priest, he argued that if all things in the world lost their "forms," they would still be formed from above and act as they now do because they would continue to be regulated by the immutable form of providence (*forma ipsa incommutabilis . . . ipsa est eorum providentia*).

And in the next section of *Free Choice,* this point is reiterated: "These two creatures," he says, "body and soul," are *formabilia,* receptive to forms. They do not form themselves. This is in keeping with his theory of causality: Nothing can give itself what it does not have. They must be given their principles of existence and operation from above by the form that is always the same (*ex illa forma subsistens, quae semper ejusmodi est*). "This is why all goods whatsoever, great or small, cannot exist unless God is their source" (*Quamobrem, quantumcumque bona, quamvis magna, quamvis minima, nisi ex Deo esse non possunt,* 2.17.46). This was written before Augustine had studied much of the Bible.

The Latin word *providentia* literally means foresight or overseeing; it was contracted into the word *prudentia.* So Augustine is telling us that eternal wisdom functions as "prudence" (practical wisdom) when humans understand that God governs all things and events wisely.[4]

This early explanation of the role of divine providence in terms of the preservation of the forms of all creatures may be compared with what Augustine explains more fully in the mature *City of God* (5.11).

> Therefore God supreme and true, with His Word and Holy Spirit (which three are one), one God omnipotent, creator and maker of every soul and of every body; by whose gift all are happy through verity and not through vanity . . . from whom is every mode, every species, every order; from whom are measure, number, weight; from whom is everything which has an existence in nature, of whatever kind it be, and of whatever value (*cujuslibet aestimationis est*); from whom are the seeds of forms and the forms of seeds . . . who has not left, not to speak of heaven and earth, angels and men, but even the entrails of the smallest and most contemptible animal, or the feather of a bird, or the little flower of a plant, or the leaf of a tree, without a harmony (*sine suarum partium convenientia*) and as it were, a mutual peace among all its parts;—that God can never be believed to have left the kingdoms of men, their dominations and servitudes, outside the laws of His providence (*a suae providentiae legibus alienas esse voluisse*).

The mention of mutual peace in the parts of living things in the quotation above brings to mind Augustine's famous description of peace (*City* 19.13) as the "tranquillity of order" (see pages 47–49 above). There it is related to the ordering of many things but especially to human societies of all kinds. The connection of order (*ordo*) with persevering toward a proper natural end (*manentia*) is brought out in section 2 at the end of the above text in book 19.[5] The Devil's perversity, Augustine explains, consisted in the fact that "he did not endure in the tranquillity of order" (*in ordine tranquillitate non mansit*). Even the bad angels were created with an innate disposition (*ordo*) toward their ends—but also with the freedom to disrupt their orderly course.

Augustine's philosophy of society, politics, and history has been the subject of many studies.[6] His terminology in this area fluctuated and is open to different interpretations.[7] Since the focus in this part of book 10 of the *Confessions* is on love—that of humans for God, and of God for humanity—it may suffice to recall what we saw earlier (see pages 47–49 above) about "two loves": one the holy love of God, which unifies the members of the city of God (*civitas Dei*); the second, selfish and foul, directed to the domination of humanity and constituting the terrestrial city headed by the Devil (*Lit Gen* 11.15.20). These loves both establish city-states (*civitates*) that are also called societies (*societates*). For Augustine, they are groups of rational beings, united in some sort of agreement (*City* 12.21), but *civitas* would not be used for a group of thieves (because of their bad end), while *societas* could designate either a good or a bad group. He also speaks of a "people" (*populus*) and a "republic" (*res publica*); these are somewhat more organized groups.

As Augustine explained in a letter to the Roman official Marcellinus (*Letter* 138.2.9):

> What is a republic unless it be the material constituent of a people (*res populi*), and so a common thing (*res communis*), certainly the constituent of a city (*res civitatis*)? What, then is a city, other than a multitude of men peacefully brought together by some sort of bond (*multitudo hominum in quodam vinculum reducta concordiae*)?

In other words, Augustine sees a number of persons gathered into some organized unity based on what their wills love; they are thus directed to a common objective. Even his social philosophy stems from an inner psychic disposition.

In the *City of God* (19.7), Augustine describes three "natural" societies: the family (*domus*), the urban city (*urbs*), and the whole of humanity (*orbis*). If one wonders about the unifying principle of the whole human race, since it includes some persons who love God and others who do not, his answer is that, good or bad, human beings are one in their origin; all are descended from Adam. As he explains in the *City of God* (12.21):

> Therefore God created one single man, certainly not that he
> might be a solitary being bereft of all society, but that by this
> means the unity of society and the bond of peace might more
> effectually be commended to Him; men being bound not only by
> similarity of nature but also by family affection.

Augustine was quite convinced that all humans are of the same basic race.[8] As far as he was concerned, it is what people will, what they do voluntarily, that makes human beings different from each other.

If peace is very important in Augustine's social philosophy, then its opposite, war, must also figure prominently in his thinking about society. We have seen the importance of order in *Confessions* 10, but war is for Augustine the ultimate social disorder. Newspaper articles at the time of the United Nations and U.S. military activities in the Persian Gulf attributed as many as seven "conditions for a just war" to Augustine. Actually, it was later commentators who developed this complicated theory of just warfare. Augustine only mentions the idea of a just war (*bellum justum*) a few times, and he can hardly be credited with—or blamed for—such justification.

The rules of just warfare first appear in a formal treatment in the canon-law literature of the twelfth century.[9] After the middle of the thirteenth century, Thomas Aquinas stated three requirements for making war justly, and he supported them with appropriate quotations from Augustine.[10] This provides us with a simple and accurate digest of Augustine's thought on the subject. The first requirement, says Aquinas, is authorization by the chief of state, by whose command the war is to be fought (*auctoritas principis, cujus mandato bellum est gerendum*). After citing Scripture (Ps. 81:4 and Rom. 13:4), Aquinas refers us to Augustine's *Reply to Faustus* (22.75), where it is stated that the natural order requires that the undertaking of warfare be only by the authority and advice of the leading men in the state (*ordo naturalis . . . hoc poscit, ut suscipiendi belli auctoritas atque consilium penes principes sit*). The second condition Aquinas enunciated is that there be a just cause (*causa justa*) for making any war. To explain, he cites Augustine's *Questions on the Heptateuch* (6, Q. 10, on Josh. 8:12), "Just wars are commonly defined as those that remedy injuries . . . or restore what has been wrongfully taken from a people or state" (*Justa bella solent definiri quae ulciscuntur injurias . . . vel reddere quod per injuriam ablatum est*). Thirdly, Aquinas required a right intention on the part of those making war (*intentio bellantium recta*), that is, either to promote some good or negate some evildoing. For this requirement, he appeals to the *City of God* (19.12; 22.74):[11] "The desire for injury, the cruelty of vengeance, the implacable and not placated intention, the ferocity of rebellion, the lust for domination, and any similar dispositions, these are the things that cast guilt on the right to make wars" (*haec sunt quae in bellis jure culpantur*). These quotations almost exhaust what Augustine had to say about warfare. In general, he regretted all wars and himself died while the Vandals were setting siege to his episcopal city, Hippo.

Analysis 27.38: One of the shortest chapters in the *Confessions,* this hymn to divine beauty is one of the few examples extant of the poetry of Augustine. It has been the despair of at least a dozen translators who have tried to put it into suitable English. The Latin text has been arranged in fourteen poetic lines by Solignac, with additional punctuation to show the lyrical cadence of this passage.[12] The opening lines: "*Sero te amavi, pulchritudo tam antiqua et tam nova, sero te amavi,*" were translated in the mid-nineteenth century by E. B. Pusey: "Too late loved I Thee, O Thou Beauty of ancient days, yet ever new! too late I loved Thee!"[13] Pierre de Labriolle put it in more prosaic French: "Tard je t'ai aimée, ô Beauté si ancienne et si nouvelle, tard je t'ai aimée."[14] The most recent English version by Henry Chadwick gets away from the second person singular, now unfamiliar to the reader of English: "Late have I loved you, beauty so old and so new: late have I loved you."[15] Perhaps it is not possible to catch the lilt of the Latin in a modern language.

The opening lines introduce the whole motif of the hymn: Augustine's mature love for divine beauty, followed by his regret that he formerly turned away (*perversio*) from the divine to the attractive but imperfect forms of mutable creatures. "Thou wert within and I was without" (*et ecce intus eras et ego foris*). We have here one of the shortest, yet most striking, descriptions of his youthful externalism contrasted to his mature interiorism. It is by introspection that the highest beauty is appreciated.

In the middle lines, there is the contrast of God's continued presence to Augustine with his own deliberate absence from God: "Thou wert with me, yet I was not with Thee" (*mecum eras, et tecum non eram*). The working of divine providence has never been more poetically expressed.

At the end, the last six English lines find Augustine doing what many later Christian mystics also attempted: he tries to describe how God appealed to him through all his senses. Divine cries burst upon his hearing; divine light illumined his sight; God's fragrance alerted his sense of smell; His taste stimulated Augustine's hunger and thirst; divine contact aroused his ardent desire for heavenly peace.

Comment: Despite its brevity, this poem embodies many features of Augustine's philosophy. Its focus on God is typical of his theocentric approach to all reality. The stress on God's dwelling within Augustine's mind gives the ultimate reason for the use of introspective methodology. Divine illumination of human understanding is implied here. God's creation of and providential care for creatures are suggested. And the final attempt to describe God's presence in terms of sensual attractiveness only serves to highlight Augustine's conviction that intellectual understanding and volitional loving are the avenues of approach to God that are available to the ordinary person. This hymn of praise epitomizes much of Augustine's love of wisdom.

I NOTES

1. The translation of *Summa contra Gentiles* 1.60 is by A. C. Pegis, book 1: *God* (Garden City, N.Y.: Doubleday, 1955), 204.

2. This is the main theme in S. J. Grabowski, *The All-Present God;* see especially chaps. 4–7.

3. For a study of this theme of divine presence from Augustine into later medieval thought, see Armand Maurer, "Reflections on Thomas Aquinas' Notion of Presence," in *Philosophy and the God of Abraham: Essays in Memory of James A. Weisheipl, O.P.*, ed. R. J. Long (Toronto: Pontifical Institute of Mediaeval Studies, 1991), 113–27.

4. Compare *Free Choice* 2.19.52, where Augustine says that prudence is possessed differently by each person, but each rational soul must consult the rule of all the virtues by turning to the truth and wisdom common to all (*in ipsa veritate sapientiaque communi*). The next book of the *Confessions* (11.6.8) speaks of the "prudently reasoning mind whose internal ear is attuned to Thy eternal Word" (*menti prudenti, cujus auris interior posita est ad aeternum verbum tuum*).

5. Cf. *The Gift of Perseverance* 1.1–9 for the view that perseverance is a divine gift.

6. See for instance Herbert A. Deane, *The Political and Social Ideas of St. Augustine* (New York: Columbia University Press, 1965); John O'Meara, *Charter of Christendom;* Henri I. Marrou, *St. Augustine and His Influence Through the Ages* (New York: Harper, 1957); J. H. S. Burleigh, *The City of God: A Study of St. Augustine's Philosophy* (London: Macmillan, 1944); Peter Brown, *Religion and Society in the Age of St. Augustine* (London: Faber & Faber, 1972).

7. Consult Jeremy D. Adams, *The* Populus *of Augustine and Jerome* (New Haven, Conn.: Yale University Press, 1971); R. T. Marshall, *Studies in the Political and Socio-Religious Terminology of the 'De Civitate Dei,'* (Washington, D.C.: Catholic University of America, 1952); T. A. Garret, "St. Augustine and the Nature of Society," *New Scholasticism* 30 (1956): 16–36.

8. Augustine himself was a Berber and may have had quite a dark complexion.

9. E. B. F. Midgley, *The Natural Law Tradition and the Theory of International Relations* (New York: Harper & Row, 1975), chap. 5 details the history of "just war" thinking.

10. See Thomas Aquinas, *Summa Theologiae,* II–II, 40,1, c.

11. For the canon-law source, see *Corpus Iuris Canonici,* ed. L. Richter (Leipzig: Tauschnitz, 1922) Gratiani, Decretum II, causa xxiii, quaestio 1, canon 6: Apud nos.

12. "Notes Complémentaires," *Les Confessions,* BA, 14:569–70. My analysis owes much to Solignac's perceptive annotations.

13. See the reprint of the Pusey version in the Everyman Edition (New York, 1927).

14. *Confessions de s. Augustin,* trans. P. de Labriolle (Paris: Les Belles Lettres, 1947), 2:268.

15. Saint Augustine, *Confessions,* trans. Henry Chadwick (Oxford-New York: Oxford University Press, 1991), 201.

At the end of his introspective study of memory, Augustine has turned to a poetic chant of praise directly addressed to God as the source of beauty, justice, wisdom, and all higher values. This hymn continues in chapters 28 through 30, with which our commentary will terminate.

Analysis 10.28.39: Throughout book 10, Augustine expresses his hopes of attaining some sort of meeting with God in a future life. His expectation of this event is described at the start of chapter 28: "When I shall cleave to Thee with all my being, sorrow and toil will no longer exist for me" (*Cum inhaesero tibi ex omni me, nusquam erit mihi dolor et labor*). He feels that he can look forward to eventual release from his earthly burdens. At present he is torn between conflicting emotions: "My joys, which are to be lamented, struggle against my sorrows, which are cause for joy, and I know not on which side victory may stand" (*contendunt maerores mei et ex qua parte stet victoria nescio*).

We are reading the admission of a man at midlife, occupying a leading position in his community, to whom many of his parishioners go for advice and settlement of their problems, and he is uncertain about the state of his own innermost feelings. "Amid adversities, I long for successes; amid successes, I fear adversities. What is the middle area?" (*prospera in adversis desidero; adversa in prosperis timeo. quis inter haec medius locus?*). The way of moderation is not easy to find, even for a thoughtful person like Augustine.

Comment: We have noticed at the start of our commentary (see Chapter Five above) how Augustine thought that time is measured by one's mind looking at the past, the momentary present, and the future. Here in chapter 28, he mentions one aspect of his expectations for a future life with God. Among other things, he anticipates a cessation of his temporal trials of sorrow and hard work (*dolor et labor*). The reader might expect that Augustine derived a good deal of satisfaction from his position as a prominent administrator in the Catholic Church of North Africa, and no doubt he did, but he continued to suffer from criticisms and attacks by adversaries both within and without his congregation. He was fiercely opposed by some of the Donatist Christians, and he knew that Christianity was being blamed for the decline of the imperial power of Rome because of its teaching of mildness and humility. In particular, some of the pagan families still important in the empire worried about the gradual weakening of Roman authority throughout the world. Within ten years of the completion of the *Confessions,* Rome itself would be sacked by invading Vandals (A.D. 411). Augustine's troubled mind around the year 400 was not simply due to personal concern; he was already worried about the future of the shaky peace (the *pax Romana*) that the empire had established throughout the Mediterranean world. He was soon to write the *City of God,* in which the first half was devoted to a defense of Christianity against the charge that it was responsible for the deterioration of imperial power and peace.

Noteworthy at the end of this chapter in book 10 is Augustine's reference to the middle place (*medius locus*) between extremes of success and adversity. Of course, this is an echo of Stoic ethics as popularized by Seneca, Marcus Aurelius, and Cicero. Among pagan moralists, both Greek and Latin, the ideal state of mind was described as the happy medium between excess and defect of the mental passions. But Augustine had also devoted much thought, as we have seen several times, to the concept of measure or moderation (*modus*) in the biblical triad of number, measure, and weight from the Book of Wisdom (11:21). This combination of Stoic moderation of feelings with biblical measure is an important feature in Augustine's ethical position.[1] It is the key to the meaning of the virtue of temperance.

Analysis 29.40: "My whole hope is nowhere but in Thy exceedingly great mercy" (*Et tota spes mea non est nisi in magna valde misericordia tua*). Of the three great Christian virtues, we have heard a good deal about faith and charity but not so much about hope (*spes*). In regard to this virtue of hope, which later writers will call a "theological" virtue, Augustine first quotes Paul (Rom. 8:24) in the *City of God* (19.4): "For we must be content to hope that we shall be saved—our salvation is not in sight, we should not have to be hoping for it, if it were—but, as I say, we must hope to be saved, since we are not saved yet—it is something we must wait for with patience." To this, Augustine adds: "As, therefore we are saved, so we are made happy by hope. And as we do not yet possess a present but look for a future salvation, so it is with our happiness." Neither Scripture nor philosophy can suggest that perfect happiness is possible in this life on earth.

After quoting the Old Testament (Book of Wisdom 8:21) to the effect that God alone can enable a person to be continent, Augustine next turns to a very different source, Neoplatonic philosophy. "Through continence," he says, "we are gathered in and returned to the One, from whom we have flowed out into the many" (*per continentiam quippe colligimur et redigimur in unum, a quo in multa defluximus*). This typically Plotinian talk will be considered in our comment.

Of course, the most striking feature of 29.40 is the prayer that bluntly requests God's assistance in controlling sexual excesses. Augustine says: "Grant what Thou dost command and command what Thou wilt" (*da quod jubes et jube quod vis*). This calls for further explanation.

Comment: Let us look first at the claim that we humans are "gathered in and returned to the One from whom we have flowed." This is one of the central themes in Neoplatonism. Augustine seems to have possessed an unusual ability to recall almost the precise words from his earlier readings. This is obvious in the many biblical phrases that enrich the language of his *Confessions* and other works. But he also remembered almost exact texts from Neoplatonic writers, as is evident in the account of the vision at Ostia in book 9. Here in book 10, however, it is the similarity to passages in Plotinus' *Enneads* that is striking. In the first *Ennead* (1.2.5), the process of psychic purification (*katharsis*) is discussed. When purified, Plotinus says, "the soul separates from the body and it gathers in all its parts into one" (sect. 5). And in section 6 he adds that a person thus purified is totally cleansed, and "sensual feelings are not moral faults." In *Ennead* 4, Plotinus asks, "What of the memory of our friends, our children, our wife" after such purification? (4.3.32). To this he responds, "The soul flees from the many (*ta polla*) and returns to the One." Since Augustine proceeds in subsequent chapters of book 10 to discuss many aspects of possible incontinence, it is rather clear that such texts from Plotinus, or his Latin followers, remained vivid in Augustine's memory.

More important, however, in chapter 29 is one of the most discussed, and criticized, statements that Augustine ever made.[2] He has just called upon God, as the divine physician, to cure his troubles (in 28.39) and now he says: "Grant what Thou dost command and command what Thou wilt." It is later repeated, and these two imperatives have all the punch of a well-known political slogan.

The prayer says to God, if obedience is expected to your restrictions on sense pleasure, then give us the power to resist such temptations.

To Pelagius (a moralist but not a priest), this seemed like a bold demand from a person too weak to fight his own battles. This sort of thing infuriated Pelagius, as Augustine recounts in *The Gift of Perseverance* (20.53, written in 428/29). When another bishop showed these words to the somewhat puritanical Pelagius, he was much disturbed and "could not bear it" (*ferre non potuit*). As Gerald Bonner describes the situation, "These words provoked a furious reaction from Pelagius. Here in the words of one of the luminaries of western Christendom was expressed all that he found most intolerable in the excuses of the slothful."[3]

Actually Augustine's prayer for help should be understood in its whole context. He is admitting his moral weakness and imperfection, particularly in regard to sexual continence. His request is not a demand that God take over all responsibility for our misdeeds. This is fully explained in the *Retractations* (1.9), where in great detail he defends his dialogue *Free Choice* against Pelagian misuse of his text. The Pelagian heretics, he says, so stress the will's decision (*voluntatis arbitrium*) that "they leave no room for God's grace" (*ut gratiae Dei non relinquunt locum*). What Augustine stood for, in this controversy, was a balanced view of our active and willing cooperation with whatever special assistance God deigned to provide. It may be said in Pelagius' defense that Augustine's rhetorical enthusiasm sometimes led him into overstatements of his criticism. But there is no doubt that Augustine was forced by the Pelagian attacks to shift his early emphasis on human freedom to a more detailed statement of the role of divine grace in the lives of humans.[4]

From the point of view of philosophical ethics (on which Augustine wrote no general treatise; his ethical writings were on special moral problems), it is more important for us to avoid making Augustinian moral theory into a legalism. Despite the attention that he paid to divine "commands," Augustine's main ethical emphasis is on the human need to develop the good qualities of character that are exemplified by the four key natural virtues of practical wisdom (*prudentia*), temperance, fortitude, and justice. These are complemented and uplifted by the Christian virtues of faith, hope, and charity. The last in each group (justice and charity) have to do with our treatment of our fellow humans. In this area of conduct, law—human and divine—is necessary, but its force is to be tempered by the merciful love that is charity. As he remarks in the *Enchiridion* (32.121), "Every precept finds its end in charity" (*omnis itaque praecepti finis est charitas*).

On Grace and Free Choice, written in 426/27, states most clearly this interplay of human freedom and divine assistance (15.31). The then elderly Augustine wrote:

> Free will (*voluntas libera*) is always present in us, but it is not always good. It is either free from righteousness, when it is in the service of sin, or when it is in the service of righteousness, then it is good. But the grace of God is always good and it brings about a good will in man who, before that, was possessed of an evil will.[5]

Analysis 30.41: The fact that Augustine is not thinking of *all* moral laws here is evident from the opening sentence of this chapter: "Thou dost command me to refrain from concupiscence of the flesh and concupiscence of the eyes and the pride of this world" (*Jubes certe, ut contineam a concupiscentia carnis et concupiscentia oculorum et ambitione saeculi*). Pelagius broadened the scope of these words of Augustine into a whole ethical attitude. Augustine was well aware that there are other fields of moral concern than that of temperance. He often complained in his letters that too much of his time as bishop was taken up with settling various problems presented by his parishioners in the area of justice and charity in interpersonal relations. What Augustine is getting at in this chapter is a review of his own imperfections, mainly in matters of sensual desire.

He starts with the problems associated with the procreation of offspring. "Thou hast commanded [restraint] from concubinage and, in regard to marriage itself, which Thou hast permitted, Thou hast advised something better" (*Jusisti a concubitu, et de ipso conjugio melius aliquid, quam concessisti, monuisti*). Roman law did not forbid concubinage, but Christianity did. Augustine was not a baptized Catholic when he lived with a woman (apparently from a lower social class) for more than a decade.[6] Now in his mid-forties, looking back on that early period in his life, he regrets his youthful conduct and points out that, while the Church approves of marriage, the celibate life which he now embraces as a bishop is held in higher esteem.

Next, in section 41, Augustine admits that he is still bothered by erotic experiences recalled from his early life. "But there still lives in my memory, and I have spoken much about it, the images of such things which habit has imprinted therein" (*sed adhuc vivunt in memoria mea, de qua multa locutus sum, talium imagines quas ibi consuetudo mea fixit*). The impact of such temptations he is able to resist when awake, but Augustine frankly admits that he has little or no rational control of his dreams. This bothers him. He asks: "Am I not myself at such times, O lord my God?" (*numquid tunc ego non sum, domine deus meus?*). This is another question that he is unable

to answer. "Where is reason at such a time, which resists such temptations when I am awake?" (*ubi est tunc ratio talibus suggestionibus
resistit vigilans?*). He concludes that "we regret, however, that it has
been done by us in some way or other" (*quod tamen in nobis quoquo
modo factum esse doleamus*).

Comment: Perhaps too much has been written about Augustine's
youthful sensuality. He was in his late teens when he fathered the
boy named "God's Gift." Monica evidently did not consider the un-
named mother a suitable person to be the wife of a rising government official, for she arranged in Milan a marriage with a young girl
on their own level in society.[7] These plans were not fulfilled, probably because of Augustine's conversion. Now, some fifteen years
later, Augustine confesses that in celibacy he has chosen a superior
spiritual life. As he says, "Thou hast advised something better" than
the contemplated matrimony.

His major complaint, after serving for four or five years as
bishop, is that he still has erotic stimulations in his dreams. These
temptations he is unable to control while asleep, and he wonders
about the absence of his use of reason (*ratio*) in such somnolent periods. It presents quite a problem in Augustinian psychology, for the
continuity of personal life seems to require some endurance
(*manentia*) of rationality throughout one's temporal career. He asks,
"Does it (*ratio*) go to sleep along with the bodily senses?" A dozen
years earlier, Augustine and Nebridius had exchanged letters (*Epist*
8 and 9) dealing with various problems connected with images experienced in dreams. Augustine admitted that he could not explain
them. He still wonders in book 10, "Am I not myself, at such times?"
In these tentative speculations, Augustine comes close to discover-
ing what some modern psychologists call the subconscious mind.[8]

Unlike Thomas Aquinas (*Summa Theologiae* I–II.6.1) and later
Scholastic thinkers, who developed a sophisticated explanation of
voluntariness and moral actions, Augustine did not have the background in Aristotle's psychology or in the writings of the early Greek
fathers (Gregory of Nyssa, Nemesius, and John Damascene) that
could have enabled him to explore the role of habits in relation to
moral responsibility.

At the end of section 41, his expression of regret at the occurrence of these uncontrollable movements of sensuality is more a
matter of intellectual frustration than real sorrow. Of these initial
responses of sensual feelings, he simply says, "It is not we who have
done this" (*nos non fecisse*).

Analysis 30.42: Continuing this examination of his moral consciousness, Augustine says that he is now confident of divine help.

"Thou wilt increase, O Lord, Thy gifts more and more within me, so that my soul, escaping from the viscous snare of concupiscence, may follow me to Thee" (*augebis, domine, magis magisque in me munera tua, ut anima mea sequatur me ad te concupiscentiae visco expedita*). This is not easy to express briefly in English. He is speaking of his *anima,* that is, his principle of bodily life, which should follow the lifting up of his *animus,* his rational soul, from the sticky grasp of fleshly lusts.

As we have seen, this matter of sexual continence is still a moral problem for Augustine. But he says, "I am still imperfect; hoping that Thou wilt perfect Thy mercies in me unto the plenitude of peace, which my interior and exterior parts will possess with Thee, when 'death is swallowed up in victory'" (*quod inconsummatus sum;* cf.1 Cor. 15:54). Augustine is looking forward to the eventual perfecting of both his spiritual and corporeal capacities.

Comment: There is an air of finality about this last quotation from Paul. It appears to put an end to Augustine's exploration of his memory, the depths of human awareness, and the remembrance of moral concerns. That is why we bring our study of this selected text from book 10 to a close at this point.

However, there are twelve more chapters in the tenth book, in which Augustine further unveils his inner thoughts and feelings. In succession he examines his failings and occasional triumphs in dealing with the pleasures of eating and drinking (he always had wine at his table, according to Possidius, but not fine foods), the attractions of objects of smell (no great problem), and the pleasures of hearing. (For a former teacher of public speaking, and possibly poetry reading, oral stimuli did provide some attractions. It is amusing that, in chapter 33 of book 10, Augustine expresses some reservations about singing at church services.) He has a good deal to say about the pleasures of sight; light was always an object of fascination to him (chap. 34). All sentient curiosity is downplayed, but Augustine admits that he finds some innocent pleasure in watching the behavior of small creatures, such as lizards and spiders (35.57). Toward the end of book 10, Augustine discusses pride in being in control of other people (as he was in his diocese) and also pride of wealth and human adulation. On the whole, he thinks that he has most of these things under control.

Chapter 40 looks back on what he has done in the tenth book. In the "hidden places" of his memory he has found so many things that he grows "pale with astonishment" (sect. 65). His closing chapters (41–43) offer a brief but powerful digest of his present religious beliefs.

▌ N O T E S

1. For the influence of Stoicism, see Sister Rita Marie Bushman, "St. Augustine's Metaphysics and Stoic Doctrine," *New Scholasticism* 26 (1951): 283–302.

2. See the comments of Peter Brown in *Augustine of Hippo,* 177–80.

3. Cf. Bonner, *St. Augustine of Hippo,* 317.

4. Portalié, *A Guide to the Thought of St. Augustine,* 177–89, is more critical of Pelagius than more recent writers, such as Bonner and Brown. However, Portalié does note (181) that Augustine admitted to the Pelagians in the mature *Predestination of the Saints* (4.8) that he had come to see the respective roles of human freedom and divine grace "better and I have corrected myself. Since you read what I have to say, why do you not go along with me?"

5. *De gratia et libero arbitrio,* 15.31; I have modified the translation by R. P. Russell (FOC 59:285) slightly. This passage is one of the few uses of the term "free will" (*voluntas libera*) in Augustine's writings. Unfortunately, the outstanding work on Augustine's ethics has not been translated into English: J. Mausbach, *Die Ethik des heiligen Augustinus.*

6. This decade of association with the mother of his son was something quite different from Chadwick's translation of *jusisti a concubitu* (*Confessions,* 203) as "sleeping with a girl-friend."

7. *Conf* 6.15.25 tells of the return to Africa of Adeodatus' mother and the plans for a marriage in Milan. Cf. Peter Brown, *Augustine of Hippo,* 88–89.

8. Compare G. W. Leibniz's "petites perceptions" in *Monadologie,* 21–22; E. von Hartmann, *Philosophy of the Unconscious;* and Sigmund Freud, *The Interpretation of Dreams.*

But what of wisdom, the love of which has given the name "philoso-phy" to one of the most important areas of human study? Wisdom is one of the key names of God in *The Trinity* (15.7.12), but what does Augustine finally say about it in the *Confessions?* One answer is found in book 12 (15.20). There he sees two levels of sapiential knowledge:

> Though we do not find time before it (for "wisdom has been cre-ated before all things," Ecclesiasticus 1:4), it is certainly not that wisdom which is absolutely co-eternal and equal with Thee, O God of ours, Its own Father, that Wisdom through which all things have been created, the principle (*principium*) in which Thou hast made heaven and earth. It is a wisdom which has been created (*sed profecto sapientia quae creata est*), an intellectual nature which is light by virtue of a contempla-tion of Light (*intellectualis natura scilicet, quae contemplatione luminis lumen est*); for it is also called wisdom, even though created. But there is a great difference between the light which is a source of illumination and that which receives it, and there is an equally great difference between the wisdom which cre-ates and that which is created.

Of course, the uncreated Wisdom of which Augustine speaks here is the second Person of the Trinity, the Word of God. As such, this eternal being is not something that is ever possessed by hu-mans. The lower-level, created wisdom would seem to be that spe-cial subjective quality of the souls of those people who achieve a high grade of intellectual and volitional perfection. This is what enables the sage to make especially good judgments and willingly to act in accord with the eternal standards of virtue. It also extends to the reasonable control of excessive impulses of passions in humans. This is obviously a level of perfection achieved but rarely by human agents. It is created in the sense that the psychic quality, or habit, of wisdom is an acquired or infused perfection of the soul, which is itself created by God. And it is created, as Augustine sees it, because God makes it possible for human intellects to attain such wisdom.

A dozen years before writing the last books of the *Confessions,* the newly baptized Augustine composed the treatise *Morals of the Catholic Church.* In it (21.38) he commented on Paul's warning: "Beware lest anyone seduce you by philosophy" (Col. 2:8). Augustine's explanation of this gives us an insight into his early understanding of the love of wisdom.

> Since the very name *philosophy,* etymologically considered, means something great that should be desired with the whole mind, for indeed philosophy is the love and pursuit of wisdom (*siquidem philosophia est amor studiumque sapientiae*), the Apostle very prudently adds, lest he seem to downgrade the love of wisdom (*ne ab amore sapientiae deterrere videretur*), "and the elements of this world." For, there are some people who have abandoned the virtues and are ignorant about what God is, and about how great is the majesty of a Nature that abides forever in the same manner (*majestas semper eodem modo manentis naturae*). These are people who think they are doing something important, if they search out, with extreme curiosity and care, this bodily mass of the universe that we call the world. This generates so much pride that they seem to dwell in the very heavens that they so frequently discuss. So the soul should restrain itself from craving for this sort of empty knowledge, if it proposes to serve God with an unsullied mind. For one is, in most cases, deceived by such love, thinking that nothing exists except the body (*at aut nihil putet esse, nisi corpus*). Or even if, compelled by authority, one admits that there is something incorporeal, one cannot think of it except in terms of bodily imagery, believing that this is the only way that reality exists, because false sense perception gives this impression. So it is in reference to this, that a person is warned to avoid false images.

Even as a newly baptized Christian, Augustine retains his respect for philosophy. It is astrology, and the people who try to seem wise by such pseudoscience, that the warning is against. He thinks that worthwhile philosophical thinking must be open to the world of the spirit and the guidance of eternal wisdom.

A quarter-century later (A.D. 412), Augustine sent a long letter to Consentius (*Epist* 120) in which he explained the relation of faith to reason and further described the nature of wisdom. At the start he said that usually faith should precede reasoning, but in some cases reason may come first. While simple religious faith is adequate for many Christians, it is incumbent on those who can do more to seek whatever understanding is possible. There are some beliefs that cannot be wholly understood, however.

Apart from religious beliefs, there are other things, such as past events of history and assured expectations for the future, that Augustine saw as requiring faith. Many things remain the objects of trust in others (*Epist* 120.9). He gives as an example Antioch, a city he never visited. Yet he has some beliefs about it without having seen it. At section 18, he explains that even among objects that are experienced there are differences:

> We have, then, three classes of objects which are seen: the first are material things, such as the heavens and earth and everything the bodily senses perceive or experience in them; the second are representations of bodily things (*simile corporalibus*).... The third class is different from both the former; it consists of things that are not corporeal and have no corporeal representation, for example, wisdom, which is perceived by the understanding, and by whose light all these other things are correctly judged (*sicut est sapientia, quae mente intellectu conspicitur, et in cujus luce de his omnibus veraciter judicatur*).

He continues his exposition of these objects of the third type, using the divine Trinity as an example. Our partial understanding of this mystery is faced with an incorporeal object, which presents special difficulty. Here Augustine introduces another level of wisdom that is neither the wisdom which is God nor the natural wisdom to which a truth-loving philosopher might aspire. This in-between quality is the gift of wisdom, a special grace given to some people (Augustine is thinking, for instance, of the Old Testament prophets) who are infused with a higher understanding and degree of virtue than that of the ordinary spiritually perfected person. As he says: "If some of His light is in us and is called *our* wisdom" (*si autem aliquis splendor ejus in nobis est, quae nostra sapientia dicitur*), then it is different from all representations of material objects.

Then (*Epist* 120.12) Augustine mentions things other than the Trinity that are on the third level of understanding. They are: wisdom, justice, charity, chastity, and other similar qualities. Is God one of these objects for us? In section 13 he speaks of the beginning of knowledge about God (*inchoatio cognitionis Dei*) and explains that if, before we have a positive knowledge of what God is, we already have a start on knowing what He is not, then such understanding is certainly to be cherished (*Non enim parva est inchoatio cognitionis Dei, si antequam possimus nosse quid sit, incipiamus jam nosse quid non sit; intellectum vero valde ama*).

Writing as late as 419, in the last book of *The Trinity* (15.7.13), Augustine gives us his mature judgment about the highest wisdom. It is certainly far beyond human understanding:

> What man, then, is there who can comprehend that wisdom by which God knows all things, in such wise that neither

what we call things past are past therein, nor what we call
things future are therein attended as coming, as though they
were absent, but both past and future with things present are
all present; nor yet are things thought severally, so that
thought passes from one to another, but all things simulta-
neously are at hand in one glance—what man, I say, is there
who comprehends that wisdom, and the like prudence, and
the like knowledge, since in truth even our own wisdom is
beyond our comprehension?

So a seventy-five-year-old Augustine not only admits that the
perfect divine wisdom cannot be grasped except dimly "in an
enigma" but even that the human wisdom to which philosophers
aspire generally eludes us. He goes on to explain (still in sect. 13)
that it is by means of memory that we think about both past and
future objects. "But we do not know past things from the future ones,
rather we grasp the future objects from past experiences, and we do
not see them in any solid knowledge" (*Nec ex futuris praeterita, sed
futura ex praeteritis, non tamen firma cognitione conspicimus*).

It is by memory, he adds, that we are able to look ahead in
speaking or singing and think of the next words that we are to utter.
Our thoughts on all things that are not presently being experienced
depend on memory. We cannot pretend to know about absent objects
or meanings instantaneously, as God does in an eternal present.
Still in section 13, he continues:

> We know, and are absolutely certain, that all this takes place
> in our mind or by our mind; but how it takes place the more
> attentively we desire to scrutinize, the more do both our very
> words break down, and our purpose itself fails (*et ipsa non
> perdurat intentio*), when by our understanding, if not our
> tongue, we would try to reach something clear in our under-
> standing.

The wisdom that Augustine loved and sought is a many-layered
thing. In its fullest realization it is God Himself, the second Person
of the divine Trinity. One can only love this highest wisdom from
afar. Our knowledge of this wisdom comes through similitudes and
negations, by analogy.[1] The gift of wisdom is one level below; it is
freely conferred by God on selected persons, such as prophets and
sages. They are not necessarily learned in the academic sense. Augustine suspected that his mother had this gift.[2] On the third level is
philosophical wisdom, a perfection of the human understanding and
will, attained by some few people who strive by natural reasoning to
see the ultimate causes for all things and events. Philosophy, for
Augustine, makes a legitimate attempt to go beyond scientific
knowledge into the domain of eternally valid truths and rules of conduct. Much of what he passed on to his readers has become part of
the heritage of values inherent in modern culture.

I NOTES

1. Commenting on the argument of Augustine's *De Trinitate,* J. Moingt says ("Notes Complémentaires," BA 16:642): "The trinity of wisdom brings us to our point of departure, to the contemplation of the immutable Good." And two paragraphs later, Moingt adds: "So we cannot go beyond likenesses in our effort to know God. But this attempt to penetrate 'into the domain of the incomprehensible' has not been in vain. It succeeded in cleansing our search" (Moingt's comments in French are translated here).

2. In *De beata vita,* 10, Augustine says his mother's summary of what the happy life is "reaches the peak of philosophy" (*Ipsam, inquam, prorsus, mater, arcem philosophiae tenuisti*). And later (16), when Monica characterizes the Academic Skeptics as "sick" people (*caducarii*), Augustine may imply that her wisdom passes judgment on at least some philosophers.

| Augustine's Works

For Augustine's works of philosophical significance, the English titles are listed alphabetically, followed by the Latin titles, plus the date of composition by Augustine, the location in J. P. Migne, Patrologia Latina (PL), still the only almost complete collected edition of the Latin now available in most libraries; and the Bibliothèque Augustinienne (BA), the Corpus Scriptorum Ecclesiasticorum Latinorum (CSEL), and the Corpus Christianorum, Series Latina (CCSL); the latter three series are still in the process of publication.

There is no complete English version of Augustine's writings; English collections that include some of Augustine's writings are:

Ancient Christian Writers. Westminster, Md.: Newman Press, 1946–
   (ACW)
Basic Writings of St. Augustine. 2 vols. New York: Random House, 1948
   (BW)
Catholic University of America Patristic Series. Washington, D.C., 1922–
   (CUAP)
The Works of Aurelius Augustinus. Edited by Marcus Dods. 15 vols.
   Edinburgh: Clark, 1871–1876 (EDIN)
Fathers of the Church. New York-Washington: Catholic University of
   America Press, 1947– (FOC)
Library of Christian Classics. London-Philadelphia: Westminster Press,
   1953–55 (LCC)
Select Library of Nicene and Post-Nicene Fathers of the Church. 1887–1902.
   Reprint. Grand Rapids, Mich.: Eerdmans, 1956 (LNPN). Other
   English translations are listed at the end of some entries.

Unless otherwise noted, the English quotations from Augustine are by the author, except for some modifications of the Dods version.

Academics, Answer to the (Contra Academicos, III) (A.D. 386): PL 32; BA 4; CSEL 63; FOC 5; ACW 12

Adimantus the Manichee, Against (Contra Adimantum Manichaeum) (A.D. 393/96): PL 42; BA 17; CSEL 25

Arians, Reply to a Sermon of the (Contra sermonem Arianorum) (A.D. 418): PL 42; BA 37

Baptism, Against the Donatists on (De baptismo contra Donatistas, VII) (A.D. 400): PL 43; BA 17; CSEL 51; BDIN 3; LNPN 4

Believing, the Profit of (De utilitate credendi) (A.D. 392): PL 42; BA 8; CSEL 25; LNPN 3; BW 1; FOC 4

Christian Combat (De agone christiano) (A.D. 396/97): PL 40; BA 1; CSEL 41; FOC 2

Christian Doctrine (De doctrina christiana, IV) (A.D. 396 and 426): PL 34; BA 11; EPIN 9; LNPN 2; FOC 2

City of God (De civitate Dei, XXII) (A.D. 413–27): PL 41; BA 33–37; CSEL 40, 1 and 2; crit. ed. Dombart & Kalb (Leipzig: Teubner, 1928/29); LNPN 2; BW 2; EDIN 12; FOC 8, 14, 24; condensed ed. (Doubleday Image, 1958); trans. H. Bettenson (Penguin, 1972)

Confessions (Confessionum, Libri XIII) (A.D. 397–401): PL 32; crit. ed. M. Skutella (Leipzig: Teubner, 1934), rev. 1969, reprinted BA 13 and 14; CSEL 33; Gibb-Montgomery ed. 1927; CC (1981); Sir Tobie Matthew (London, 1620); William Watts (1631); A. Woodhead (1660); Bishop Challoner (1739); R. Hudleston (1954), E. B. Pusey (1838); J. G. Pilkington in LNPN 1, reprint BW 1; V. J. Bourke (1953); F. Sheed (1954); A. C. Outler (1955); J. K. Ryan (1960); R. Pine-Coffin (1961); R. Warner (1963); H. Chadwick (1991)

Continence (De continentia) (A.D. 395): PL 40, BA 3; CSEL 41; FOC 16

Cresconius, Against (Contra Cresconium, IV) (A.D. 406): PL 43; BA 30; CSEL 52

Dead, Care for the (De cura pro mortuis gerenda) (A.D. 421): PL 40; BA 2; CSEL 41; LNPN 3; FOC 27

Donatists after the Meeting, Against the (Contra Donatistas post collationem) (A.D. 412): PL 43; BA 31

Donatists, Brief of Meeting with (Breviculus collationis cum Donatistas) (A.D. 411): PL 43; BA 31; CSEL 53

Donatists, Correcting the (De correctione Donatistarum, Epist 185) (A.D. 417): PL 33; BA 44; CSEL 57

Donatus, Chant against the Sect of (Contra partem Donati) (A.D. 393/96): PL 43; BA 27; CSEL 51, 53

Emeritus, a Donatist Bishop, Reply to (Contra Emeritum Donat. Episcopum) (A.D. 418): PL 43; BA 31

Emeritus, Proceedings with (Gesta cum Emerito) (A.D. 418): PL 43; BA 31; CSEL 53

Enchiridion, a Manual for Laurentius (Enchiridion ad Laurentium, De fide, spe et caritate) (A.D. 421): PL 40; BA 9; ACW 3; FOC 2; EDIN 9; LNPN 3; BW 1

Errors, on Philosophical (De erroribus philosophiae) (A.D. 410): PL 33; BA 38; CSEL 44 (*Epist* 118); FOC 18

Faith and the Creed, Sermon (De fide et symbolo, sermo) (A.D. 393): PL 40; BA 9; CSEL 41; FOC 27

Faith and Works (De fide et operibus) (A.D. 413): PL 40; BA 8; CSEL 41; FOC 27

Faith in Things Unseen (De fide rerum quae non videntur) (A.D. 400): PL 40; BA 8; LNPN 3; FOC 4; CUAP 84

Faustus the Manichaean, Reply to (Contra Faustum Manichaeum, XXII) (A.D. 397/98): PL 42; BA 18; CSEL 25; EDIN 5; LNPN 4

Felix the Manichaean, Reply to (Contra Felicem Manichaeum, II) (A.D. 404): PL 42; BA 17; CSEL 25

Fortunatus the Manichaean, Debate with (Contra Fortunatum Manichaeum, Disputatio) (A.D. 392): PL 42; BA 17; CSEL 25

Free Choice of the Will (De libero arbitrio voluntatis, III) (A.D. 388–95): PL 32; BA 6; CSEL 74; LCC 6; FOC 59

Fundamental Manichaean Letter, Against the (Contra epistulam quam vocant Fundamenti) (A.D. 397): PL 42; BA 17; CSEL 25

Galatians, Explanation of Epistle to (Expositio Epistulae ad Galatas) (A.D. 394): PL 35; BA series 7.

Gaudentius a Donatist, Against (Contra Gaudentium Donatistarum episcopum) (A.D. 420): PL 43; BA 31; CSEL 53

Genesis against the Manichaeans, On (De Genesi contra Manichaeos, II) (A.D. 388/89): PL 34; BA series 7; FOC 84

Genesis, Incomplete Literal Commentary on (De Genesi ad litteram, imperfectus liber) (A.D. 393 and 426): PL 34; BA series 7; CSEL 28; FOC 84

Genesis, Literal Commentary on (De Genesi ad litteram, XII) (A.D. 401–15): PL 34; BA 48–49; CSEL 28, 1; Bk. 12, Latin and English trans. J. H. Taylor, St. Louis University Diss., 1948

God, Seeing (De videndo Deo, Epist 147) (A.D. 413): PL 33; BA 41; CSEL 44; FOC 20

God, Presence of (De praesentia Dei, Epist 187) (A.D. 417): PL 33; BA 23; CSEL 57; FOC 30

Gospel of St. John, On the (In Joannis Evangelium, Tractatus) (A.D. 414–17): PL 35; BA 71, 72; EDIN 10, 11; LNPN 7

Gospel Writers, Agreement among the (De consensu evangelistarum, IV) (A.D. 400): PL 34; BA series 7; CSEL 43

Gospels, Questions on the (Quaestiones Evangeliorum, Mat et Luc) (A.D. 397–400): PL 35; BA series 7

Grace and Free Choice (De gratia et libero arbitrio, ad Valentinum) (A.D. 426/27): PL 44; BA 23; EDIN 15; LNPN 5; BW 1; FOC 59

Grace of Christ and Original Sin (De gratia Christi et peccato originali, II) (A.D. 418): PL 44; BA 21; CSEL 42; EDIN 12; LNPN 5

Grace, Rebuke and (De correptione et gratia) (A.D. 426/27): PL 44; BA 23; EDIN 15; LNPN 5; FOC 2

Heresies, for Quodvuldeus (De haeresibus ad Quodvultdeum) (A.D. 429): PL 42; BA 37; CUAP 90

Happy Life, The (De beata vita) (A.D. 386): PL 32; BA 4; CSEL 63; trans. F. E. Tourscher (1933); FOC 5; CUAP 72

Heptateuch, Discourses on the (Locutiones in Heptateuchum, VII) (A.D. 419): PL 34; BA series 7; CSEL 28

Heptateuch, Questions on the (Quaestiones in Heptateuchum, VII) (A.D. 419): PL 34; BA series 7; CSEL 28

Homilies on St. John to the Parthians (Tractatus 124 in Joannem) (A.D. 416/17): PL 35; BA 72; LNPN 7; LCC 8

Immortality of the Soul (De immortalitate animae) (A.D. 387): PL 32; BA 5; BW 1; FOC 4

Instructing the Unlearned (De catechizandis rudibus) (A.D. 400): PL 40; BA 11; LNPN 3; EDIN 9; ACW 2; CUAP 8

Jews, Answer to the (Adversus Judaeos) (A.D. 428): PL 42; BA 37; FOC 27

Julian, Against (Contra Julianum, VI) (A.D. 421): PL 44; BA 24; FOC 35

Law, Against Adversaries of the (Contra adversarium Legis) (A.D. 420): PL 42; BA 37

Letters (Epistulae, 270 including some to Augustine) (A.D. 386–430): PL 33; BA 38–44; CSEL 34, 44, 57, 58; LNPN 1; EDIN 6, 11; FOC 12, 18, 20, 30, 32

Lying, On (De mendacio) (A.D. 395): PL 40; BA 2; CSEL 41; FOC 16

Lying, Against (Contra mendacium) (A.D. 420–22): PL 40; BA 2; CSEL 41; FOC 16

Magnitude of the Soul (De quantitate animae) (A.D. 387/88): PL 32; BA 5; FOC 4; ACW 9

Marriage and Concupiscence (De nuptiis et concupiscentia, II) (A.D. 419/20): PL 44; BA 22; CSEL 42; EDIN 12

Marriage, on Adulterous (De conjugiis adulterinis) (A.D. 419): PL 40; BA 2; CSEL 41; FOC 27

Maximinus an Arian Bishop, Reply to (Contra Maximinum Arianorum episcopum) (A.D. 428): PL 42; BA 37

Mirror of Holy Scripture (Speculum de Scriptura sacra) (A.D. 427): PL 33; BA series 7; CSEL 12

Monks, the Work of (De opere monachorum) (A.D. 400): PL 33; BA 3; CSEL 42; FOC 16

Morals of the Catholic Church and the Manichaeans (De moribus ecclesiae catholicae et manichaeorum, II) (A.D. 387/89): PL 32; BA 1; EDIN 5; LNPN 4; BW 1; FOC 56

Music, On (De musica, VI) (A.D. 388–91): PL 32; BA 7; FOC 4; trans. of bk. 6 by T. P. Maher, St. Louis University M.A. Thesis, 1939; FOC 4

Nature and Grace (De natura et gratia) (A.D. 413/15): PL 44; BA 20; CSEL 60; EDIN 4; LNPN 5; BW 1

Order, On (De ordine, II) (A.D. 386): PL 32; BA 4; CSEL 63; FOC 5

Pagans, Criticism of (Contra Paganos, Epist 102) (A.D. 408/9): PL 33; BA 41; CSEL 34; FOC 18

Parmenianus, Against the Letter of (Contra epistulam Parmeniani, III) (A.D. 400): PL 43; BA 27; CSEL 5

Patience, a Sermon (De patientia, sermo) (A.D. 418): PL 40; BA 2; CSEL 41; LNPN 5; FOC 16

Pelagians, Against Two Letters of (Contra duas epistulas Pelagianorum, IV) (A.D. 420): PL 44; BA 22; CSEL 60

Pelagius, Proceedings with (De gestis Pelagii) (A.D. 417): PL 44; BA 20; CSEL 42; EDIN 4; LNPN 5

Perseverance, Gift of (De dono perseverantiae) (A.D. 428/29): PL 44; BA 23; EDIN 15; LNPN 5; CUAP 91

Petilianus, Reply to the Letters of (Contra litteras Petiliani, III) (A.D. 400/402): PL 43; BA 29; CSEL 52

Predestination of the Saints (De praedestinatione sanctorum) (A.D. 428/29): PL 44; BA 23; EDIN 15; LNPN 5; BW 1

Priscillianists, Reply to the (Contra Priscillianistas) (A.D. 415): PL 42; BA 17; CSEL 25

Psalms, Expositions of the (Enarrationes in Psalmos) (A.D. 394?–418/20): Maurist ed. (Venice, 1730 reprint) vol. 4, cols. 1–1700; PL 36, 37; BA series 7; partial trans. LNPN 8; ACW 29, 30 (on Ps. 1–37).

Questions, Eighty-three Various (Quaestionibus LXXXIII, de diversis) (A.D. 388–95): PL 40; BA 10; partial trans. by V. J. Bourke: Q. 18 and 45, in *A's View of Reality*, 53–55; Q. 46 and 48 in *TEA*, 62–63 and 221–22.

Questions for Simplicianus (*Quaestiones VII ad Simplicianum,* II) (A.D. 395/97): PL 40; BA 10; LCC 6

Questions from Dulcitius (*Quaestiones VIII Dulcitii*) (A.D. 422–25): PL 40; BA 10; FOC 16

Religion, True (*De vera religione*) (A.D. 389–91): PL 34; BA 8; CCSL (1962); trans. J. H. S. Burleigh, in *Augustine, Earlier Writings* (Chicago: Regnery, 1959)

Questions on the Heptateuch (*Quaestiones in Heptateuchum, libri VII*) (A.D. 419): PL 34; BA series 7; CSEL 28

Retractations: Reviewing His Writings (*Retractationes,* II) (A.D. 426/27): PL 32; BA 12; CSEL 36; FOC 60

Righteousness, Man's Perfection in (*De perfectione justitiae hominis*) (A.D. 415): PL 44; BA 20; CSEL 42; EDIN 4; LNPN 5

Romans, Explanation of Epistle to the (*Expositio quarumdam propositionum ex Epistula ad Romanos*) (A.D. 393/96): PL 35; BA series 7

Romans, Incomplete Explanation of the Epistle to the (*Epistulae ad Romanos, inchoata expositio*) (A.D. 393/96): PL 35; BA series 7

Rome, Fall of the City of (*De Urbis excidio*) (A.D. 410): PL 40; BA 32

Rule for Religious (*Regula ad Sanctimoniales, Epist* 211) (A.D. 423): PL 33; BA 39; CSEL 57; FOC 32

Secundinus the Manichaean, Reply to (*Contra Secundinum Manichaeum*) (A.D. 405/6): PL 42; BA 17; CSEL 25

Sermon on the Mount, the Lord's (*De sermone Domini in monte,* II) (A.D. 393/6): PL 34; BA series 7; EDIN 8; LNPN 6; FOC 11; ACW 5

Sermons (*Sermones Augustini*) (A.D. 393–430): PL 38–39, 46–47; BA series 10; *Sermones post Maurinos reperti,* ed. G. Morin in *Miscellanea Agostiniana,* vol. 1 (Rome, 1930); *Sermones de vetere testamento,* ed. C. Lambot, CC 41; *Selected Sermons,* FOC 11; *Sermons for Christmas and the Epiphany,* ACW 15; *Selected Sermons of St. Augustine,* trans. Quincy Howe (New York: Holt, Rinehart and Winston, 1966)

Sermons on the Life and Works of Clerics (*Sermones de vita et operibus clericorum,* i.e., nos. 355, 356) (A.D. 425/26): PL 39, cols. 1568–82.

Sins, Punishment and Remission, and the Baptism of Infants (*De peccatorum meritis et remissione et baptismo parvulorum,* III) (A.D. 412): PL 44; BA 19; CSEL 60

Soliloquies (*Soliloquia,* II) (A.D. 386/87): PL 32; BA 5; LNPN 7; FOC 5; BW 1; CC 6

Soul, Its Origin, a Letter (*De origine animae, Epist* 166) (A.D. 415): PL 33; BA 38; CSEL 44; FOC 44

Soul and Its Origin, The (*De anima et ejus origine,* II) (A.D. 419–20): PL 44; BA 21; CSEL 60; EDIN 12; LNPN 5

Spirit and the Letter (*De spiritu et littera*) (A.D. 412): PL 44; BA 19; CSEL 60; EDIN 4; LBPN 5; LCC 8

Teacher, The (*De magistro*) (A.D. 389): PL 32; BA 6; ACW 9; LCC 6; FOC 59; BW 1; trans. G. G. Leckie (New York, 1938)

Trinity, The (*De Trinitate,* XV) (A.D. 399–419): PL 42; BA 15, 16; crit. ed. W. J. Mountain and F. Glorie, CC 50 (L and La); LNPN 3; BW 2; LCC 8; FOC 45

Two Souls, Against the Manichaeans (*De duabus animabus contra manichaeos*) (A.D. 392/93): PL 42; BA 17; CSEL 25; LNPN 4

Unity of the Church (*De unitate ecclesiae*) (A.D. 402): PL 43; BA 27

Virginity, Holy (De sancta virginitate) (A.D. 401): PL 40; BA 3; CSEL 41; LNPN 3; FOC 27
Widowhood, the Good of (De bono viduitatis) (A.D. 414): PL 40; BA 2; CSEL 41; FOC 16
World, On the End of the (De fine saeculi, Epist 199) (A.D. 419): PL 33; BA 41; CSEL 57; FOC 30

I Secondary Studies

I Bibliographies

Augustine Bibliography: *Reproduction des fichiers bibliographiques de l'Institut des Etudes Augustiniennes.* 2 vols. Boston, Mass.: G. R. Hall & Co. 1972.

Bavel, T. van, *Répertoire Bibliographique de saint Augustin, 1950–1960.* New York: Oxford University Press, 1963.

Miethe, Terry L. *Augustinian Bibliography, 1970–1980.* Westport, Conn.: Greenwood Press, 1982.

Nebreda, E. *Bibliographia Augustiniana.* Rome: Tipografia Cuore di Maria, 1928.

Revue des Etudes Augustiniennes (Paris) contains annual surveys of Augustine studies.

I Books and Articles

Adams, Jeremy D. *The* Populus *of Augustine and Jerome.* New Haven, Conn.: Yale University Press, 1971.

Alfaric, Prosper. *L'evolution intellectuelle de Saint Augustin.* Paris: Nourry, 1918.

Arendt, Hannah. *Der Liebensbegriff bei Augustinus.* Berlin: J. Springer, 1925.

Armstrong, A. H. *Saint Augustine and Christian Platonism.* Villanova, Pa.: Villanova University Press, 1967.

Battenhouse, R. *A Companion to the Study of St. Augustine.* New York: Oxford University Press, 1955.

Bonner, Gerald, *St. Augustine of Hippo: Life and Controversies.* Philadelphia, Pa.: The Westminster Press, 1963. Rev. ed. Norwich, 1986.

Bourke, V. J. "Augustine of Hippo: The Approach of the Soul to God." In *The Spirituality of Western Christendom,* edited by E. R. Elder, 1–12; 189–91. Kalamazoo, Mich.: Cistercian Publications, Inc.

———. *Augustine's Quest of Wisdom.* Milwaukee, Wis.: Bruce, 1945.

———. *Augustine's View of Reality.* Villanova, Pa.: Villanova University Press, 1964.

———. "The Body-Soul Relation in the Early Augustine." In *Collectanea Augustiniana,* edited by J. C. Schnaubelt and F. Van Fleteren, 435–50. Bern: Peter Lang, 1990.

———. *The Essential Augustine.* New York: Mentor-Omega, 1964.

———. *Wisdom from St. Augustine: Collected Essays.* Houston, Tex.: University of St. Thomas, 1984.

Boyer, Charles. *L'ideé de vérité dans la philosophie de saint Augustin.* Paris: Beauchesne, 21. Reprint. 1960.

Brown, Peter. *Augustine of Hippo: A Biography.* Berkeley and Los Angeles: University of California Press, 1967.

——. *Religion and Society in the Age of St. Augustine.* London: Faber & Faber, 1972.

Burkitt, F. C. *The Religion of the Manichees.* Cambridge: Cambridge University Press, 1925.

Burleigh, J. H. S. *The City of God: A Study of St. Augustine's Philosophy.* London: Macmillan, 1944.

Burnaby, John. *Amor Dei: Augustine on the Love of God as the Motive of Christian Life.* 2d ed. London: Hodder & Stoughton, 1947.

——. "Augustine of Hippo and Augustinian Ethics." *Dictionary of Christian Ethics,* edited by J. Macquarrie, 22–24. Philadelphia, Pa.: Westminster Press, 1967.

Bushman, Sister Rita Marie. "St. Augustine's Metaphysics and Stoic Doctrine." *New Scholasticism* 26 (1951): 283–302.

Callahan, John. *Augustine and the Greek Philosophers.* Villanova, Pa.: Villanova University Press, 1967.

——. *Four Views of Time in Ancient Philosophy.* Cambridge, Mass.: Harvard University Press, 1948.

——. "Basil of Caesarea: A New Source for St. Augustine's Theory of Time." *Harvard Studies in Classical Philology* 63 (1958): 437–54.

Carruthers, Mary J. *The Book of Memory: A Study of Memory in Medieval Culture.* New York: Cambridge University Press, 1990.

Cayré, Fulbert. *Initiation à la philosophie de s. Augustin.* Paris: Desclée de Brouwer, 1947.

Chadwick, Henry. *Augustine.* Oxford: Oxford University Press, 1986.

Chapman, Emmanuel. *Saint Augustine's Philosophy of Beauty.* New York: Sheed & Ward, 1939.

Chroust, A. M. "The Fundamental Ideas in St. Augustine's Philosophy of Law." *American Journal of Jurisprudence* 18 (1973): 57–79.

Clark, Mary T. *Augustine: Philosopher of Freedom.* New York: Desclée Co., 1958.

Cooke, Bernard. "The Mutability-Immutability Principle in St. Augustine's Metaphysics." *The Modern Schoolman* 23 (1946): 175–93; 24 (1946): 37–49.

Courcelle, Pierre. *Les Confessions de s. Augustin dans la tradition littéraire.* Paris: Etudes Augustiniennes, 1963.

——. *Recherches sur les Confessions de s. Augustin.* Paris: de Boccard, 1950.

Crouse, R. D. "In multa defluximus: Confessions X, 29–43." In *Neoplatonism and Early Christian Thought,* edited by H. J. Blumenthal and R. A. Markus, 180–85. London: Cambridge University Press, 1981.

——. "Recurrens in te unum: The Patterns of St. Augustine's Confessions." *Studia Patristica (Texte und Untersuchungen)* 14 (1975): 385–92.

Deanne, Herbert A. *The Political and Social Ideas of St. Augustine.* New York: Columbia University Press, 1965.

Deman, Thomas. *Le traitement scientifique de la morale chrétienne selon s. Augustin.* Montreal: Institut d'Etudes Médiévales, 1957.

Evans, G. R. *Augustine on Evil.* London: Cambridge University Press, 1982.

Figgis, John N. *The Political Aspects of St. Augustine's "City of God."* London: Longmans, 1921.

Gassert, R. G. "The Meaning of cogitatio in St. Augustine." *The Modern Schoolman* 25 (1948): 238–45.

Gilson, Etienne. *History of Christian Philosophy in the Middle Ages.* New York: Random House, 1955.

———. *The Christian Philosophy of St. Augustine.* Translated by L. Lynch. New York: Random House, 1960. (Originally *Introduction à l'étude de s. Augustin.* Paris: Vrin, 1929. Reprint. 1949.)

Grabowski, S. J. *The All-Present God: A Study in St. Augustine.* St. Louis, Mo.: Herder, 1954.

Green, W. M. *Augustine on the Teaching of History.* Berkeley and Los Angeles: University of California Press, 1944.

Guitton, Jean. *Le temps et l'éternité chez saint Augustin.* Paris: Aubier, 1956.

Henry, Paul. "Augustine and Plotinus." *Journal of Theological Studies* 38 (1937): 1–23.

———. *St. Augustine on Personality.* New York: Macmillan, 1960.

Holte, Ragnar. *Béatitude et sagesse: Saint Augustin et la fin de l'homme.* Paris: Etudes Augustiniennes, 1962.

Huddleston, B. *A Commentary on Augustine's Confessions X–XI.* Washington, D.C.: Catholic University of America Press, 1972.

Hugo, J. J. *St. Augustine on Nature, Sex and Marriage.* Chicago, Ill.: Scepter, 1969.

Jackson, B. D. "The Theory of Signs in St. Augustine's *De doctrina christiana.*" In *Augustine: A Collection of Critical Essays,* edited by R. A. Markus, 92–147. Garden City, N.Y.: Doubleday, 1972.

Jansen, L. F. "The Divine Ideas in the Writings of St. Augustine." *The Modern Schoolman* 22 (1945): 117–31.

Jordan, R. "Time and Contingency in St. Augustine." In *Augustine: A Collection of Critical Essays,* edited by R. A. Markus, 255–79. Garden City, N.Y.: Doubleday, 1972.

Keeler, Leo W. "St. Augustine on the Problem of Error." *Thought* 8 (1933): 410ff.; reprinted in Keeler, *The Problem of Error from Plato to Kant.* Rome: Pontificia Universitas Gregoriana, 1934.

———. *Sancti Augustini doctrina de cognitione: Textus selectus.* Rome: Pontificia Universitas Gregoriana, 1934.

Kertész, A. N. *Doctrine S. Augustini de memoria mentis.* Rome: Pontificia Universitas Gregoriana, 1944.

King, E. B., and J. T. Schaefer, eds. *Saint Augustine and His Influence in the Middle Ages.* Sewanee Mediaeval Studies, vol. 3. Louvain: Peeters, 1988.

Kirwan, Christopher. *Augustine.* London: Routledge, 1989.

Koterski, Joseph W. "St. Augustine on the Moral Law." *Augustinian Studies* 11 (1980): 65–78.

Le Blond, Jean-Marie. *Les conversions de saint Augustin.* Paris: Aubier, 1950.

McKeough, M. J. *The Meaning of the rationes seminales in St. Augustine.* Washington, D.C.: Catholic University of America Press, 1926.

Markus, R. A., ed. *Augustine. A Collection of Critical Essays.* Garden City, N.Y.: Doubleday, 1972.

———. *Saeculum: History and Society in the Theology of St. Augustine.* London: Cambridge University Press, 1970.

———. "St. Augustine on Signs." In *Augustine: A Collection of Critical Essays,* edited by R. A. Markus, 61–91. Garden City, N.Y.: Doubleday, 1972.

Marrou, Henri I. *St. Augustine and His Influence Through the Ages.* New York: Harper, 1957.

———. *The Resurrection and St. Augustine's Theology of Human Values.* Villanova, Pa.: Villanova University Press, 1966.

Martin, F. X., and J. A. Richmond, eds. *From Augustine to Eriugena: Essays on Neoplatonism and Christianity.* Baltimore, Md.: Catholic University of America Press, 1984.

Marshall, R. T. *Studies in the Political and Socio-Religious Terminology of the 'De civitate Dei.'* Patristic Studies, vol. 86. Washington, D.C.: Catholic University of America Press, 1952.

Maurer, A. A. "Orestes Brownson and St. Augustine." *The Modern Schoolman* 69 (1992).

Mausbach, Joseph. *Die Ethik des heiligen Augustinus.* 2d ed. 2 vols. Freiburg i. B: Herder, 1929.

Meer, F. van der. *Augustine the Bishop.* Translated by B. Battershaw. London: Sheed & Ward, 1961.

Moingt, J. "Notes Complémentaires" to *De Trinitate.* BA 16:608–11.

Mourant, John. *Introduction to the Philosophy of St. Augustine: Selected Readings.* University Park: The Pennsylvania State University Press, 1964.

———. *Saint Augustine on Memory.* Villanova, Pa.: Villanova University Press, 1980.

Nash, R. H. *The Light of the Mind: St. Augustine's Theory of Knowledge.* Lexington: University Press of Kentucky, 1969.

O'Connell, R. J. *Art, Aesthetics and the Christian Intelligence in the Works of St. Augustine.* Oxford: Blackwell, 1978.

———. *St. Augustine's Confessions: The Odyssey of Soul.* Cambridge, Mass.: Harvard University Press, 1969.

O'Meara, John J. *Charter of Christendom: The Significance of the City of God.* New York: Macmillan, 1961.

———. *Porphyry's Philosophy from Oracles in Augustine.* Paris: Etudes Augustiniennes, 1959.

———. *The Young Augustine.* Paris: Etudes Augustiniennes, 1954. 2d ed. London: Longmans, Green, 1980.

O'Toole, C. J. *The Philosophy of Creation in the Writings of St. Augustine.* Washington, D.C.: Catholic University of America Press, 1944.

Owens, Joseph. "Deo Intus Pandente (Augustine, *De magistro, 40*)." *The Modern Schoolman* 69 (1992).

Pegis, Anton C. "The Mind of St. Augustine." *Mediaeval Studies* 6 (1944): 1–61.

Pellegrino, Michel. *Les Confessions de saint Augustin.* Paris: Etudes Augustiniennes, 1960. Revised translation of *Le Confessioni di Sant' Agostino.* Rome: Studium, 1956.

Perler, Othmar. *Les voyages de saint Augustin.* Paris: Etudes Augustiniennes, 1969.

Pétré, Hélène. *Caritas: Etude sur le vocabulaire latin de la charité chrétienne.* Specilegium Sacrum Lovaniense, vol. 22. Louvain: Institut Supérieur de Philosophie, 1948.

Portalié, Eugène. *A Guide to the Thought of St. Augustine.* Translated by R. J. Bastian. Chicago: Regnery, 1960.

Rief, Josef. *Der Ordobegriff des jungen Augustinus.* Paderborn: Schöningh, 1962.

Rist, J. M. *Platonism and Its Christian Heritage.* London: Oxford University Press, 1985.

Roland-Gosselin, Bernard. *La morale de saint Augustin*. Paris: Rivière, 1925.

Schmaus, M. *Die psychologische Trinitätslehre des heiligen Augustinus*. Münster: Aschendorff, 1927.

Schmitt, A. "Mathematik und Zahlenmystik." In *Aurelius Augustinus,* edited by M. Grabmann and J. Mausbach, 353–66. Cologne: Aschendorff, 1930.

Schnaubelt, J. C., and F. Van Fleteren, eds. *Collectanea Augustiniana*. Bern: Peter Lang, 1990.

Schuetzinger, Caroline E. *The German Controversy on Augustine's Illumination Theory*. New York: Pageant Press, 1960.

Sohngen, Gunther. "Der Aufbau der augustinischen Gedächtnislehre, *Conf,* X, 6–27." In *Aurelius Augustinus,* edited by M. Grabmann and J. Mausbach. Cologne: Aschendorff, 1930.

Solignac, A. "Introduction," 1–267; and "Notes Complémentaires" to *Les Confessions,* 1:647–98, 2:529–634. BA vols. 13, 14. Paris: Desclée de Brouwer, 1962.

Svoboda, K. *L'esthétique de saint Augustin et ses sources*. Brno-Paris: Les Belles Lettres, 1933.

Switalski, Bruno. *Plotinus and the Ethics of St. Augustine*. New York: Polish Institute of Arts & Sciences, 1946.

Testard, Maurice. *Saint Augustin et Cicéron*. Paris: Etudes Augustiniennes, 1958, 1:20–34.

Thonnard, F. J. "Notes Complémentaires" to *De magistro* and *De libero arbitrio*. BA 6:475–76. Paris: Desclée de Brouwer, 1952.

Torchia, N. J. "The Significance of the Moral Concept of Virtue in St. Augustine's Ethics." *The Modern Schoolman* 68 (1990): 1–17.

Woods, H. *Augustine and Evolution: A Study in the De Genesi ad litteram*. New York: Universal Knowledge Foundation, 1924.

I N D E X

I Index of Subjects

Wisdom *(continue)*
  highest, 145, 148, 191; how known, 130, 132, 212; humans born without, 172, 173; and human perfection, 146, 210–11; knowledge *(scientia)* and, 121; is life, 122, 129; love of, 3, 21, 41, 200; philosophical, 173, 180, 213; and philosophy, 210, 211; supreme, 119, 192, 212; three kinds of, 212, 213; and virtue, 190, 210–11

Word *(verbum, logos)*, 17, 18

World soul, 20, 144

Zoroastrianism, 12

| Index of Names